INSTRUCTOR'S

ESSENTIALS OF ORGANIZATIONAL BEHAVIOR

INSTRUCTOR'S MANUAL

JIM DUPREE
GROVE CITY COLLEGE

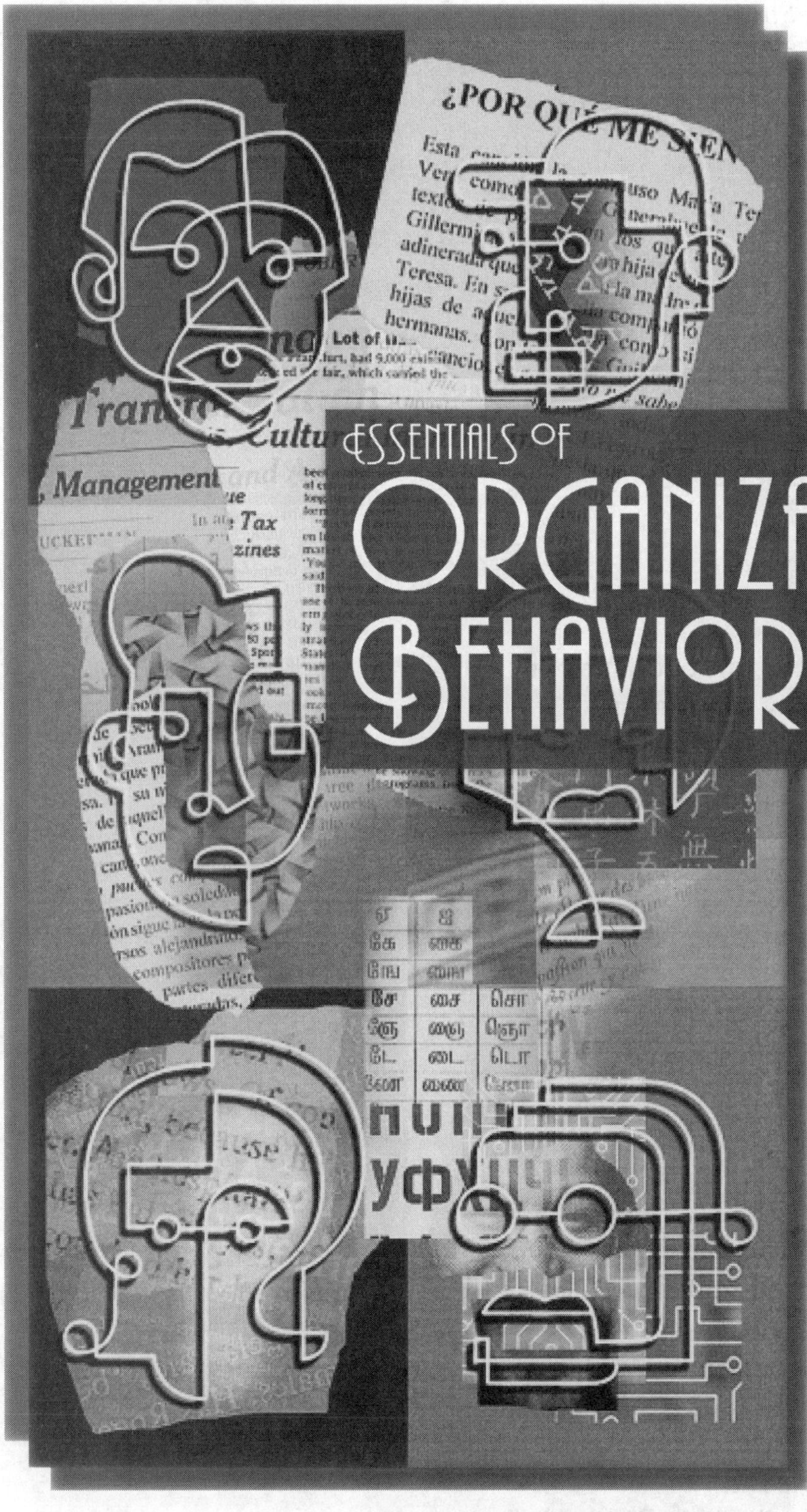

SIXTH EDITION

ESSENTIALS OF ORGANIZATIONAL BEHAVIOR

STEPHEN P. **ROBBINS**

PRENTICE HALL
UPPER SADDLE RIVER, NEW JERSEY 07458

Acquisitions editor: David Shafer
Associate editor: Michele Foresta
Project editor: Joan Waxman
Manufacturer: Victor Graphics, Inc.

Printed in the United States of America

10 9 8 7 6 5 4 3 2 1

ISBN 0-13-012442-7

Prentice-Hall International (UK) Limited, *London*
Prentice-Hall of Australia Pty. Limited, *Sydney*
Prentice-Hall Canada Inc., *Toronto*
Prentice-Hall Hispanoamericana, S.A., *Mexico*
Prentice-Hall of India Private Limited, *New Delhi*
Prentice-Hall of Japan, Inc., *Tokyo*
Prentice-Hall (Singapore) Pte Ltd
Editora Prentice-Hall do Brasil, Ltda., *Rio de Janeiro*

TABLE OF CONTENTS

CHAPTER 1 - INTRODUCTION TO ORGANIZATIONAL BEHAVIOR

CHAPTER OBJECTIVES

After reading this chapter students should be able to:

1 Define organizational behavior (OB).
2 Identify the primary behavioral disciplines contributing to OB.
3 Describe the three goals of OB.
4 List the major challenges and opportunities for managers to use OB concepts.
5 Explain the key elements in total quality management (TQM).
6 Discuss why work force diversity has become an important issue in management.
7 Explain how managers and organizations are responding to the problem of employee ethical dilemmas.

LECTURE OUTLINE

I. THE FIELD OF ORGANIZATIONAL BEHAVIOR

- A. Definition
    1. Organizational behavior (OB) is the systematic study of the actions and attitudes that people exhibit within organizations.
    2. Key parts of the definition
        - a) Systematic study
            - (1) The use of scientific evidence gathered under controlled conditions and measured and interpreted in a reasonably rigorous manner to attribute cause and effect.
            - (2) OB--its theories and conclusions--is based on a large number of systematically designed research studies.
        - b) Systematic study of actions (or behaviors) and attitudes in three areas: productivity, absenteeism, and turnover.
            - (1) Managers clearly are concerned with the quantity and quality of output that each employee generates.
            - (2) Absence and turnover--particularly excessively high rates---can adversely affect this output.
            - (3) Organizational behavior is also concerned with employee job satisfaction, which is an attitude.
            - (4) A concern for three reasons.
                - (a) First, there may be a link between satisfaction and productivity.
                - (b) Second, satisfaction appears to be negatively related to absenteeism and turnover.
                - (c) Finally, it can be argued that managers have a humanistic responsibility to provide their employees with jobs that are challenging, intrinsically rewarding, and satisfying.
        - c) Systematic study within an organization.
            - (1) OB is specifically concerned with work-related behavior.
            - (2) An organization is a formal structure of planned coordination, involving two or more people who share a common purpose.
            - (3) Its characterized by formal roles that define and shape the behavior of its members.

- B. Contributing Disciplines
    1. Organizational behavior is applied behavioral science.

   a) The predominant contributing disciplines are psychology, sociology, social psychology, anthropology, and political science.
2. Psychology is the science that seeks to measure, explain, and sometimes change the behavior of humans and other animals.
   a) Psychologists concern themselves with studying and attempting to understand individual behavior.
   b) Contributors are learning theorists, personality theorists, counseling psychologists, and, most important, industrial and organizational psychologists.
   c) Early industrial psychologists concerned themselves with problems of fatigue, boredom, and any other factor relevant to working conditions that could impede efficient work performance.
   d) More recently, their contributions have been expanded to include learning, perception, personality, emotions, training, leadership effectiveness, needs and motivational forces, job satisfaction, decision-making processes, performance appraisals, attitude measurement, employee-selection techniques, job design, and work stress.
3. Sociology studies people in relation to their fellow human beings.
   a) Greatest contribution through their study of group behavior in organizations, particularly formal and complex organizations.
   b) Areas of valuable input include group dynamics, design of work teams, organizational culture, formal organization theory and structure, bureaucracy, communications, status, power, and conflict.
4. Social Psychology is an area within psychology, blending concepts from psychology and sociology.
   a) It focuses on the influence of people on one another.
   b) A major area of concern--change--how to implement it and how to reduce barriers to its acceptance.
   c) Areas of significant contributions are in measuring, understanding, and changing attitudes, communication patterns, the ways in which group activities can satisfy individual needs, and group decision-making processes.
5. Anthropology is the study of societies to learn about human beings and their activities.
   a) This has helped us understand differences in fundamental values, attitudes, and behavior between people in different countries and within organizations.
6. Political Science is frequently overlooked-- the study of the behavior of individuals and groups within a political environment.
   a) Specific topics of concern to political scientists include structuring conflict, allocation of power, and how people manipulate power for individual self-interest.

II. GOALS OF ORGANIZATIONAL BEHAVIOR

A. What does OB seek to do?

B. Explanation

1. Seek to answer why an individual or a group of individuals did something.
2. The least important of the three goals, from a management perspective, because it occurs after the fact.

C. Prediction

1. The goal of prediction focuses on future events to determine what outcomes will result from a given action.

2. There are various ways to implement a major change, so the manager is likely to assess employee responses to several change interventions. And use that information in making the decision as to which change effort to use.

D. Control
1. The most controversial goal is to control behavior. Because most of us live in democratic societies, which are built upon the concept of personal freedom.
2. OB does offer technologies that facilitate the control of people.
   a) Whether those technologies should be used in organizations becomes an ethical question.

III. CHALLENGES AND OPPORTUNITIES FOR OB: A MANAGERIAL PERSPECTIVE

A. The ability to explain, predict, and control organizational behavior has never been more important to managers.

B. Improving Quality and Productivity
1. William French manages in a tough business. He is the director of manufacturing at Alcatel Network Systems plant, which makes broadband telecommunication and data network products and those products face, a multitude of aggressive competitors.
   a) By using self-directed work teams, streamlining processes, and implementing continuous improvement programs, this Alcatel plant is now a model of manufacturing efficiency.
2. Managers are confronting the challenges that William French is facing and to improve quality and productivity, they are implementing programs such as total quality management and reengineering-programs that require extensive employee involvement.
   a) See Exhibit 1-2. What Is Total Quality Management?
3. Reengineering asks managers to reconsider how work would be done and their organization structured if they were to start over?
   a) Example of in-line skates as a reengineering approach to roller-skates.
   b) The goal was to come up with a skating device that could improve skating speed, mobility, and control.

C. Improving People Skills
1. People skills are critical to managerial effectiveness.
2. There are specific people skills that managers can use on the job.
   a) The text will raise this as you read.

D. Managing Work Force Diversity
1. A key challenge currently facing North American organizations.
2. Workforce diversity means that organizations are becoming more heterogeneous in terms of gender, race, and ethnicity.
   a) Encompasses anyone who varies from the "norm." In addition to the more obvious groups--women, African Americans, Hispanic Americans, and Asian Americans--it also includes the physically disabled, gays and lesbians, and the elderly.
3. Traditional melting pot approach to differences in organizations assumed that people who were different would somehow automatically want to assimilate.
4. Now the challenge for organizations is to make themselves more accommodating to diverse groups.
5. Diverse groups were such a small percentage of the U.S. workforce.
   a) The bulk of the pre-1980s workforce was male Caucasians working full time to support a nonemployed wife and school-aged children.

b) Currently, 46 percent of the U.S. labor force are women. Minorities and immigrants make up 23 percent.

6. Workforce diversity has important implications for management practice.
   a) Managers need to recognize differences and respond to them.
      (1) Diversity, if positively managed, can increase creativity and innovation in organizations as well as improve decision making by providing different perspectives on problems.

E. Responding to Globalization
   1. Management is no longer constrained by national borders.
      a) A British firm owns Burger King.
      b) Exxon receives almost 75 percent of its revenues from sales outside the U.S.
   2. Globalization affects a manager's people skills in at least two ways.
      a) First, if you are a manager, you are increasingly likely to find yourself in a foreign assignment.
      b) Second, even in your own country, you are going to find yourself working with bosses, peers, and subordinates who were born and raised in different cultures.

F. Empowering People
   1. The reshaping of the relationship between managers and those they are supposedly responsible for managing.
      a) Decision-making is being pushed down to the operating level.
      b) Managers are allowing employees full control of their work.
      c) An increasing number of organizations are using self-managed teams.
   2. Managers are empowering employees.
   3. Managers are having to learn how to give up control, and employees are having to learn how to take responsibility for their work and make appropriate decisions.

G. Stimulating Innovation and Change
   1. Today's successful organizations must foster innovation and master the art of change or they will become candidates for extinction.
   2. Victory will go to those organizations that maintain their flexibility, continually improve their quality, and beat their competition to the marketplace with a constant stream of innovative products and services.
   3. The challenge for managers is to stimulate employee creativity and tolerance for change.
      a) The field of OB provides a wealth of ideas and techniques to aid in realizing these goals.

H. Coping with "Temporariness"
   1. Managers have always been concerned with change. What is different is the amount of time between change implementations.
   2. Today, change is an ongoing activity for most managers. The concept of continuous improvement, for instance, implies constant change.
   3. Managing used to be characterized by long periods of stability interrupted occasionally by short periods of change.
      a) That is reversed today.
   4. Managers and employees face a world of permanent "temporariness."
      a) Workers need to continually update their knowledge and skills to perform new job requirements.

b) Work groups are also increasingly in a state of flux. In the past, employees were assigned to a specific department, and that assignment was relatively permanent.
c) Organizations themselves are in a state of flux. They continually reorganize their various divisions, sell off poorly performing businesses, downsize operations, and replace permanent employees with temporaries.
5. Today's managers and employees must learn to learn to live with flexibility, spontaneity, and unpredictability.

I. Declining Employee Loyalty
1. Corporate employees used to believe that their employers would reward loyalty and good work with job security, generous benefits, and steady pay increases.
2. That changed beginning in the mid-1980s as corporations sought to become "lean and mean" by closing factories, moving operations to less-expensive countries, selling off or closing down less-profitable businesses, eliminating entire levels of management, replacing permanent employees with temporaries, and substituting performance-based pay systems for seniority-based programs.
3. European companies are also doing this.
4. These changes have resulted in a sharp decline in employee loyalty.

J. Improving Ethical Behavior
1. In today's organizational world its not surprising that many employees feel pressured to cut corners, break rules, and engage in other forms of questionable practices.
2. Members of organizations are increasingly finding themselves facing ethical dilemmas, situations in which they are required to define right and wrong conduct.
3. Good ethical behavior has never been clearly defined.
a) In recent years the line differentiating right from wrong has become even more blurred.
b) Employees see people all around them engaging in unethical practices--elected officials, high-powered lawyers, successful executives, and employees in other companies.
4. A variety of responses to this problem.
a) Writing and distributing codes of ethics to guide employees through ethical dilemmas.
b) Offering seminars, workshops, and similar training programs to try to improve ethical behaviors.
c) Providing in-house advisors whom can be contacted, in many cases anonymously, for assistance in dealing with ethical issues.
d) Creating protection mechanisms for employees who reveal internal unethical practices.
5. Today's manager needs to create an ethically healthy climate in which his or her employees can do their work productively and confront a minimal degree of ambiguity regarding what constitutes right and wrong behaviors.

IV. THE PLAN OF THIS BOOK
A. A building block approach.
1. See Exhibit 1-3.
2. Chapters 2 through 6 deal with the individual in the organization.
a) The foundations of individual behavior--values, attitudes, perception, and learning.
b) The role of personality and emotions in individual behavior.
c) Conclude with motivation issues and individual decision making.
3. Chapters 7 through 12 address group behavior.

a) Introduce a group behavior model.
b) Discuss ways to make teams more effective.
c) Consider communication issues and group decision-making.
d) Investigate leadership and the issues of trust, power, politics, and conflict and negotiation.

4. Organizational behavior reaches its highest level of sophistication when we add the formal organization system to our knowledge of individual and group behavior. Chapters 13 through 17, discuss:
   a) How an organization's structure, work design, and technology affect behavior.
   b) The effect that an organization's formal performance appraisal and reward system has on people.
   c) How each organization has its own culture that acts to shape the behavior of its members.
   d) The various organizational change and development techniques that managers can use to affect behavior for the organization's benefit.

SUMMARY

1 Organizational behavior (OB) is the systematic study of the actions and attitudes that people exhibit within organizations.

2 Organizational behavior is applied behavioral science. The predominant contributing disciplines are psychology, sociology, social psychology, anthropology, and political science.

3 The three primary goals of OB are to explain why an individual or a group of individuals do something; to predict future events--to determine what outcomes will result from a given action; and to control behavior, the most controversial goal of the three. OB does offer technologies that facilitate the control of people. Whether those technologies should be used in organizations becomes an ethical question.

4 The major challenges and opportunities for managers to use OB concepts occur in the areas of improving quality and productivity through the use of TQM, reengineering and other techniques; improving people skills; managing work force diversity--a key challenge since organizations are becoming more heterogeneous in terms of gender, race, and ethnicity; responding to globalization; empowering people by the reshaping of the relationship between managers and those they're supposedly responsible for managing; stimulating innovation and change; coping with temporariness as the work force becomes more part time and contingency based; dealing with declining employee loyalty; and improving ethical behavior.

5 The plan of the book is built on a building-block approach. Chapters 2 through 6 deal with the individual in the organization. Chapters 7 through 12 address group behavior. Chapters 13 through 17, discuss how an organization's structure, work design, and technology affect behavior, the effect that an organization's formal performance appraisal and reward system has on people, how each organization has its own culture that acts to shape the behavior of its members, and the various organizational change and development techniques that managers can use to affect behavior for the organization's benefit.

DISCUSSION QUESTIONS

1 Define organizational behavior (OB).
Answer - Organizational behavior (OB) is the systematic study of the actions and attitudes that people exhibit within organizations. Key parts: systematic study--the use of scientific evidence gathered under controlled conditions and measured and interpreted in a reasonably rigorous manner to attribute cause and effect; systematic study of actions (or behaviors) and attitudes in three areas: productivity, absenteeism, and turnover; systematic study within an organization--OB is specifically concerned with work-related behavior--and that takes place in organizations.

2 Identify the primary behavioral disciplines contributing to OB.
Answer - Organizational behavior is applied behavioral science. Psychology is the science that seeks to measure, explain, and sometimes change the behavior of humans and other animals. Sociology studies people in relation to their fellow human beings. Greatest contribution was through their study of group behavior in organizations, particularly formal and complex organizations. Social Psychology is an area within psychology, blending concepts from psychology and sociology. It focuses on the influence of people on one another. Anthropology is the study of societies to learn about human beings and their activities. This has helped us understand differences in fundamental values, attitudes, and behavior between people in different countries and within organizations. Political Science is frequently overlooked-- the study of the behavior of individuals and groups within a political environment.

3 Describe the three goals of OB.
Answer - Explanation--seeking to answer why an individual or a group of individuals did something. The least important of the three goals, from a management perspective, because it occurs after the fact. Prediction--focusing on future events to determine what outcomes will result from a given action. Control--The most controversial goal is to control behavior. Because most of us live in democratic societies, which are built upon the concept of personal freedom. OB does offer technologies that facilitate the control of people. Whether those technologies should be used in organizations becomes an ethical question.

4 List the major challenges and opportunities for managers to use OB concepts.
Answer - Improving quality and productivity through the use of TQM, reengineering and other techniques; improving people skills; managing work force diversity--a key challenge since organizations are becoming more heterogeneous in terms of gender, race, and ethnicity; responding to globalization; empowering people by the reshaping of the relationship between managers and those they are supposedly responsible for managing; stimulating innovation and change; coping with temporariness as the work force becomes more part time and contingency based; dealing with declining employee loyalty; and improving ethical behavior.

5 Explain the key elements in total quality management (TQM).
Answer - See Exhibit 1-2. What Is Total Quality Management?

6 Discuss why work force diversity has become an important issue in management.
Answer - Workforce diversity means that organizations are becoming more heterogeneous in terms of gender, race, and ethnicity. Encompasses anyone who varies from the "norm." In addition to the more obvious groups--women, African Americans, Hispanic Americans, and Asian Americans--it also includes the physically disabled, the elderly, etc. Traditional melting pot approach to differences in organizations assumed that people who were different would somehow automatically want to assimilate. Now diverse groups were such a small percentage of the U.S. workforce--currently, 46 percent of the U.S. labor force are women. Minorities and immigrants make up 23 percent.

7 Explain how managers and organizations are responding to the problem of employee ethical dilemmas.
Answer - Writing and distributing codes of ethics to guide employees through ethical dilemmas. Offering seminars, workshops, and similar training programs to try to improve ethical behaviors. Providing in-house advisers whom can be contacted, in many cases anonymously, for assistance in dealing with ethical issues. Creating protection mechanisms for employees who reveal internal unethical practices. Today's manager needs to create an ethically healthy climate in which his or her

employees can do their work productively and confront a minimal degree of ambiguity regarding what constitutes right and wrong behaviors.

EXERCISE

Have students introduce themselves by giving their name, and any other information you deem appropriate, and by offering one short 1-3 minute story about an experience they had with an organization. Give students several minutes to think about their story; keep time, and stop students who go too long. Use the stories to introduce the importance of OB to them.

CHAPTER 2 - FOUNDATIONS OF INDIVIDUAL BEHAVIOR

CHAPTER OBJECTIVES

After reading this chapter, students should be able to:

1 List the dominant values in today's workforce.
2 Describe the relationship between satisfaction and productivity.
3 Explain the theory of cognitive dissonance.
4 Summarize the relationship between attitudes and behavior.
5 Explain how two people can see the same thing and interpret it differently.
6 Summarize attribution theory.
7 Outline the learning process.

LECTURE OUTLINE

I. VALUES

A. Introduction

1. Values represent basic convictions that a specific mode of conduct or end-state of existence is personally or socially preferable to an opposite or converse mode of conduct or end-state of existence.
2. They contain a moral flavor in that they carry an individual's ideas as to what is right, good, or desirable.
3. Value systems represent a prioritizing of individual values.
4. They are identified by the relative importance an individual assigns to such values as freedom, pleasure, self-respect, honesty, obedience, and equality.

B. Types of Values

1. Rokeach Value Survey
   a) Milton Rokeach created the Rokeach Value Survey (RVS).
   b) The RVS consists of two sets of values, with each set containing 18 individual value items.
   c) One set, terminal values, refers to desirable end-states of existence. These are the goals that a person would like to achieve during his or her lifetime.
   d) The other set, instrumental values, refers to preferable modes of behavior or means of achieving the terminal value.
      (1) Exhibit 2-1 gives common examples for each of these sets.
   e) RVS values vary among groups.
      (1) People in the same occupations or categories (e.g., corporate managers, union members, parents, and students) tend to hold similar values.
2. Contemporary Work Cohorts
   a) A four-stage model that attempts to capture the unique values of different cohorts or generations in the U.S. workforce.
      (1) Exhibit 2-2 proposes that employees can be segmented by the era in which they entered the work force
      (2) Because most people start work between the ages of 18 and 23, the eras also correlate closely with the chronological age of employees.
   b) Workers who grew up influenced by the Great Depression, etc., who entered the workforce from the mid-1940s through the late-1950s:
      (1) believe the Protestant work ethic.
      (2) once hired, they tend to be loyal to their employer.
      (3) are likely to place the greatest importance on a comfortable life and family security.

c) Employees who entered the workforce during the 1960s through the mid-1970s were influenced heavily by John F. Kennedy, etc.
(1) They brought with them the "hippie ethic" and existential philosophy.
(2) They have more concern for the quality of their lives than with the amount of money and possessions they can accumulate.
(3) A desire for autonomy, directs their loyalty toward themselves.

d) Individuals who entered the workforce from the mid-1970s through the mid-1980s reflect the society's return to more traditional values but with far greater emphasis on achievement and material success.
(1) Strongly influenced by Reagan conservatism, etc.
(2) These workers are pragmatists who believe that ends can justify means.
(3) Organizations that employ them are merely vehicles for their careers.
(4) Ttheir terminal values such as a sense of accomplishment and social recognition rank high with them.

e) Generation X has been shaped by globalization, the fall of communism, MTV, etc.:
(1) Value flexibility, life options, and job satisfaction.
(2) Family and relationships are very important to this cohort.
(3) Money is important as an indicator of career performance.
(4) Willing to trade off salary increases, rifles, security, and promotions for increased leisure time and expanded lifestyle options.
(5) On the RVS, they rate high on friendship, happiness, and pleasure.

3. An understanding that individuals' values differ but tend to reflect the societal values of the period in which they grew up can be a valuable aid in explaining and predicting behavior.

C. Values, Loyalty, and Ethical Behavior

1. If ethical standards have fallen, perhaps we should look to our four-stage model of work cohort values for a possible explanation.
   a) See Exhibit 2-2.
2. Through the mid-1970s, the managerial ranks were dominated by Protestant-work-ethic types (Stage I) whose loyalties were to their employer. When faced with ethical dilemmas, their decisions were made in terms of what was best for their organization.
3. Beginning in the mid-to-late 1970s, individuals with existential values began to rise into the upper levels of management. They were soon followed by pragmatic types.
4. By the late 1980s, a large portion of middle and top management positions in business organizations were held by people from Stages II and III.
   a) The loyalty of existentials and pragmatics is to self and careers, respectively. Their focus is inward and their primary concern is with looking out for Number One.
   b) Such self-centered values would be consistent with a decline in ethical standards.
5. The potential good news in this analysis is that recent entrants to the work force, tomorrow's managers, appear to be less self-centered.
6. We might look forward to higher ethical standards in business over the next decade or two merely as a result of changing values within the managerial ranks.

D. Values Across Cultures

1. A comparison of American and Japanese cultures.
   a) American children are taught early the values of individuality and uniqueness.
   b) A significant part of an American student's education is to learn to think, analyze, and question.
   c) Japanese children are indoctrinated to be "team players," to work within the group, and to conform.

d) Japanese counterparts are rewarded for recounting facts.
e) The average U.S. worker is more competitive and self-focused than the Japanese worker.

2. A Framework for Assessing Cultures.
   a) A widely referenced approach for analyzing variations among cultures has been done by Geert Hofstede.
      (1) He found that managers and employees vary on the following five value dimensions of national culture:
   b) Power distance.
      (1) The degree to which people in a country accept that power in institutions and organizations is distributed unequally.
   c) Individualism vs. collectivism.
      (1) Individualism is the degree to which people in a country prefer to act as individuals rather than as members of groups.
      (2) Collectivism is the opposite or the equivalent of low individualism.
   d) Quantity of life vs. quality of life.
      (1) Quantity of life is the degree to which values like assertiveness, the acquisition of money and material goods, and competition prevail.
      (2) Quality of life is the degree to which people value relationships and show sensitivity and concern for the welfare of others.
   e) Uncertainty avoidance.
      (1) The degree to which people in a country prefer structured over unstructured situations.
   f) Long-term vs. short-term orientation.
      (1) People in long-term orientation countries look to the future and value thrift and persistence.
      (2) A short-term orientation values the past and present and emphasizes respect for tradition and social obligations.
   g) Exhibit 2-3 summarizes how a number of countries rate on these five dimensions.
3. Implications for OB.
   a) Most of the concepts that currently make up organizational behavior have been developed by Americans using American subjects within domestic contexts.
      (1) Therefore not all OB theories and concepts are universally applicable to managing people around the world.

II. ATTITUDES

A. Introduction

1. Attitudes are evaluative statements---either favorable or unfavorable--concerning objects, people, or events.
2. They reflect how one feels about something.
3. OB focuses on a very limited number of job-related attitudes--job satisfaction, job involvement (the degree to which a person identifies with his or her job and actively participates in it), and organizational commitment (an indicator of loyalty to, and identification with, the organization).
   a) Job satisfaction has received the bulk of attention.

B. Job Satisfaction

1. Job satisfaction refers to an individual's general attitude toward his or her job.
   a) A person with a high level of job satisfaction holds positive attitudes toward the job.
   b) A person who is dissatisfied with his or her job holds negative attitudes about that job and has a low level of satisfaction.

2. What Determines Job Satisfaction?
   a) The most important factors conducive to job satisfaction are mentally challenging work, equitable pay and other rewards, supportive working conditions and supportive colleagues.
   b) Employees tend to prefer jobs that give them opportunities to use their skills and abilities and offer a variety of tasks, freedom, and feedback on how well they are doing.
   c) Employees want pay systems and promotion policies that they perceive as just, unambiguous, and in line with their expectations.
   d) Employees are concerned with their work environment for both personal comfort and job facilitation.
      (1) They prefer physical surroundings that are safe, comfortable, clean, and with a minimum degree of distractions.
   e) For most employees, work also fills the need for social interaction, therefore, friendly and supportive co-workers leads to increased job satisfaction.
3. Satisfaction and Productivity
   a) This topic has attracted a lot of attention and interest.
   b) The early views were "a happy worker is a productive worker."
   c) A more careful analysis indicates that if satisfaction does have a positive effect on productivity, that effect is fairly small.
      (1) The introduction of moderating variables, however, has improved the relationship.
   d) Currently, on the basis of a comprehensive review of the evidence, it appears that productivity is more likely to lead to satisfaction rather than the other way around.

C. Reducing Dissonance
1. Cognitive dissonance occurs when there are inconsistencies between two or more of a person's attitudes or between a person's behavior and attitudes.
   a) The theory of cognitive dissonance suggests that people seek to minimize dissonance and the discomfort it causes.
2. A person's desire to reduce dissonance is determined by the importance of the elements creating the dissonance, the degree of influence the individual believes he or she has over the elements, and the rewards that may be involved in dissonance.
   a) If the elements creating the dissonance are relatively unimportant, the pressure to correct this imbalance will be low.
   b) The degree of influence that individuals believe they have over the elements involved will have an impact on how they will react to the dissonance.
   c) If they perceive the dissonance to be an uncontrollable result--something that they can't change--they are not likely to be receptive to attitude change.
3. Rewards also influence the degree to which individuals are motivated to reduce dissonance.
   a) The tension inherent in high dissonance may be reduced if accompanied by a high reward.
4. Organizational implications.
   a) It can help to predict the propensity to engage in both attitudinal and behavioral change.
   b) The greater the dissonance after it has been moderated by importance, choice, and reward factors---the greater the pressure to reduce it.

D. The Attitude-Behavior Relationship
1. The early research on the relationship between attitudes and behavior assumed a casual relationship; that is, the attitudes people hold determine what they do.
2. In the late 1960s, however, this assumed relationship between attitudes and behavior (A-B) was challenged by a review of the research.
    a) A reviewer of a number of studies concluded that attitudes were either unrelated to behavior or, at best, only slightly related.
    b) More recent research has demonstrated that there is indeed a measurable relationship if moderating contingency variables are taken into consideration.
3. Concentration on both specific attitudes and specific behaviors improves our chances of finding significant A-B relationships.
    a) The more specific the attitude we are measuring and the more specific we are in identifying a related behavior, the greater the probability that we can show a relationship between A and B.
4. Social constraints also moderate behavior.
    a) Discrepancies between attitudes and behavior may occur because the social pressures on the individual to behave in a certain way are exceptionally powerful.
5. Of course, A and B may be at odds for other reasons.
    a) Individuals can and do hold contradictory attitudes at a given time.

III. PERCEPTION
A. Introduction
1. Perception is a process by which individuals organize and interpret their sensory impressions in order to give meaning to their environment.
2. Research consistently demonstrates that different individuals may look at the same thing yet perceive it differently.

B. Factors Influencing Perception
1. A number of factors operate to shape and sometimes distort perception.
2. These factors can reside in the perceiver, in the object or target being perceived, or in the context of the situation in which the perception is made.
3. Personal characteristics affecting perception include attitudes, personality, motives, interests, past experiences, and expectations.
4. Characteristics of the target being observed can affect what is perceived.
5. Because targets are not looked at in isolation, the relationship of a target to its background influences perception as does our tendency to group similar or nearby objects together.

C. Attribution Theory
1. Much of the research on perception is directed at inanimate objects.
    a) OB is concern with human perception.
    b) Our perception and judgment of a person's actions will be significantly influenced by the assumptions we make about that person's internal state.
2. Attribution theory develops explanations of how we judge people differently depending on what meaning we attribute to a given behavior.
3. The theory suggests that when we observe an individual's behavior, we attempt to determine whether it was internally or externally caused.
    a) That determination depends on three factors: (1) distinctiveness, (2) consensus, and (3) consistency.
    b) Internally caused behaviors are believed to be under the personal control of the individual.

c) Externally caused behavior results from outside causes; that is, the person is seen as forced into the behavior by the situation.
4. Distinctiveness refers to whether an individual displays different behaviors in different situations.
   a) What we want to know is whether this behavior is unusual.
   b) If it is, the observer is likely to give the behavior an external attribution.
   c) If this action is not unique, it will probably be judged as internal.
5. Consensus. If everyone who is faced with a similar situation responds in the same way, we can say the behavior shows consensus.
   a) From an attribution perspective, if consensus is high, you would be expected to give an external attribution to the employee's tardiness.
   b) if other employees who took the same route made it to work on time, you would conclude the tardiness had an internal cause.
6. Consistency. Does the person respond the same way over time?
   a) The more consistent the behavior, the more the observer is inclined to attribute it to internal causes.
7. We look at actions and judge them within their situational context.
   a) If you have a reputation as a good student yet fail one test in a course, the instructor is likely to disregard the poor exam.
   b) Why? He or she will attribute the cause of this unusual performance to external conditions.
8. Another important finding from attribution theory is that errors or biases distort attributions.
   a) There is substantial evidence that when we judge the behavior of other people, we tend to underestimate the influence of external factors and overestimate the influence of internal or personal factors.
      (1) This is called the fundamental attribution error.
   b) Individuals also tend to attribute their own successes to internal factors such as ability or effort while putting the blame for failure on external factors such as luck.
      (1) This is called the self-serving bias and suggests that feedback provided to employees in performance reviews will be predictably distorted by recipients depending on whether it is positive or negative.

D. Shortcuts to Judging Others
1. Making judgments about others is done all the time by people in organizations.
   a) To make the task easier, individuals take shortcuts.
2. Individuals cannot assimilate all they observe, so they use selectivity.
   a) Selective perception allows us to "speed read" others but not without the risk of drawing an inaccurate picture.
3. Assumed similarity, or the "like me' effect, results in an individual's perception of others being influenced more by what the observer is like than by what the person being observed is actually like.
4. When we judge someone on the basis of our perception of the group to which he or she belongs, we are using the shortcut called stereotyping.
5. When we draw a general impression about an individual on the basis of a single characteristic such as intelligence, sociability, or appearance, a halo effect is operating.

IV. LEARNING

A. Introduction
1. Almost all complex human behavior is learned. If we want to explain, predict, or control behavior, we need to understand how people learn.

2. A more accurate definition of learning is any relatively permanent change in behavior that occurs as a result of experience.
   a) Exhibit 2-4 summarizes the learning process.
3. First, learning helps us adapt to, and master, our environment.
   a) By changing our behavior to accommodate changing conditions, we become responsible citizens and productive employees.
4. Learning is built upon the law of effect, which says that behavior is a function of its consequences.
   a) Behavior that is followed by a favorable consequence tends to be repeated; behavior followed by an unfavorable consequence tends not to be repeated.
   b) Consequence, in this terminology, refers to anything a person considers rewarding (i.e., money, praise, promotions, a smile).
5. Two theories, or explanations, of how we learn.
   a) Shaping
   b) Modeling
6. When learning takes place in graduated steps, it is shaped.
   a) Much of our learning has been done by shaping.
   b) When we speak of "learning by mistakes," we are referring to shaping. We try, we fail, and we try again.
7. In addition, much of what we have learned is the result of observing others and modeling our behavior after them.
   a) Modeling can produce complex behavioral changes quite rapidly.

V. IMPLICATIONS FOR MANAGERS

A. Introduction

1. Exhibit 2-5 summarizes the discussion of individual behavior.
   a) Although they are not permanently fixed, an employee's values, attitudes, and personality are essentially givens at the time he or she enters an organization.
   b) Also added ability to our model to acknowledge that an individual's behavior is influenced by the talents and skills that person holds when he or she joins the organization.

B. Values

1. Knowledge of an individual's value system can provide insight into his or her attitudes.
2. Given that people's values differ, managers can use the Rokeach Value Survey to evaluate job applicants and determine if their values align with the dominant values of the organization.
   a) An employee's performance and satisfaction are likely to be higher if his or her values fit well with the organization.
3. Managers are more likely to appreciate, evaluate positively, and allocate rewards to employees who "fit in," and employees are more likely to be satisfied if they perceive that they do "fit in."

C. Attitudes

1. Managers should be interested in their employees' attitudes because attitudes influence behavior.
2. Research on the satisfaction-productivity relationship suggests that the goal of making employees happy on the assumption that doing so will lead to high productivity is probably misdirected.
   a) Managers would get better results by directing their attention primarily to what will help employees become more productive.

3. Managers should also be aware that employees will try to reduce cognitive dissonance.
    a) If employees are required to engage in activities that appear inconsistent to them or are at odds with their attitudes, the pressures to reduce the resulting dissonance are lessened when the employee perceives the dissonance as externally imposed and thus beyond his or her control or if the rewards are significant enough to offset the dissonance.

D. Perception
1. Managers need to recognize that their employees react to perceptions, not to reality.
2. Employees naturally organize and interpret what they see; inherent in this process is the potential for perceptual distortion.
3. Managers need to pay close attention to how employees perceive both their jobs and management practices.

E. Learning
1. The issue is whether managers are going to let employee learning occur randomly or whether they are going to manage learning--through the rewards they allocate and the examples they set.
2. If marginal employees are rewarded with pay raises and promotions, they will have little reason to change their behavior.
3. Similarly, managers should realize that employees will look to them as models.

SUMMARY

1 The dominant values in today's workforce vary with the work cohort the individual belongs to: Protestant work ethic, existential, pragmatic, or generation X. Exhibit 2-2 outlines the values for each group.

2 Job satisfaction refers to an individual's general attitude toward his or her job. There has been a lot of discussion about job satisfaction and productivity. The early views were "a happy worker is a productive worker." A more careful analysis indicates that if satisfaction does have a positive effect on productivity, that effect is fairly small. Currently, on the basis of a comprehensive review of the evidence, it appears that productivity is more likely to lead to satisfaction rather than the other way around.

3 Cognitive dissonance occurs when there are inconsistencies between two or more of a person's attitudes or between a person's behavior and attitudes. The theory of cognitive dissonance suggests that people seek to minimize dissonance and the discomfort it causes. A person's desire to reduce dissonance is determined by the importance of the elements creating the dissonance, the degree of influence the individual believes he or she has over the elements, and the rewards that may be involved in dissonance.

4 Early research on the relationship between attitudes and behavior assumed a casual relationship; that is, the attitudes people hold determine what they do. In the late 1960s a reviewer of a number of studies concluded that attitudes were either unrelated to behavior or, at best, only slightly related. More recent research has demonstrated that there is indeed a measurable relationship if moderating contingency variables are taken into consideration.

5 Two people can see the same thing and interpret it differently because a number of factors operate to shape and sometimes distort perception. These factors can reside in the perceiver, in the object or target being perceived, or in the context of the situation in which the perception is made. Personal characteristics affecting perception include attitudes, personality, motives, interests, past experiences, and expectations. Characteristics of the target being observed can also affect what is perceived.

6 Attribution theory develops explanations of how we judge people differently depending on what meaning we attribute to a given behavior. The theory suggests that when we observe an individual's behavior, we attempt to determine whether it was internally or externally caused and that

determination depends on three factors: (1) distinctiveness, (2) consensus, and (3) consistency. Another important finding from attribution theory is that errors or biases distort attributions. This is called the fundamental attribution error.

7 Almost all complex human behavior is learned. If we want to explain, predict, or control behavior, we need to understand how people learn. An accurate definition of learning is any relatively permanent change in behavior that occurs as a result of experience. Exhibit 2-4 summarizes the learning process.

DISCUSSION QUESTIONS

1 What is the Rokeach Value Survey?
Answer - The Rokeach Value Survey was developed by Milton Rokeach. The RVS consists of two sets of values, with each set containing 18 individual value items. One set, terminal values, refers to desirable end-states of existence. These are the goals that a person would like to achieve during his or her lifetime. The other set, instrumental values, refers to preferable modes of behavior or means of achieving the terminal value. Exhibit 2-1 gives common examples for each of these sets.

2 What are the dominant values in today's workforce as segmented by work cohort and why is understanding them important for managers?
Answer - A four-stage model can be used to show the unique values of the different "workforces." Exhibit 2-2 shows how employees can be segmented by the era in which they entered the work force. Workers who grew up influenced by the Great Depression, etc., who entered the workforce from the mid-1940s through the late-1950s: believe the Protestant work ethic. Once hired, they tend to be loyal to their employer, are likely to place the greatest importance on a comfortable life and family security. Employees who entered the workforce during the 1960s through the mid-1970s were influenced heavily by John F. Kennedy, etc. They brought with them the "hippie ethic" and existential philosophy, with more concern for the quality of their lives than with the amount of money and possessions they can accumulate, a desire for autonomy, and their loyalty is towards themselves. Individuals who entered the workforce from the mid-1970s through the mid-1980s reflect the society's return to more traditional values but with far greater emphasis on achievement and material success. Strongly influenced by Reagan conservatism, etc., these workers are pragmatists who believe that ends can justify means, organizations that employ them are merely vehicles for their careers, and their terminal values such as a sense of accomplishment and social recognition rank high with them. Generation X has been shaped by globalization, the fall of communism, MTV, etc. They value flexibility, life options, and job satisfaction, family and relationships are very important to this cohort, money is important as an indicator of career performance, and they are willing to trade off salary increases, rifles, security, and promotions for increased leisure time and expanded lifestyle options. An understanding that individuals' values differ but tend to reflect the societal values of the period in which they grew up can be a valuable aid in explaining and predicting behavior.

3 Describe the relationship between satisfaction and productivity.
Answer - The relationship of job satisfaction and productivity has attracted a lot of attention and interest. The early views were "a happy worker is a productive worker." A more careful analysis indicates that if satisfaction does have a positive effect on productivity, that effect is fairly small. The introduction of moderating variables, however, has improved the relationship. Currently, on the basis of a comprehensive review of the evidence, it appears that productivity is more likely to lead to satisfaction rather than the other way around.

4 Explain the theory of cognitive dissonance and its implications for organizations.
Answer - Cognitive dissonance occurs when there are inconsistencies between two or more of a person's attitudes or between a person's behavior and attitudes. The theory of cognitive dissonance suggests that people seek to minimize dissonance and the discomfort it causes. A person's desire to reduce dissonance is determined by the importance of the elements creating the dissonance, the

degree of influence the individual believes he or she has over the elements, and the rewards that may be involved in dissonance. If the elements creating the dissonance are relatively unimportant, the pressure to correct this imbalance will be low. The degree of influence that individuals believe they have over the elements involved will have an impact on how they will react to the dissonance. If they perceive the dissonance to be an uncontrollable result--something that they can't change--they are not likely to be receptive to attitude change. Rewards also influence the degree to which individuals are motivated to reduce dissonance. The tension inherent in high dissonance may be reduced if accompanied by a high reward. The organizational implications are: it can help to predict the propensity to engage in both attitudinal and behavioral change and the greater the dissonance after it has been moderated by importance, choice, and reward factors---the greater the pressure to reduce it.

5 Summarize the relationship between attitudes and behavior.
Answer - Early research on the relationship between attitudes and behavior assumed a casual relationship; that is, the attitudes people hold determine what they do. In the late 1960s, however, this assumed relationship between attitudes and behavior (A-B) was challenged by a review of the research. More recent research has demonstrated that there is indeed a measurable relationship if moderating contingency variables are taken into consideration. Concentration on both specific attitudes and specific behaviors improves our chances of finding significant A-B relationships. The more specific the attitude we are measuring and the more specific we are in identifying a related behavior, the greater the probability that we can show a relationship between A and B. Social constraints also moderate behavior. Discrepancies between attitudes and behavior may occur because the social pressures on the individual to behave in a certain way are exceptionally powerful.

6 Explain how two people can see the same thing and interpret it differently.
Answer - Perception is a process by which individuals organize and interpret their sensory impressions in order to give meaning to their environment. Research consistently demonstrates that different individuals may look at the same thing yet perceive it differently. There are a number of factors that influence perception and sometimes distort perception. These factors can reside in the perceiver, in the object or target being perceived, or in the context of the situation in which the perception is made. Personal characteristics affecting perception include attitudes, personality, motives, interests, past experiences, and expectations. Characteristics of the target being observed can affect what is perceived. Because targets are not looked at in isolation, the relationship of a target to its background influences perception as does our tendency to group similar or nearby objects together.

7 Summarize attribution theory.
Answer - Attribution theory develops explanations of how we judge people differently depending on what meaning we attribute to a given behavior. The theory suggests that when we observe an individual's behavior, we attempt to determine whether it was internally or externally caused. That determination depends on three factors: (1) distinctiveness, (2) consensus, and (3) consistency.

8 Explain the various "shortcuts" we use to evaluate people and their potential problems.
Answer - Making judgments about others is done all the time by people in organizations. To make the task easier, individuals take shortcuts. Individuals cannot assimilate all they observe, so they use selectivity. Selective perception allows us to "speed read" others but not without the risk of drawing an inaccurate picture. Assumed similarity, or the "like me' effect, results in an individual's perception of others being influenced more by what the observer is like than by what the person being observed is actually like. When we judge someone on the basis of our perception of the group to which he or she belongs, we are using the shortcut called stereotyping. When we draw a general impression about an individual on the basis of a single characteristic such as intelligence, sociability, or appearance, a halo effect is operating.

9 Explain the learning process.
Answer - Almost all complex human behavior is learned. If we want to explain, predict, or control behavior, we need to understand how people learn. A more accurate definition of learning is any relatively permanent change in behavior that occurs as a result of experience. Exhibit 2-4 summarizes the learning process. First, learning helps us adapt to, and master, our environment. Learning is built upon the law of effect, which says that behavior is a function of its consequences. There are two theories of how we learn; through shaping and through modeling. When learning takes place in graduated steps, it is shaped. When we speak of "learning by mistakes," we are referring to shaping. We try, we fail, and we try again. In addition, much of what we have learned is the result of observing others and modeling our behavior after them. Modeling can produce complex behavioral changes quite rapidly.

EXERCISE

Interviewing Cohorts

The purpose of this exercise is to show to the students how much work values really vary. The students will develop an interview instrument and use it to interview 3-5 people who are clearly in different age categories, i.e., work cohorts.

1. Put students into small groups.
2. As separate groups, brainstorm questions for an interview regarding job satisfaction, life goals, etc.
3. As a class discuss the questions and ideas and narrow them to a list of 5-10 questions, something that could be administered in an oral interview in 30 minutes.
4. Each group should assign one member to each cohort.
   - Workers who grew up influenced by the Great Depression, etc., who entered the workforce from the mid-1940s through the late-1950s.
   - Employees who entered the workforce during the 1960s through the mid-1970s were influenced heavily by John F. Kennedy, etc.
   - Individuals who entered the workforce from the mid-1970s through the mid-1980s reflect the society's return to more traditional values but with far greater emphasis on achievement and material success.
   - Generation X has been shaped by globalization, the fall of communism, MTV, etc.
5. The interviewer should identify an individual and conduct an interview using the questionnaire created in class.
   - Students might consider scouting the local McDonald's or Wal-Mart. These types of businesses hire across the age spectrum and would make it easier to find candidates to interview.
6. Groups should meet and consolidate their information into a report, either a 10 minute oral or a 3-5 page written report.
   - As part of their report they should discuss a practical implication for managing an individual from each of the cohorts.
   - How would they manage them differently based on the information they've found?
7. Groups should present and discuss their findings in class.
   - Students will find information that will support and conflict with what the text says.
   - Students will discover that workers have very different views of the nature of work, life goals, etc.

CHAPTER 3 - PERSONALITY AND EMOTIONS

CHAPTER OBJECTIVES

After reading this chapter, students should be able to

1 Describe the eight categories in the MBTI personality framework.
2 Identify the "Big Five" personality variables and their relationship to behavior in organizations.
3 Describe the impact of job typology on the personality-job performance relationship.
4 Differentiate felt from displayed emotions.
5 Identify the six universal emotions.
6 Explain whether it is possible for a person to be emotionless.
7 Describe ways in which emotions influence work-related behavior

LECTURE OUTLINE

I. PERSONALITY

A. Introduction

1. When we describe people in terms of characteristics such as quiet, passive, loud, etc., we are categorizing them in terms of personality traits.
2. An individual's personality, therefore, is the combination of psychological traits we use to classify that person.
3. Sixteen primary personality traits have been identified.
    a) See Exhibit 3-1.
    b) Each trait is bipolar--it has two extremes.
    c) These sixteen traits have been found to be steady and constant sources of behavior, allowing prediction of an individual's behavior in specific situations.

B. The Myers-Briggs Type Indicator

1. One of the most widely used personality frameworks.
2. Essentially a 100-question personality test that asks people how they usually feel or act in particular situations.
3. Individuals are classified as:
    a) extroverted or introverted (E or I).
    b) sensing or intuitive (S or N).
    c) thinking or feeling (T or F).
    d) perceiving or judging (P or J).
4. These classifications are then combined into sixteen personality types.
    a) A recent book that profiled thirteen contemporary business people who created super-successful firms such as Apple Computer, Federal Express, Honda Motors, Microsoft, Price Club, and Sony found all thirteen to be intuitive thinkers (NTs).
    b) This finding is particularly interesting because intuitive thinkers represent only about five percent of the population.
5. More than two million people a year take the MBTI in the United States alone.
6. There is no hard evidence that the MBTI is a valid measure of personality. But lack of such evidence does not seem to deter organizations from using it.

C. The Big-Five Model

1. An impressive body of research supports that five basic personality dimensions underlie all others.
2. Factors in the Big-Five Model are:
    a) Extroversion--sociable, talkative, assertive.
    b) Agreeableness---Good-natured, cooperative, and trusting.

c) Conscientiousness--Responsible, dependable, persistent, and achievement oriented.
d) Emotional stability--Calm, enthusiastic, secure (positive) as opposed to tense, nervous, depressed, and insecure (negative).
e) Openness to experience--Imaginative, artistically sensitive, and intellectual.

3. Research on the Big Five found important relationships between these personality dimensions and job performance.
   a) Five categories of occupations were examined: professionals (including engineers, architects, accountants, attorneys), police, managers, sales, and semiskilled and skilled employees.
   b) Job performance was defined in terms of performance ratings, training proficiency (performance during training programs), and personnel data such as salary level.
   c) Conscientiousness predicted job performance for all five occupational groups.
   d) For the other personality dimensions, predictability depended on both the performance criterion and occupational group.

D. Other Key Personality Attributes

1. Six additional personality attributes have been identified that appear to have more direct relevance for explaining and predicting behavior in organizations.
   a) Locus of control
   b) Authoritarianism
   c) Machiavellianism
   d) Self-monitoring
   e) Risk propensity
   f) Type A personality
2. Locus of Control
   a) Some people believe they are masters of their own fate.
   b) Other people see themselves as pawns of fate.
   c) Locus of control in the first case is internal, those who see their life as being controlled by outsiders are externals.
      (1) Employees who rate high in externality are less satisfied with their jobs, more alienated from the work setting, and less involved in their jobs than are internals.
3. Authoritarianism is the belief that there should be status and power differences among people in organizations.
   a) The extremely high authoritarian personality is intellectually rigid, judgmental of others, deferential to those above and exploitative of those below, distrustful, and resistant to change.
4. Machiavellianism
   a) Is close to authoritarianism, named after Niccolo Machiavelli, who wrote in the sixteenth-century on how to gain and use power.
   b) An individual exhibiting strong Machiavellian tendencies is manipulative, maintains emotional distance, and believes that ends can justify means.
      (1) "If it works, use it" is consistent with a high Mach perspective.
   c) High Machs are more likely to engage in behavior that is ethically questionable than are low Machs.
   d) In jobs that require bargaining skills or where there are substantial rewards for winning, high Machs will be productive.
5. Self-monitoring
   a) Some people are much better than others at adjusting their behavior to changing situations.
   b) High self-monitors are sensitive to external cues and can behave differently in different situations.

        (1) They are chameleons able to change to fit the situation and to hide their true selves.
    c) On the other hand, low self-monitors are consistent.
        (1) They display their true dispositions and attitudes in every situation.
    d) High self-monitors tend to pay closer attention to the behavior of others and are capable of conforming.
    e) High self-monitors also tend to be better at playing organizational politics.
6. Risk propensity
    a) Individuals with a high-risk propensity make more rapid decisions and use less information in making their choices than individuals with low risk propensity.
7. Type A personality
    a) Excessively competitive and always seem to be experiencing a chronic sense of urgency.
    b) Type A's are characterized by an incessant struggle to achieve more and more in less and less time.
    c) They are impatient, cope poorly with leisure time, and create a life of self-imposed deadlines.
        (1) In the North American culture, such characteristics tend to be highly prized and positively associated with ambition and the successful acquisition of material goods.
    d) In terms of work behavior, Type A's are fast workers.
        (1) They emphasize quantity over quality.
        (2) Type A's are rarely creative.

E. Personality and National Culture
1. There are certainly no common personality types for a given country.
2. Yet a country's culture should influence the dominant personality characteristics of its population.
    a) Let's build this case by looking at two personality attributes--locus of control and the Type A personality.
3. Cultures differ in terms of people's relationship to their environment.
    a) In North America, people believe that they can dominate their environment.
    b) People in other societies, such as Middle Eastern countries, believe that life is essentially preordained.
        (1) Notice the close parallel to internal and external locus of control.
4. The prevalence of Type A personalities
    a) There will be more in capitalistic countries, where achievement and material success are highly valued.
        (1) It is estimated that about 50 percent of the North American population is Type A.
        (2) In cultures such as Sweden and France, where materialism is less revered, we would predict a smaller proportion of Type A personalities.

F. Matching Personalities and Jobs
1. Efforts have been made to match personalities with the proper jobs.
2. The most researched personality-job-fit theory is the six-personality-types model.
3. This model states that an employee's satisfaction with and propensity to leave his or her job depend on the degree to which the individual's personality matches his or her occupational environment.
    a) The six major personality types are listed in Exhibit 3-2, along with their compatible occupations.
4. A Vocational Preference Inventory questionnaire

a) 160 occupational titles
b) Respondents indicate which of these occupations they like or dislike, and their answers are used to form personality profiles.
c) Research strongly supports the hexagonal diagram in Exhibit 3-3.

5. The theory argues that satisfaction is highest and turnover lowest where personality and occupation are in agreement.

II. EMOTIONS

A. Introduction

1. Example of a 37-year-old U.S. postal worker in Milwaukee shooting co-workers.
2. Emotions are an important factor in employee behavior.
3. Until very recently, the topic of emotions had been given little or no attention within the field of OB.
   a) The myth of rationality was one hindrance.
      (1) Since the late nineteenth century, organizations have been essentially designed with the objective of trying to control emotions.
      (2) It was believed that a well-run organization was one that successfully eliminated frustration, anger, love, hate, joy, grief and similar feelings.
   b) The second factor that acted to keep emotions out of OB was the belief that emotions of any kind were disruptive.
      (1) When emotions were considered, the discussion focused on strong negative emotions--especially anger--which interfered with an employee's ability to do his or her job effectively.
      (2) Emotions were rarely viewed as being constructive or able to stimulate performance-enhancing behaviors.

B. What Are Emotions?

1. Need to clarify three terms that are closely intertwined--affect, emotions, and moods.
2. Affect is a generic term that covers a broad range of feelings that people experience.
   a) Its an umbrella concept that encompasses both emotions and moods.
3. Emotions are intense feelings that are directed at someone or something.
4. Moods are feelings that tend to be less intense than emotions and they lack a contextual stimulus.
5. Emotions are reactions to an object, not a trait.
   a) They are object specific.
   b) Moods, on the other hand, are not directed at an object.
   c) Emotions can turn into moods when you lose focus on the contextual object.
6. Emotional labor
   a) Most jobs also require emotional labor.
   b) This is when an employee expresses organizationally desired emotions during interpersonal transactions.
   c) The concept was originally developed in relation to service jobs.
   d) Today, the concept of emotional labor seems relevant to almost every job.

C. Felt vs. Displayed Emotions

1. Emotional labor creates dilemmas for employees when their job requires them to exhibit emotions that are incongruous with their actual feelings.
2. Emotions can be separated into felt versus displayed.
   a) Felt emotions are an individual's actual emotions.
   b) In contrast, displayed emotions are those that are organizationally required and considered appropriate in a given job.

(1) They're not innate; they're learned.

3. The key point here is that felt and displayed emotions are often different.
   a) Many people have problems working with others simply because they naively assume that the emotions they see others display are what those others actually feel.

D. The Six Universal Emotions

1. Research has identified six universal emotions: anger, fear, sadness, happiness, disgust, and surprise.
   a) Exhibit 3-4 illustrates that these six emotions can be conceptualized as existing along a continuum.
   b) The closer any two emotions are to each other on this continuum, the more likely people are to confuse them.
2. These six basic emotions surface in the workplace.

E. Can People Be Emotionless?

1. Some people have severe difficulty in expressing their emotions and understanding the emotions of others.
   a) Psychologists call this alexithymia (which is Greek for "lack of emotion").
   b) People who suffer from alexithymia rarely cry and are often seen by others as bland and cold.
   c) Their own feelings make them uncomfortable, and they are not able to discriminate among their different emotions.
   d) They are often at a complete loss to understand what others around them feel.
2. People who suffer from alexithymia are not necessarily poor work performers.
   a) People who lack emotion need to be in jobs that require little or no emotional labor.

F. Gender and Emotions

1. Its widely assumed that women are more "in touch" with their feelings than men.
   a) The evidence does confirm differences between men and women when it comes to emotional reactions and ability to read others.
2. Women show greater emotional expression than men.
   a) They experience emotions more intensely and they display more frequent expressions of both positive and negative emotions, except anger.
   b) They have more comfort in expressing emotions.
   c) They are better at reading nonverbal cues than are men.
3. Three possible answers to explain these differences.
   a) The different ways men and women have been socialized.
   b) Women may have more innate ability to read others and present their emotions than men do.
   c) Women may have a greater need for social approval and, thus, a higher propensity to show positive emotions like happiness.

G. Emotions and National Culture

1. Cultural norms in the United States dictate that employees in service organizations should smile and act friendly when interacting with customers.
2. But this norm does not apply worldwide.
   a) In Israel, smiling by supermarket cashiers is seen as a sign of inexperience, so cashiers are encouraged to look somber.
   b) In Moslem cultures, smiling is frequently taken as a sign of sexual attraction, so women are socialized not to smile at men.

3. This illustrates the need to consider cultural factors as influencing what is or is not considered as emotionally appropriate.
    a) There tends to be high agreement on what emotions mean within cultures but not between cultures.

H. OB Applications
1. Ability and Selection
    a) People who know their own emotions and are good at reading others' emotions may be more effective in their jobs.
    b) Emotional intelligence (EI) refers to an assortment of noncognitive skills, capabilities, and competencies that influence a person's ability to succeed in coping with environmental demands and pressures.
    c) Its composed of five dimensions:
        (1) Self-awareness--The ability to know what you are feeling.
        (2) Self-management--The ability to manage one's own emotions and impulses.
        (3) Self-motivation--The ability to persist in the face of setbacks and failures.
        (4) Empathy--The ability to sense how others are feeling.
        (5) Social skills--The ability to handle the emotions of others.
2. EI may play an important role in job performance.
    a) The implications from the initial evidence on EI is that employers should consider it as a factor in selection, especially in jobs that demand a high degree of social interaction.
3. Decision-Making
    a) Traditional approaches to the study of decision making in organizations have emphasized rationality.
    b) Its naive to assume that decision choices aren't influenced by one's feelings at a particular moment.
    c) You can improve your understanding of decision making by considering the heart as well as "the head." People use emotions as well as rational and intuitive processes in making decisions.
4. Motivation
    a) Like decision making, the dominant approaches to the study of motivation reflect an over rationalized view of individuals.
    b) Motivation theories basically propose that individuals are motivated to the degree they expect to receive desired outcomes.
    c) People's perceptions and calculations of situations are filled with emotional content that significantly influences how much effort they exert.
5. Leadership
    a) The ability to lead others is a fundamental quality sought by organizations.
    b) Almost all effective leaders rely on the expression of feelings to help convey their messages.
    c) Corporate executives know that emotional content is critical if employees are to buy into their vision of their company's future and accept change.
        (1) By arousing emotions and linking them to an appealing vision, leaders increase the likelihood that managers and employees alike will accept change.
6. Interpersonal Conflict
    a) Whenever conflicts arise, you can be fairly certain that emotions are also surfacing.
    b) A manager's success in trying to resolve conflicts, in fact, is often largely due to his or her ability to identify the emotional elements in the conflict.

III. IMPLICATIONS FOR MANAGERS

A. Personality

1. The importance of a manager's understanding of personality differences probably lies in selection.
2. You are likely to have higher-performing and more-satisfied employees if consideration is given to matching personality types with compatible jobs.
3. In addition, managers can expect that individuals with an external locus of control may be less satisfied with their jobs than internals, and also that they may be less willing to accept responsibility for their actions.

B. Emotions

1. Emotions are a natural part of an individual's make-up.
2. Managers often err by ignoring the emotional elements in organizational behavior and assessing individual behavior as if it were completely rational.
3. As one consultant aptly put it, "You can not divorce emotions from the workplace because you can not divorce emotions from people."
4. Managers who understand the role of emotions will significantly improve their ability to explain and predict individual behavior.
5. Emotions effect job performance.
   a) They can hinder performance, especially negative emotions.
   b) Emotions can also enhance performance in two ways.
      (1) Emotions can increase arousal levels, thus acting as motivators to higher performance.
      (2) Emotional labor recognizes that feelings can be part of a job's required behavior. For instance, the ability to effectively manage emotions in leadership and sales positions may be critical to success in those positions.

SUMMARY

1 The MBTI personality framework is one of the most widely used personality frameworks. It is essentially a 100-question personality test that asks people how they usually feel or act in particular situations. The results classify people into sixteen personality types.

2 An impressive body of research supports that five basic personality dimensions underlie all others. This "Big Five" Model has five key factors: Extroversion--sociable, talkative, assertive, agreeableness---Good-natured, cooperative, and trusting, conscientiousness--Responsible, dependable, persistent, and achievement oriented, emotional stability--Calm, enthusiastic, secure (positive) as opposed to tense, nervous, depressed, and insecure (negative), and openness to experience--Imaginative, artistically sensitive, and intellectual.

3 Six additional personality attributes have been identified that appear to have more direct relevance for explaining and predicting behavior in organizations: locus of control, authoritarianism, machiavellianism, self-monitoring, risk propensity, and type A personality.

4 Research shows that national culture does have some impact on personality. While there are no common personality types for a given country a country's culture should influence the dominant personality characteristics of its population.

5 Efforts have been made to match personalities with the proper jobs. The most researched personality-job-fit theory is the six-personality-types model. This model states that an employee's satisfaction with and propensity to leave his or her job depend on the degree to which the individual's personality matches his or her occupational environment. The six major personality types are listed in Exhibit 3-2, along with their compatible occupations.

6 Until very recently, the topic of emotions had been given little or no attention within the field of OB. The myth of rationality was one hindrance. The second factor that acted to keep emotions out of OB was the belief that emotions of any kind were disruptive. To understand emotions we need to

understand three terms that are closely intertwined--affect, emotions, and moods. Emotions are reactions to an object, not a trait. Research has identified six universal emotions: anger, fear, sadness, happiness, disgust, and surprise.

7 Some people have severe difficulty in expressing their emotions and understanding the emotions of others. Psychologists call this alexithymia (which is Greek for "lack of emotion"). People who suffer from alexithymia rarely cry and are often seen by others as bland and cold.

8 It is widely assumed that women are more "in touch" with their feelings than men. The evidence does confirm differences between men and women when it comes to emotional reactions and ability to read others. Women show greater emotional expression than men.

9 Cultural norms as to the appropriate expression of emotion vary across cultures. There tends to be high agreement on what emotions mean within cultures but not between cultures.

10 These various findings regarding emotions can be applied in a number of organizational behavioral contexts: selection, decision-making, motivation, leadership, and in managing interpersonal conflict.

DISCUSSION QUESTIONS

1 Describe the eight categories in the MBTI personality framework.
Answer - The MBTI is essentially a 100-question personality test that asks people how they usually feel or act in particular situations. Individuals are classified as: extroverted or introverted (E or I), sensing or intuitive (S or N), thinking or feeling (T or F), perceiving or judging (P or J). These classifications are then combined into sixteen personality types.

2 What is the value of the "Big Five" personality model for organizations?
Answer - The Big-Five model has five key factors: Extroversion--sociable, talkative, assertive, agreeableness---Good-natured, cooperative, and trusting, conscientiousness--Responsible, dependable, persistent, and achievement oriented, Emotional stability--calm, enthusiastic, secure (positive) as opposed to tense, nervous, depressed, and insecure (negative), and openness to experience--Imaginative, artistically sensitive, and intellectual. Research on the Big Five found important relationships between these personality dimensions and job performance. Five categories of occupations were examined: professionals (including engineers, architects, accountants, attorneys), police, managers, sales, and semiskilled and skilled employees. Job performance was defined in terms of performance ratings, training proficiency (performance during training programs), and personnel data such as salary level. Conscientiousness predicted job performance for all five occupational groups. For the other personality dimensions, predictability depended on both the performance criterion and occupational group.

3 Identify and describe the six additional personality attributes that appear to have more direct relevance for explaining and predicting behavior in organizations than other measures.
Answer - Locus of control--Some people believe they are masters of their own fate. Other people see themselves as pawns of fate. Locus of control in the first case is internal, those who see their life as being controlled by outsiders are externals. Authoritarianism is the belief that there should be status and power differences among people in organizations. Machiavellianism is close to authoritarianism. An individual exhibiting strong Machiavellian tendencies is manipulative, maintains emotional distance, and believes that ends can justify means. Self-monitoring--some people are much better than others at adjusting their behavior to changing situations. High self-monitors are sensitive to external cues and can behave differently in different situations. On the other hand, low self-monitors are consistent. They display their true dispositions and attitudes in every situation. Risk propensity--individuals with a high risk propensity make more rapid decisions and use less information in making their choices than individuals with low risk propensity. Type A personality--excessively competitive and always seem to be experiencing a chronic sense of urgency. Type A's are characterized by an incessant struggle to achieve more and more in less and less time.

4 What is the relationship of national culture and individual personality?
Answer - Research shows that national culture does have some impact on personality. While there are no common personality types for a given country a country's culture should influence the dominant personality characteristics of its population.

5 What is the value of matching personality with vocation?
Answer - Efforts have been made to match personalities with the proper jobs. The most researched personality-job-fit theory is the six-personality-types model. This model states that an employee's satisfaction with and propensity to leave his or her job depend on the degree to which the individual's personality matches his or her occupational environment. The six major personality types are listed in Exhibit 3-2, along with their compatible occupations.

6 Differentiate felt from displayed emotions.
Answer - Emotional labor creates dilemmas for employees when their job requires them to exhibit emotions that are incongruous with their actual feelings. Emotions can be separated into felt versus displayed. Felt emotions are an individual's actual emotions. In contrast, displayed emotions are those that are organizationally required and considered appropriate in a given job. They are not innate; They are learned. The key point here is that felt and displayed emotions are often different. Many people have problems working with others simply because they naively assume that the emotions they see others display are what those others actually feel.

7 Identify the six universal emotions.
Answer - Research has identified six universal emotions: anger, fear, sadness, happiness, disgust, and surprise. Exhibit 3-4 illustrates that these six emotions can be conceptualized as existing along a continuum. The closer any two emotions are to each other on this continuum, the more likely people are to confuse them.

8 Explain whether it is possible for a person to be emotionless.
Answer - Some people have severe difficulty in expressing their emotions and understanding the emotions of others. Psychologists call this alexithymia (which is Greek for "lack of emotion"). People who suffer from alexithymia rarely cry and are often seen by others as bland and cold. Their own feelings make them uncomfortable, and they are not able to discriminate among their different emotions. People who suffer from alexithymia are not necessarily poor work performers they simply need to be in jobs that require little or no emotional labor.

9 What is the relationship of national culture and the expression of emotions?
Answer - Cultural norms in the United States dictate that employees in service organizations should smile and act friendly when interacting with customers. But this norm does not apply worldwide. In Israel, smiling by supermarket cashiers is seen as a sign of inexperience, so cashiers are encouraged to look somber. This illustrates the need to consider cultural factors as influencing what is or is not considered as emotionally appropriate. There tends to be high agreement on what emotions mean within cultures but not between cultures.

10 Describe ways in which emotions influence work-related behavior.
Answer - There are a number of OB applications of the research on emotions. Selection--People who know their own emotions and are good at reading others' emotions may be more effective in their jobs. Emotional intelligence (EI) refers to an assortment of noncognitive skills, capabilities, and competencies that influence a person's ability to succeed in coping with environmental demands and pressures. Decision-Making--Traditional approaches to the study of decision making in organizations have emphasized rationality. You can improve your understanding of decision making by considering the heart as well as the head. People use emotions as well as rational and intuitive processes in

making decisions. Motivation--Motivation theories basically propose that individuals are motivated to the degree they expect to receive desired outcomes. People's perceptions and calculations of situations are filled with emotional content that significantly influences how much effort they exert. Leadership--The ability to lead others is a fundamental quality sought by organizations. Effective leaders almost all rely on the expression of feelings to help convey their messages. By arousing emotions and linking them to an appealing vision, leaders increase the likelihood that managers and employees alike will accept change. Interpersonal Conflict--Whenever conflicts arise, you can be fairly certain that emotions are also surfacing. A manager's success in trying to resolve conflicts, in fact, is often largely due to his or her ability to identify the emotional elements in the conflict.

EXERCISE

Dyad discussion

The purpose of this exercise is to facilitate understanding between male and female students through the discussion of emotions. This can be done in pairs, in a group of four, half women and half men, or in a "fish bowl," a mixed pair discussing in the center of the class with fellow students watching.

1. Select the partners.
2. Individually they should complete the following questions:
   a. When I graduate I will ____________
   b. When I'm out with my friends having a pizza we talk about _________
   c. The things that make me happy or joyful are ____________
   d. Things that make me angry or sad are ___________
   e. When a professor treats me unfairly I _________
   f. When my parents are unjustly angry with me I ___________
   g. When my girlfriend(boyfriend) is upset I _________
   h. When I'm happy or joyful I ____________
   i. When I'm sad or angry I ___________
3. Once the questions are answered students should come together in their pairs/groups and discuss their answers to the questions.
4. Once they've discussed all the previous questions, using questions h and i. students should discuss how they show these feelings.
5. The students or observers should note how congruent their previous behavior was with what they said about how they manage feelings of joy, sadness, or anger.
6. Coming back together as a class, have volunteers share what they learned. Discuss how their learning, especially in terms of gender, match or disagree with course content.

CHAPTER 4 - BASIC MOTIVATION CONCEPTS

CHAPTER OBJECTIVES

After reading this chapter, you should be able to:

1 Outline the basic motivation process.
2 Describe Maslow's hierarchy of needs theory.
3 Contrast Theory X and Theory Y.
4 Differentiate motivators from hygiene factors.
5 List the characteristics that high achievers prefer in a job.
6 Summarize the types of goals that increase performance.
7 Contrast reinforcement and goal-setting theories.
8 Explain equity theory.
9 Clarify the key relationships in expectancy theory.

LECTURE OUTLINE

I. WHAT IS MOTIVATION?
 A. Definition
  1. May be defined in terms of some outward behavior.
   a) People who are motivated exert a greater effort to perform than those who are not motivated.
  2. A more descriptive but less substantive definition.
   a) Motivation is the willingness to do something and is conditioned by this action's ability to satisfy some need for the individual.
   b) A need, in our terminology, is a physiological or psychological deficiency that makes certain outcomes appear attractive.
   c) The motivation process - Exhibit 4-1.

 B. Needs and drives
  1. An unsatisfied need creates tension, which stimulates drives within the individual.
  2. These drives generate a search for particular goals that, if attained, will satisfy the need and lead to the reduction of tension.
  3. Motivated employees are in a state of tension.
   a) To relieve this tension, they engage in activity.
   b) The greater the tension, the more activity will be needed to bring about relief.

II. EARLY THEORIES OF MOTIVATION
 A. Hierarchy of Needs Theory
  1. The best-known approach to motivation is Abraham Maslow's hierarchy of needs theory.
  2. He hypothesized that every human being has an internal hierarchy of five needs.
   a) Physiological needs--hunger, thirst, shelter, sex, and other bodily needs
   b) Safety needs--security and protection from physical and emotional harm
   c) Social needs--affection, a sense of belonging, acceptance, and friendship
   d) Esteem need--internal factors such as self-respect, autonomy, and achievement and external factors such as status, recognition, and attention
   e) Self-actualization needs--the drive to become what one is capable of becoming; includes growth, achieving one's potential, and self-fulfillment
  3. As each is satisfied, the next need becomes dominant.
   a) See Exhibit 4-2 for the hierarchy.
   b) A substantially satisfied need no longer motivates.
  4. Maslow separated the five needs into higher and lower orders.

a) Physiological and safety needs were lower order and were predominately satisfied externally.
b) Social, esteem, and self-actualization were categorized as higher-order needs and are satisfied internally.
c) The natural conclusion is that, in times of economic plenty, almost all permanently employed workers will have their lower-order needs substantially met.

5. Maslow's need theory has received wide recognition, particularly among practicing managers.
   a) This acceptance is due to the logic and ease with which the theory is intuitively understood.
   b) However, research does not generally validate the theory.
      (1) There is little support for the prediction that need structures are organized along the dimensions proposed.
      (2) Nor does the prediction that the substantial satisfaction of a given need leads to the activation of the next higher need seem true.

B. Theory X and Theory Y

1. Douglas McGregor proposed two distinct views of human beings.
   a) One basically negative, labeled Theory X.
   b) The other basically positive, labeled Theory Y.
2. Theory X--four assumptions
   a) Employees inherently dislike work and, whenever possible, will attempt to avoid it.
   b) Since employees dislike work, they must be coerced, controlled, or threatened with punishment to achieve desired goals.
   c) Employees will shirk responsibilities and seek formal direction whenever possible.
   d) Most workers place security above all other factors associated with work and will display little ambition.
3. Theory Y--four contrasting assumptions
   a) Employees can view work as being as natural as rest or play.
   b) A person who is committed to the objectives will exercise self-direction and self-control.
   c) The average person can learn to accept, and even seek responsibility.
   d) Creativity---that is, the ability to make good decisions--is widely dispersed throughout the population and not necessarily the sole province of those in management.
4. Implications if you accept McGregor's analysis.
   a) Theory X assumes that lower-order needs dominate individuals.
   b) Theory Y assumes that higher-order needs dominate individuals.
5. Unfortunately, no evidence confirms that either set of assumptions is valid.

C. Two-Factor Theory

1. The two-factor theory--motivation-hygiene theory--was proposed by psychologist Frederick Herzberg.
2. Herzberg investigated the question, "What do people want from their jobs?"
3. Research showed people replied significantly differently based on whether they felt good or bad about their jobs.
4. He isolated certain characteristics.
   a) Exhibit 4-3.
   b) Some consistently related to job satisfaction--internal factors--such as advancement, recognition, responsibility, and achievement.

c) Others related to job dissatisfaction--extrinsic factors--such as supervision, pay, company policies, and working conditions.

5. The opposite of satisfaction is not dissatisfaction--removing dissatisfying characteristics from a job does not necessarily make the job satisfying.
   a) Managers who seek to eliminate factors that can create job dissatisfaction will be placating their work force rather than motivating them.
   b) Conditions surrounding the job such as quality of supervision, pay, company policies, etc., were characterized as hygiene factors.
   c) When they are adequate, people will not be dissatisfied; neither will they be satisfied.
   d) To motivate people, Herzberg suggested emphasizing factors associated with the work itself or to outcomes directly derived from it, such as promotional opportunities, opportunities for personal growth, etc.
   e) These are the characteristics that people find intrinsically rewarding.
6. Criticisms of the theory.
   a) The procedure that Herzberg used is limited by its methodology.
   b) The reliability of Herzberg's methodology is questionable.
   c) No overall measure of satisfaction was utilized.
   d) The theory is inconsistent with previous research, it ignores situational variables.
   e) Herzberg assumed a relationship between satisfaction and productivity, but his research methodology looked only at satisfaction, not at productivity.
7. Regardless of criticisms, Herzberg's theory has been widely popularized, and few managers are unfamiliar with his recommendations.

III. CONTEMPORARY THEORIES OF MOTIVATION

A. McClelland's Theory of Needs

1. David McClelland and others have proposed three major relevant motives or needs in the workplace--McClelland's Theory of Needs.
   a) The need for achievement (nAch)--the drive to excel, to achieve in relation to a set of standards, to strive to succeed
   b) The need for power (nPow)--the need to make others behave in a way they would not have behaved otherwise
   c) The need for affiliation (nAff)--the desire for friendly and close interpersonal relationships.
2. Some people have a compelling drive to succeed, but they are striving for personal achievement rather than the rewards of success.
   a) This drive is the need for achievement.
   b) McClelland found that high achievers differentiate themselves from others by their desire to do things better.
   c) They seek situations in which they can attain personal responsibility for finding solutions to problems, receive rapid and unambiguous feedback on their performance, and set moderately challenging goals.
   d) They prefer working at a challenging problem and accepting the personal responsibility for success or failure rather than leaving the outcome to chance or the actions of others.
   e) High achievers perform best when they perceive their probability of success 50--50.
   f) They like to set realistic but difficult goals that require stretching themselves a little.
3. The need for power is the desire to have an impact, to be influential, and to control others.
   a) Individuals high in nPow enjoy being in charge, strive for influence over others, prefer competitive and status-oriented situations, and tend to be more concerned with gaining prestige and influence over others than with effective performance.

4. The third need is the need for affiliation.
   a) This need has received the least attention of researchers.
   b) Individuals with a high nAff strive for friendship, prefer cooperative situations rather than competitive ones, and desire relationships involving a high degree of mutual understanding.
5. All three motives are typically measured through a projective test in which subjects respond to a set of pictures.
6. Predictions can be made on the basis of the relationship between achievement need and job performance.
   a) Individuals with a high need to achieve prefer job situations with personal responsibility, feedback, and an intermediate degree of risk.
      (1) High achievers are successful in entrepreneurial activities such as running their own business, managing a self-contained unit within a large organization, and many sales positions.
   b) A high need to achieve does not necessarily lead to being a good manager.
   c) The needs for affiliation and power tend to be closely related to managerial success.
      (1) The best managers are high in the need for power and low in their need for affiliation.
   d) Employees have been successfully trained to stimulate their achievement need.

B. Goal-Setting Theory
1. Considerable evidence supports goal-setting theory.
2. Intentions--expressed as goals---can be a major source of work motivation.
3. Difficult-to-achieve goals produce a higher level of output than a generalized goal of "do your best."
4. The specificity of the goal itself acts as an internal stimulus.
5. If factors such as ability and acceptance of the goals are held constant, we can also state that the more difficult the goals, the higher the level of performance.
6. If employees have the opportunity to participate in the setting of their own goals, will they try harder?
   a) The evidence is mixed.
   b) A major advantage of participation may be in increasing acceptance of the goal itself as a desirable one.
   c) Participative goals may have no superiority over assigned goals when acceptance is taken as a given, participation does increase the probability that more difficult goals will be agreed to and acted upon.
7. Studies testing goal-setting theory have demonstrated the superiority of specific and challenging goals as motivating forces.
8. There appears to be a contradiction between the findings on achievement motivation and goal setting.
   a) It is not actually a contradiction.
   b) First, goal-setting theory deals with people in general.
   c) The conclusions on achievement motivation are based only on people who have a high nAch, and probably fewer than 10 to 20 percent of North Americans are naturally high achievers.
   d) Second, goal setting's conclusions apply to those who accept, and are committed to, the goals. Difficult goals will lead to higher performance only if they are accepted.

C. Reinforcement Theory
1. A counterpoint to goal-setting theory is reinforcement theory.

a) The former is a cognitive approach, proposing that an individual's purposes direct his or her actions.
b) Reinforcement theory uses a behavioristic approach, which argues that reinforcement conditions behavior.

2. The two theories are clearly at odds philosophically.
   a) Reinforcement theorists see behavior as environmentally caused. What controls behavior are reinforcers--any consequences that, when immediately following a response, increase the probability that the behavior will be repeated.
3. Reinforcement theory ignores the inner state of the individual and concentrates solely on what happens to a person when he or she takes some action.
   a) Because it does not concern itself with what initiates behavior, it is not, strictly speaking, a theory of motivation.
4. Chapter 2 introduced the law of effect (behavior is a function of its consequences) and showed that reinforcers (consequences) condition behavior and explains how people learn.
   a) Research indicates that people will exert more effort on tasks that are reinforced than on tasks that are not.
   b) But reinforcement is not the single explanation for differences in employee motivation.
   c) Goals, for instance, have an impact on motivation; so, too, do levels of achievement motivation, inequities in rewards, and expectations.

D. Equity Theory

1. Employees make comparisons.
   a) The issue centers around relative rewards and what you believe is fair.
   b) Employees compare their own job inputs and outcomes with those of others and those inequities can influence the degree of effort that employees exert.
2. Equity theory says that employees weigh what they put into a job situation (input) against what they get from it (outcome) and then compare their input-outcome ratio with the input-outcome ratio of relevant others.
   a) If they perceive equity, they feel that their situation is fair, that justice prevails.
   b) If the ratios are unequal, inequity exists; that is, the employees tend to view themselves as underrewarded or overrewarded.
3. When inequities occur, employees will attempt to correct them.
   a) The referent that employees choose to compare themselves against is an important variable in equity theory.
4. The three referent categories have been classified as "other," "system," and "self."
   a) The other category includes other individuals with similar jobs in the same organization and also includes friends, neighbors, or professional associates.
   b) The system category considers organizational pay policies and procedures as well as the administration of this system.
   c) The self category refers to input-outcome ratios that are unique to the individual. This category is influenced by such criteria as past jobs or family commitments.
5. The choice of a particular set of referents is related to the information available about referents as well as to their perceived relevance.
6. When employees envision an inequity, they may make one or more of five choices:
   a) Distort either their own or others' inputs or outcomes.
   b) Behave so as to induce others to change their inputs or outcomes.
   c) Behave so as to change their own inputs or outcomes.
   d) Choose a different comparison referent.
   e) Quit their job.

7. Equity theory recognizes that individuals are concerned with both the absolute amount of rewards and the relationship of that amount to what others receive.
8. Inputs, such as effort, experience, education, and competence, are compared with outcomes such as salary levels, raises, recognition, and other factors.
9. Specifically, the theory establishes four propositions relating to inequitable pay:
    a) Given payment by time, overrewarded employees will produce more than equitably paid employees.
    b) Given payment by quantity of production, overrewarded employees will produce fewer but higher-quality units than equitably paid employees.
    c) Given payment by time, underrewarded employees will produce less or a poorer quality of output.
    d) Given payment by quantity of production, underrewarded employees will produce a large number of low-quality units in comparison with equitably paid employees.
10. A review of the recent research tends to consistently confirm the equity thesis:
    a) Employee motivation is influenced significantly by relative rewards as well as by absolute rewards.
    b) When employees perceive inequity, they will act to correct the situation.
11. Problems with the theory.
    a) Some key issues unclear.
        (1) How do employees decide who is included in the "other" referent category?
        (2) How do they define inputs and outcomes?
        (3) How do they combine and weigh their inputs and outcomes to arrive at totals?
        (4) When and how do the factors change over time?
12. Regardless of these problems, equity theory has an impressive amount of research support and offers us some important insights into employee motivation.

E. Expectancy Theory
1. The most comprehensive explanation of motivation is expectancy theory.
2. Expectancy theory argues that the strength of a tendency to act in a certain way depends on the strength of an expectation that the act will be followed by a given outcome and on the attractiveness of that outcome to the individual.
3. Three variables:
    a) Attractiveness--the importance the individual places on the potential outcome or reward that can be achieved on the job.
    b) Performance-reward linkage--the degree to which the individual believes that performing at a particular level will lead to the attainment of a desired outcome.
    c) Effort-performance linkage--the probability perceived by the individual that exerting a given amount of effort will lead to performance.
    d) Exhibit 4-4 simplifies expectancy theory into its major contentions.
4. The strength of a person's motivation to perform (effort) depends on how strongly she believes she can achieve what she attempts.
5. Four steps inherent in the theory.
    a) First, what perceived outcomes does the job offer the employee--positive or negative?
    b) Second, how attractive do employees consider these outcomes? Are they valued positively, negatively, or neutrally?
    c) Third, what kind of behavior must the employee exhibit in order to achieve these outcomes? The outcomes are not likely to have any effect on the individual employee's performance unless the employee knows, clearly and unambiguously, what she must do in order to achieve them.
    d) Fourth, how does the employee view her chances of doing what is asked of her?

6. Issues
    a) It emphasizes payoffs or rewards. As a result, rewards need to align with what the employee wants.
        (1) This requires an understanding and knowledge of what value the individual puts on organizational payoffs.
    b) Second, expectancy theory emphasizes expected behaviors.
    c) Finally, the theory is concerned with the individual's expectations.

IV. DON'T FORGET: MOTIVATION THEORIES ARE CULTURE BOUND

A. Most current motivation theories were developed in the United States by Americans and about Americans.
1. The pro-American characteristic in these theories is the strong emphasis on individualism and quantity-of-life factors.
2. Maslow's hierarchy of needs theory argues that people start at the physiological level and then move progressively up the hierarchy in this order: physiological, safety, social, esteem, and self-actualization.
    a) This hierarchy aligns with American culture.
3. Another motivation concept with a U.S. bias is the achievement need.
4. Goal-setting theory is also certainly culture bound.
    a) It assumes that subordinates will be reasonably independent (not too high a score on power distance), managers and subordinates will seek challenging goals (low in uncertainty avoidance), and performance is considered important by both (high in quantity of life).
    b) Goal-setting theory's recommendations are not likely to increase motivation in countries in which the opposite conditions exist, such as France, Portugal, and Chile.

V. IMPLICATIONS FOR MANAGERS

1. Many of the theories presented in this chapter have demonstrated reasonably strong predictive value.
2. How does a manager concerned with motivating employees apply these theories?
3. Certain general suggestions can be extracted for application, at least for managers in North America. For instance, the following recommendations are consistent with the findings in this chapter:
    a) Recognize individual differences.
    b) Match people to jobs.
    c) Use goals.
    d) Ensure that goals are perceived as attainable.
    e) Individualize rewards.
    f) Link rewards to performance.
    g) Check the system for equity.
4. These suggestions, of course, would need to be modified to reflect cultural differences outside of North America.
5. The importance of motivating employees today justifies more specifics than the concepts we have just offered.
6. The next chapter builds on the concepts we have presented here, providing a review of the more popular motivation techniques and programs.

SUMMARY

1 Motivation may be defined in terms of some outward behavior. It is the willingness to do something and is conditioned by this action's ability to satisfy some need for the individual.

2 An unsatisfied need creates tension, which stimulates drives within the individual. These drives generate a search for particular goals that, if attained, will satisfy the need and lead to the reduction of tension.

3 The best-known approach to motivation is Abraham Maslow's hierarchy of needs theory. He hypothesized that every human being has an internal hierarchy of five needs--physiological needs, safety needs, social needs, esteem needs, and self-actualization needs. Maslow separated the five needs into higher and lower orders. Maslow's need theory has received wide recognition, particularly among practicing managers. Research does not generally validate the theory.

4 Douglas McGregor proposed two distinct views of human beings. One basically negative, labeled Theory X and the other basically positive, labeled Theory Y. If you accept McGregor's analysis: Theory X assumes that lower-order needs dominate individuals and Theory Y assumes that higher-order needs dominate individuals. Unfortunately, no evidence confirms that either set of assumptions is valid.

5 The two-factor theory--motivation-hygiene theory--was proposed by psychologist Frederick Herzberg. He isolated certain characteristics, some consistently related to job satisfaction--internal factors--such as advancement, recognition, responsibility, and achievement. Others related to job dissatisfaction--extrinsic factors--such as supervision, pay, company policies, and working conditions. His theory has been criticized for its methodology and reliability. Regardless of criticisms, Herzberg's theory has been widely popularized, and few managers are unfamiliar with his recommendations.

6 David McClelland and others have proposed three major relevant motives or needs in the workplace--McClelland's Theory of Needs. The need for achievement (hAth)--the drive to excel, to achieve in relation to a set of standards, to strive to succeed. The need for power (nPow)--the need to make others behave in a way they would not have behaved otherwise. The need for affiliation (nAff)--the desire for friendly and close interpersonal relationships.

7 Goal-setting theory is well supported by research. Intentions--expressed as goals---can be a major source of work motivation. The specificity of the goal itself acts as an internal stimulus. Studies testing goal-setting theory have demonstrated the superiority of specific and challenging goals as motivating forces.

8 A counterpoint to goal-setting theory is reinforcement theory. Reinforcement theory uses a behavioristic approach, which argues that reinforcement conditions behavior. Reinforcement theory ignores the inner state of the individual and concentrates solely on what happens to a person when he or she takes some action.

9 Equity theory proposes that employees make comparisons. Employees compare their own job inputs and outcomes with those of others and any inequities can influence the degree of effort that employees exert. Equity theory says that employees weigh what they put into a job situation (input) against what they get from it (outcome) and then compare their input-outcome ratio with the input-outcome ratio of relevant others. If they perceive equity, they feel that their situation is fair, and that justice prevails. If the ratios are unequal, inequity exists; that is, the employees tend to view themselves as underrewarded or overrewarded. Equity theory recognizes that individuals are concerned with both the absolute amount of rewards and the relationship of that amount to what others receive. A review of the recent research tends to consistently confirm the equity thesis.

10 The most comprehensive explanation of motivation is expectancy theory. Expectancy theory argues that the strength of a tendency to act in a certain way depends on the strength of an expectation that the act will be followed by a given outcome and on the attractiveness of that outcome to the individual. There are three variables: attractiveness--the importance the individual places on the potential outcome or reward that can be achieved on the job; performance-reward linkage--the degree to which the individual believes that performing at a particular level will lead to the attainment of a desired outcome; effort-performance linkage--the probability perceived by the individual that exerting a given amount of effort will lead to performance.

DISCUSSION QUESTIONS

1 Outline the basic motivation process.
Answer - See Exhibit 4-1, page 44.

2 Describe Maslow's hierarchy of needs theory.
Answer - Maslow's hierarchy of needs theory is the best-known approach to motivation. He hypothesized that every human being has an internal hierarchy of five needs. As each is satisfied, the next need becomes dominant. A substantially satisfied need no longer motivates. Maslow separated the five needs into higher and lower orders. Physiological and safety needs were lower order and were predominately satisfied externally. Social, esteem, and self-actualization were categorized as higher-order needs and are satisfied internally. The natural conclusion is that, in times of economic plenty, almost all permanently employed workers will have their lower-order needs substantially met. Maslow's need theory has received wide recognition, particularly among practicing managers. This acceptance is due to the logic and ease with which the theory is intuitively understood. However, research does not generally validate the theory. There is little support found for the prediction that need structures are organized along the dimensions proposed.

3 Contrast Theory X and Theory Y.
Answer - Douglas McGregor proposed two distinct views of human beings, one basically negative, labeled Theory X, and the other basically positive, labeled Theory Y. Each has four assumptions which tend to be the opposite of each other. Theory X assumptions: 1) Employees inherently dislike work and, whenever possible, will attempt to avoid it. 2) Since employees dislike work, they must be coerced, controlled, or threatened with punishment to achieve desired goals. 3) Employees will shirk responsibilities and seek formal direction whenever possible. 4) Most workers place security above all other factors associated with work and will display little ambition. Theory Y contrasting assumptions: 1) Employees can view work as being as natural as rest or play. 2) A person who is committed to the objectives will exercise self-direction and self-control. 3) The average person can learn to accept, even seek, responsibility. 4) Creativity---that is, the ability to make good decisions--is widely dispersed throughout the population and not necessarily the sole province of those in management. Theory X assumes that lower-order needs dominate individuals. Theory Y assumes that higher-order needs dominate individuals.

4 Differentiate motivators from hygiene factors.
Answer - The two-factor theory--motivation-hygiene theory--was proposed by psychologist Frederick Herzberg. He investigated the question, "What do people want from their jobs?" Research showed people replied significantly differently based on whether they felt good or bad about their jobs. Some characteristics consistently related to job satisfaction--internal factors--such as advancement, recognition, responsibility, and achievement seem to be related to job satisfaction. Others related to job dissatisfaction--extrinsic factors--such as supervision, pay, company policies, and working conditions. The opposite of satisfaction is not dissatisfaction--removing dissatisfying characteristics from a job does not necessarily make the job satisfying. Managers who seek to eliminate factors that can create job dissatisfaction will be placating their work force rather than motivating them. Conditions surrounding the job such as quality of supervision, pay, company policies, etc., were characterized as hygiene factors. When they are adequate, people will not be dissatisfied; neither will they be satisfied. To motivate people Herzberg suggested emphasizing factors associated with the work itself or to outcomes directly derived from it, such as promotional opportunities, opportunities for personal growth, etc.

5 List the characteristics that high achievers prefer in a job.
Answer - Some people have a compelling drive to succeed, but they are striving for personal achievement rather than the rewards of success. This drive is the need for achievement. McClelland

found that high achievers differentiate themselves from others by their desire to do things better. They seek situations in which they can attain personal responsibility for finding solutions to problems, receive rapid and unambiguous feedback on their performance, and set moderately challenging goals. They prefer working at a challenging problem and accepting the personal responsibility for success or failure rather than leaving the outcome to chance or the actions of others. High achievers perform best when they perceive their probability of success as being 50--50. They like to set realistic but difficult goals that require stretching themselves a little.

6 Summarize the types of goals that increase performance.
Answer - Intentions--expressed as goals---can be a major source of work motivation. Difficult-to-achieve goals produce a higher level of output than a generalized goal of "do your best." The specificity of the goal itself acts as an internal stimulus. If factors such as ability and acceptance of the goals are held constant, we can also state that the more difficult the goals, the higher the level of performance. Participative goals may have no superiority over assigned goals when acceptance is taken as a given. Participation does increase the probability that more difficult goals will be agreed to and acted upon. Studies testing goal-setting theory have demonstrated the superiority of specific and challenging goals as motivating forces.

7 Contrast reinforcement and goal-setting theories.
Answer - A counterpoint to goal-setting theory is reinforcement theory. The former is a cognitive approach, proposing that an individual's purposes direct his or her actions. Reinforcement theory uses a behavioristic approach, which argues that reinforcement conditions behavior. The two theories are clearly at odds philosophically. Reinforcement theorists see behavior as environmentally caused. What controls behavior are reinforcers--any consequences that, when immediately following a response, increase the probability that the behavior will be repeated. Reinforcement theory ignores the inner state of the individual and concentrates solely on what happens to a person when he or she takes some action. Because it does not concern itself with what initiates behavior, it is not, strictly speaking, a theory of motivation. But reinforcement is not the single explanation for differences in employee motivation. Goals, for instance, have an impact on motivation; so, too, do levels of achievement, inequities in rewards, and expectations.

8 Explain equity theory.
Answer - Equity theory says that employees weigh what they put into a job situation (input) against what they get from it (outcome) and then compare their input-outcome ratio with the input-outcome ratio of relevant others. If they perceive equity, they feel that their situation is fair, that justice prevails. If the ratios are unequal, inequity exists; that is, the employees tend to view themselves as underrewarded or overrewarded. When inequities occur, employees will attempt to correct them. The referent that employees choose to compare themselves against is an important variable in equity theory. The three referent categories have been classified as "other," "system," and "self."

- The "other" category includes other individuals with similar jobs in the same organization and also includes friends, neighbors, or professional associates.
- The "system" category considers organizational pay policies and procedures as well as the administration of this system.
- The "self" category refers to input-outcome ratios that are unique to the individual. This category is influenced by such criteria as past jobs or family commitments.

Equity theory recognizes that individuals are concerned with both the absolute amount of rewards and the relationship of that amount to what others receive. Inputs, such as effort, experience, education, and competence, are compared with outcomes such as salary levels, raises, recognition, and other factors. Specifically, the theory establishes four propositions relating to inequitable pay:

- Given payment by time, overrewarded employees will produce more than equitably paid employees.

- Given payment by quantity of production, overrewarded employees will produce fewer but higher-quality units than equitably paid employees.
- Given payment by time, underrewarded employees will produce less or a poorer quality of output.
- Given payment by quantity of production, underrewarded employees will produce a large number of low-quality units in comparison with equitably paid employees.

9 Clarify the key relationships in expectancy theory.
Answer - The most comprehensive explanation of motivation is expectancy theory. Expectancy theory argues that the strength of a tendency to act in a certain way depends on the strength of an expectation that the act will be followed by a given outcome and on the attractiveness of that outcome to the individual. Three variables: attractiveness--the importance the individual places on the potential outcome or reward that can be achieved on the job, performance-reward linkage--the degree to which the individual believes that performing at a particular level will lead to the attainment of a desired outcome, effort-performance linkage--the probability perceived by the individual that exerting a given amount of effort will lead to performance. Exhibit 4-4 simplifies expectancy theory into its major contentions. Four steps inherent in the theory.
- First, what perceived outcomes does the job offer the employee--positive or negative?
- Second, how attractive do employees consider these outcomes? Are they valued positively, negatively, or neutrally?
- Third, what kind of behavior must the employee exhibit in order to achieve these outcomes? The outcomes are not likely to have any effect on the individual employee's performance unless the employee knows, clearly and unambiguously, what she must do in order to achieve them.
- Fourth, how does the employee view her chances of doing what is asked of her?

EXERCISE

<u>What motivates me</u>?

The goal of this exercise is to have students realize the complexity of motivation and how as managers they will probably use several different approaches. It should also give students insight into the different styles of their professors.

1. Ask students to take 5 minutes and to individually write down how they would motivate students to study, turn in assignments on time, and treat each other with respect in class.
2. Begin a class discussion, noting on the board the suggestions.
3. Next have the students individually categorize the suggestions by theory.
4. Lead a class discussion, noting on the board the general consensus as to which ideas belong to which theoretical approaches.
5. Finally, as a class, discuss how motivating each suggestion would be to them individually. Help students note that what some students think is motivational would not be to others. [Also, you will probably discover that some students will want to "motivate" others in ways they themselves would not like to be motivated.]

CHAPTER 5 - MOTIVATION: FROM CONCEPTS TO APPLICATIONS

CHAPTER OBJECTIVES

After reading this chapter, you should be able to:

1. Identify the four ingredients common to MBO programs.
2. Outline the five-step problem-solving model in OB Mod.
3. Explain why managers might want to use employee involvement programs.
4. Define quality circles.
5. Explain how ESOPs can increase employee motivation.
6. Describe the link between skill-based pay plans and motivation theories.

LECTURE OUTLINE

I. MANAGEMENT BY OBJECTIVES

A. Goal-setting theory
   1. An impressive base of research support.
   2. How do you make goal setting operational?
      a) Install a management by objectives (MBO) program.

B. What Is MBO?
   1. Management by objectives (MBO) emphasizes participatively set goals that are tangible, verifiable, and measurable.
      a) Originally proposed by Peter Drucker 45 years ago as a means of using goals to motivate people rather than to control them.
   2. Its appeal--the emphasis on converting overall organizational objectives into specific objectives for organizational units and individual members.
      a) See Exhibit 5-1 for the process by which objectives cascade down through the organization.
   3. MBO works from the "bottom up" as well as from the "top down."
      a) The hierarchy of objectives that links objectives at one level to those at the next level.
      b) If all the individuals achieve their goals, then their unit's goals will be attained and the organization's overall objectives will become a reality.
   4. Four ingredients common to MBO programs: goal specificity, participative decision making, an explicit time period, and performance feedback.
      a) The objectives in MBO should be concise statements of expected accomplishments.
      b) MBO replaces imposed goals with participatively determined goals.
      c) Each objective has a specific time period in which it is to be completed. Typically, the time period is three months, six months, or a year.
      d) MBO seeks to give continuous feedback on progress toward goals so that individuals can monitor and correct their own actions.
         (1) Continuous feedback, supplemented by more formal periodic managerial evaluations, takes place at the top of the organization as well as at the bottom.

C. Linking MBO and Goal-Setting Theory
   1. Goal-setting theory demonstrates:
      a) Hard goals result in a higher level of individual performance.
      b) Feedback on one's performance leads to higher performance.
   2. MBO directly advocates:
      a) Specific goals and feedback.
      b) MBO implies, rather than explicitly states, that goals must be perceived as feasible.

c) Consistent with goal setting theory, MBO would be most effective when the goals are difficult enough to require the person to do some stretching.

3. The only area of possible disagreement between MBO and goal-setting theory is related to the issue of participation.
   a) MBO strongly advocates it.
   b) Goal-setting theory demonstrates that assigning goals to subordinates frequently works just as well.

D. MBO in Practice

1. Reviews of studies suggest that it is a popular technique.
   a) MBO programs are in business, health care, educational, government, and nonprofit organizations.
2. MBO's popularity should not be construed to mean that it always works.
   a) There are a number of documented cases in which MBO was implemented but failed to meet management's expectations.
   b) The problems rarely lie with MBO's basic components.
   c) The causes tend to be: unrealistic expectations, lack of top-management commitment, and an inability or unwillingness by management to allocate rewards based on goal accomplishment.

II. BEHAVIOR MODIFICATION

A. Emery Air Freight Study

1. 20 years ago with freight packers at Emery Air Freight (now part of Federal Express)
   a) Management wanted packers to aggregate shipments into freight containers rather than handle many separate items.
   b) Packers claimed 90 percent of shipments were put in containers.
   c) Analysis showed container use rate was only 45 percent.
   d) In order to encourage employees to use containers, management established a program of feedback and positive reinforcement.
   e) Container use jumped to more than 90 percent on the first day of the program and held to that level.
   f) This simple program saved the company $2 million over a three-year period.
2. The Emery Air Freight study illustrates the use of behavior modification [OB Mod].

B. What Is OB Mod?

1. See Exhibit 5-2.
2. A five-step problem-solving model:
   a) Identify performance-related behaviors.
   b) Measure the behaviors.
   c) Identify behavioral contingencies.
   d) Develop and implement an intervention strategy.
   e) Evaluate performance improvement.
3. Identify the behaviors that have a significant impact on the employee's job performance.
   a) These are those 5 to 10 percent of behaviors that may account for up to 70 or 80 percent of each employee's performance.
4. The manager then develops some baseline performance information.
   a) The number of times the identified behavior is occurring under present conditions.
5. The third step is to perform a functional analysis to identify the behavioral contingencies or consequences of performance.
   a) This tells the manager which cues emit the behavior and which consequences are currently maintaining it.

6. Now, the manager is ready to develop and implement an intervention strategy to strengthen desirable performance behaviors and weaken undesirable behaviors.
    a) The appropriate strategy will entail changing some element of the performance-reward linkage--structure, processes, technology, groups, or the task with the goal of making high-level performance more rewarding.
7. The final step in OB Mod is to evaluate performance improvement.

C. Linking OB Mod and Reinforcement Theory
1. Reinforcement theory relies on positive reinforcement, shaping, and recognizing the impact of different schedules of reinforcement on behavior.
2. OB Mod uses these concepts.

D. OB Mod in Practice
1. OB Mod has been used to improve employee productivity and to reduce errors, absenteeism, tardiness, and accident rates.
    a) General Electric
    b) Weyerhauser
    c) The city of Detroit
    d) Xerox

III. EMPLOYEE RECOGNITION PROGRAMS

A. The Laura Schendell Example
1. Organizations are increasingly recognizing what Laura Schendell is acknowledging: Recognition can be a potent motivator.

B. What Are Employee Recognition Programs?
1. Numerous forms
2. The best use multiple sources and recognize both individual and group accomplishments.
    a) Convex Computer Corporation provides an excellent illustration.

C. Linking Recognition Programs and Reinforcement Theory
1. A survey of 1,500 employees regarding the most powerful workplace motivator.
    a) Their answer was recognition, recognition, and more recognition.
2. Consistent with reinforcement theory, rewarding a behavior with recognition immediately following that behavior is likely to encourage its repetition.
3. And that recognition can take many forms.
    a) Personally congratulate an employee in private for a good job.
    b) Send a handwritten note or an e-mail message.
    c) Publicly recognize accomplishments.
    d) And to enhance group cohesiveness and motivation, you can celebrate team successes.

D. Employee Recognition Programs in Practice
1. Today's cost pressures make recognition programs particularly attractive.
    a) Recognizing an employee's superior performance often costs little or no money.
2. One of the most well-known and widely-used recognition devices is a suggestion system.
    a) Employees offer suggestions for improving processes or cutting costs and are recognized with small cash awards.
3. The Japanese have been especially effective at making suggestion systems work.

a) A typical high-performing Japanese plant in the auto components business generates 47 suggestions per employee a year and pays approximately the equivalent of U.S. $35 per suggestion.
b) In contrast, a comparable Western factory generates about one suggestion per employee per year but pays out $90 per suggestion.

IV. EMPLOYEE INVOLVEMENT PROGRAMS

A. Example

1. Teams perform many tasks and assume many of the responsibilities once handled by their supervisors.

B. What Is Employee Involvement?

1. Employee involvement has become a convenient catchall term to cover a variety of techniques.
    a) Employee participation or participative management
    b) Workplace democracy
    c) Empowerment
    d) Employee ownership
2. Employee involvement is a participative process that uses the entire capacity of employees and is designed to encourage increased commitment to the organization's success.
    a) The underlying logic--involving workers in decisions that will affect them and increasing their autonomy and control will result in higher motivation, greater commitment, more productivity, and more satisfaction.
3. Are participation and employee involvement synonyms?
    a) No.
    b) Participation is a more limited term.
    c) It is a subset within the larger framework of employee involvement.

C. Examples of Employee Involvement Programs

1. Four forms of employee involvement
2. Participative Management
    a) Characteristic of all participative management programs is joint decision making.
    b) Has been promoted as a panacea for poor morale and low productivity.
    c) Not always appropriate. For it to work:
        (1) there must be adequate time to participate.
        (2) the issues must be relevant to the employees.
        (3) employees must have the ability to participate.
        (4) the organization's culture must support employee involvement.
    d) Dozens of studies have been conducted on the participation-performance relationship.
        (1) Mixed findings.
3. Representative Participation
    a) Rather than participating directly in decisions, workers are represented by a small group of employees who actually participate.
        (1) The most widely legislated form of employee involvement around the world.
4. The goal of representative participation is to redistribute power within an organization.
5. The two most common forms that representative participation takes are works councils and board representatives.

a) Works councils link employees with management. They are groups of nominated or elected employees who must be consulted when management makes decisions involving personnel.
b) Board representatives are employees who sit on a company's board of directors and represent the interests of the firm's employees. In some countries, large companies may be legally required to make sure that employee representatives have the same number of board seats as stockholder representatives.

6. The overall influence of representative participation on working employees seems to be minimal.
   a) Works councils are dominated by management and have little impact on employees or the organization.
   b) The greatest value of representative participation is symbolic.
7. Quality Circles
   a) The most widely discussed and undertaken formal style of employee involvement.
   b) The quality circle concept is frequently tied to Japanese manufacturing success.
   c) Originally used in the United States and exported to Japan in the 1950s, the quality circle became quite popular in North America and Europe during the 1980s.
   d) It is a work group of eight to ten employees and supervisors who share an area of responsibility.
      (1) Meet regularly--typically once a week, on company time and on company premises.
      (2) Discuss their quality problems, investigate causes of the problems, recommend solutions, and take corrective actions.
      (3) Take over the responsibility for solving quality problems, and they generate and evaluate their own feedback.
      (4) Management typically retains control over the final decision regarding implementation of recommended solutions.
   e) Exhibit 5-3 describes a typical quality-circle process.
8. Do quality circles improve employee productivity and satisfaction?
   a) They are highly likely to positively affect productivity.
   b) They tend to have little or no effect on employee satisfaction.
   c) The failure of many quality-circle programs to produce measurable benefits has caused a large number of them to discontinued.
9. Employee Stock Ownership Plans.
   a) Company-established benefit plans in which employees acquire stock as part of their benefits.
      (1) Approximately 20 percent of Polaroid, forty percent of Canadian-based Spruce Falls, Inc., 71 percent of Avis Corporation and 100 percent of Weirton Steel are owned by employees.
   b) In the typical ESOP, an employee stock ownership trust is created.
   c) Companies contribute either stock or cash to buy stock for the trust and allocate the stock to employees.
   d) Employees usually cannot take physical possession of their shares or sell them as long as they're still employed at the company.
   e) ESOPs increase employee satisfaction and frequently result in higher performance.

D. Linking Employee Involvement Program and Motivation Theories
   1. Employee involvement draws on several motivation theories.
      a) Theory Y is consistent with participative management.
      b) Theory X aligns with the more traditional autocratic style of managing people.

c) Two-factor theory relates to employee involvement programs that provide employees with intrinsic motivation by increasing opportunities for growth, responsibility, and involvement in the work itself.

E. Employee Involvement Programs in Practice
1. Germany, France, the Netherlands, and the Scandinavian countries have firmly established the principle of industrial democracy in Europe, and other nations, including Japan and Israel, have traditionally practiced some form of representative participation for decades.
2. Participative management and representative participation were much slower to gain ground in North American organizations.
   a) Now, employee involvement programs stressing participation are the norm.
3. Quality circles.
   a) The list of companies that have used quality circles reads like a Who's Who of corporate America: Hewlett-Packard, General Electric, Texas Instruments, Xerox, Eastman Kodak, Polaroid, Procter & Gamble, General Motors, Ford, IBM, Motorola, American Airlines.
   b) But the success of quality circles has been far from overwhelming.
4. ESOPs.
   a) They are becoming a popular employee involvement program-having grown to around 10,000, covering more than 10 million employees.

V. VARIABLE-PAY PROGRAMS

A. Examples
1. Nucor Steel has had an incentive compensation plan in place that pays bonuses of as much as 150 percent of base to employees.
2. Rick Benson, an investment banker with Merrill Lynch, earned $1.4 million in 1998--more than six times his base salary.
3. George Fisher, GEO of Eastman Kodak, saw his annual salary and bonus drop from $3.98 million to $2.0 million in 1997.

B. What Are Variable-Pay Programs?
1. Piece-rate plans, wage incentives, profit sharing, bonuses, and gainsharing are all forms of variable-pay programs.
2. Differ from traditional programs in that a person is paid not only for time on the job or seniority but for some individual or organizational measure of performance or both.
3. Variable pay is not an annuity.
   a) With variable pay, earnings fluctuate with the measure of performance.
4. This fluctuation makes these programs attractive to management.
   a) Part of an organization's fixed labor costs become a variable cost.
   b) In addition, when pay is tied to performance, earnings recognize contribution rather than being a form of entitlement.
5. Four of the more widely used of the variable-pay programs.
   a) Piece-rate wages have been around for nearly a century.
      (1) Popular as a means for compensating production workers.
      (2) Workers are paid a fixed sum for each unit of production completed.
      (3) A system in which an employee gets no base salary and is paid only for what he or she produces is a pure piece-rate plan.
      (4) Many organizations use a modified piece-rate plan, in which employees earn a base hourly wage plus a piece-rate differential.
   b) Bonuses can be paid exclusively to executives or to all employees.

(1) Increasingly, bonus plans are taking on a larger net within organizations to include lower-ranking employees.

c) Profit-sharing plans are organization-wide programs that distribute compensation based on some established formula designed around a company's profitability.

(1) These can be direct cash outlays or, particularly in the case of top managers, allocated as stock options.

d) The variable-pay program that has gotten the most attention in recent years is undoubtedly gainsharing.

(1) A formula-based group incentive plan. Improvements in group productivity--from one period to another---determine the total amount of money to be allocated.

(2) The productivity savings can be split between the company and employees in any number of ways, but 50-50 is pretty typical.

e) Gainsharing is similar to profit sharing, not the same.

(1) By focusing on productivity gains rather than on profits, gainsharing rewards specific behaviors that are less influenced by external factors than profits are.

(2) Employees in a gainsharing plan can receive incentive awards even when the organization isn't profitable.

6. Variable-pay programs increase motivation and productivity.

a) Gainsharing has been found to improve productivity in most cases and often has a positive impact on employee attitudes.

C. Linking Variable-Pay Programs and Expectancy Theory

1. Variable pay is compatible with expectancy theory predictions.
2. The evidence supports the importance of this linkage, especially for operative employees working under piece-rate systems.
3. Group and organization-wide incentives encourage employees to sublimate personal goals in the best interests of their department or the organization.
4. Group-based performance incentives help build a strong team ethic.

D. Variable-Pay Programs in Practice

1. Variable pay is rapidly replacing the annual cost-of-living raise because of:

a) its motivational power.
b) the cost implications.
c) the need to avoid the fixed expense of permanent salary boosts.

2. Pay-for-performance has been important for compensating managers for more than a decade.
3. The new trend has been to expand this practice to nonmanagerial employees.

a) In 1995, nearly 50 percent of all U.S. companies had some form of variable pay plan for nonexecutives.

4. Variable-pay plans that use bonuses are also becoming increasingly popular in Canada.

a) In 1996 senior executives could expect bonuses equal to 18.5 percent of their salaries, double their 1995 bonuses.
b) The average bonus for an hourly worker during the same time period went from 1.1 percent of base pay to 5.8 percent.
c) About 35 percent of Canadian companies now have companywide variable-pay incentive plans.

5. Gainsharing's popularity seems to be restricted to large, unionized manufacturing companies.

VI. SKILL-BASED PAY PLANS

A. What Are Skill-Based Pay Plans

1. Skill-based pay is an alternative to job-based pay.
2. Skill-based pay (also called competency-based pay) sets pay levels on the basis of how many skills employees have or how many jobs they can do.
3. The appeal of skill-based pay plans is flexibility.
   a) Filling staffing needs is easier when employee skills are interchangeable.
   b) It facilitates communication throughout the organization because people gain a better understanding of others' jobs.
   c) It lessens dysfunctional "protection of territory" behavior.
   d) Skill-based pay also helps meet the needs of ambitious employees who confront minimal advancement opportunities.
   e) Skill-based pay appears to lead to performance improvements.
4. Downside of skill-based pay.
   a) People can "top out" relearning all the skills the program calls for them to learn.
   b) Skills can also become obsolete.
   c) Skill-based plans do not address level of performance, only whether someone can perform the skill.

B. Linking Skill-Based Pay Plans to Motivation Theories

1. Skill-based pay plans are consistent with several motivation theories.
2. Because they encourage employees to learn, expand their skills, and grow, they are consistent with Maslow's hierarchy of needs theory.
3. Paying people to expand their skill levels is also consistent with research on the achievement need.
   a) High achievers have a compelling drive to do things better or more efficiently.
4. There is also a link between reinforcement theory and skill-based pay.
   a) Skill-based pay encourages employees to develop their flexibility, to continue to learn, to cross train, to be generalists rather than specialists, and to work cooperatively with others in the organization.
5. Skill-based pay may also have equity implications.
   a) When employees make their input-outcome comparisons, skills may provide a fairer input criterion for determining pay.

C. Skill-Based Pay in Practice

1. The overall conclusion of studies, is that the use of skill-based pay is expanding and that it generally leads to higher employee performance and satisfaction.

VII. IMPLICATIONS FOR MANAGERS

1. Organizations have introduced a number of programs designed to increase employee motivation, productivity, and satisfaction. Importantly, these programs are grounded on basic motivation theories.
2. It is easy to criticize educators and researchers for their focus on building theories. Students and practitioners often consider these theories unrealistic or irrelevant to solving real-life problems. This chapter makes a good rebuttal to those critics. It illustrates how tens of thousands of organizations and millions of managers, in countries around the globe, are using motivation theories to build practical incentive programs.
3. The six motivation programs we discussed in this chapter are not applicable to every organization or every manager's needs. But an understanding of these programs will help you design internal systems that can increase employee productivity and satisfaction.

SUMMARY

1. Management by objectives (MBO) emphasizes participatively set goals that are tangible, verifiable, and measurable. Its appeal is its ability to convert overall organizational objectives into specific objectives for organizational units and individual members. MBO works from the "bottom up" as well as from the "top down." There are four ingredients common to MBO programs: goal specificity, participative decision making, an explicit time period, and performance feedback.
2. MBO and goal-setting theory are complementary. Goal-setting theory demonstrates that hard goals result in a higher level of individual performance and that feedback on one's performance leads to higher performance. MBO advocates specific goals and feedback. Consistent with goal setting theory, MBO would be most effective when the goals are difficult enough to require the person to do some stretching. MBO and goal-setting theory differ in terms of participation; MBO strongly advocates it, while goal-setting theory demonstrates that assigning goals to subordinates frequently works just as well.
3. The five-step problem-solving model in OB modification model includes identifying performance-related behaviors, measuring the behaviors, identifying behavioral contingencies, developing and implementing an intervention strategy, and evaluating performance improvement. It requires the identification of the behaviors that have a significant impact on the employee's job performance.
4. Employee involvement has become a convenient catchall term to cover a variety of techniques: employee participation or participative management, workplace democracy, empowerment, and employee ownership. Employee involvement is a participative process that uses the entire capacity of employees and is designed to encourage increased commitment to the organization's success. The underlying logic--involving workers in decisions that will affect them and increasing their autonomy and control will result in higher motivation, greater commitment, more productivity, and more satisfaction.
5. There are four primary types of employee involvement programs. Participative management involves joint decision making and is often promoted as a panacea for poor morale and low productivity. Representative participation, involves workers being represented by a small group of employees who actually participate. Quality circles, the most widely discussed and undertaken formal style of employee involvement. And ESOPs or employee stock ownership plans, company-established benefit plans in which employees acquire stock as part of their benefits.
6. Employee involvement programs are practiced around the world. Germany, France, the Netherlands, and the Scandinavian countries have firmly established the principle of industrial democracy in Europe, and other nations, including Japan and Israel, have traditionally practiced some form of representative participation for decades.
7. ESOPs can increase employee motivation. They tend to increase employee satisfaction and frequently result in higher performance. They are company-established benefit plans in which employees acquire stock as part of their benefits. Employees usually cannot take physical possession of their shares or sell them as long as they're still employed at the company.
8. Variable-pay programs are another way to motivate employees through piece-rate plans, wage incentives, profit sharing, bonuses, and gainsharing are all forms of variable-pay programs. These differ from traditional programs in that a person is paid not only for time on the job or seniority but for some individual or organizational measure of performance or both.
9. Variable pay is compatible with expectancy theory predictions. The evidence supports the importance of this linkage, especially for operative employees working under piece-rate systems. Group and organization-wide incentives encourage employees to sublimate personal goals in the best interests of their department or the organization.
10. Skill-based pay is an alternative to job-based pay. Its sets pay levels on the basis of how many skills employees have or how many jobs they can do. The appeal of skill-based pay plans is flexibility. There are some downsides however; people can "top out" relearning all the skills the program calls for them to learn, skills can also become obsolete, etc.

DISCUSSION QUESTIONS

1. How does management by objectives work?
   Answer - MBO emphasizes participatively set goals that are tangible, verifiable, and measurable. Its appeal is in the emphasis on converting overall organizational objectives into specific objectives for organizational units and individual members. Exhibit 5-1 shows the process by which objectives cascade down through the organization. MBO works from the "bottom up" as well as from the "top down." The hierarchy of objectives that links objectives at one level to those at the next level.

2. Describe the characteristics of an effective MBO program.
   Answer - There are four common characteristics; goal specificity, participative decision making, an explicit time period, and performance feedback. The objectives in MBO should be concise statements of expected accomplishments. MBO replaces imposed goals with participatively determined goals. Each objective has a specific time period in which it is to be completed. Typically, the time period is three months, six months, or a year. MBO seeks to give continuous feedback on progress toward goals so that individuals can monitor and correct their own actions. Continuous feedback, supplemented by more formal periodic managerial evaluations, takes place at the top of the organization as well as at the bottom.

3. Design a behavior modification program for training bank tellers in customer service.
   Answer - Students answers will vary but they should cover the basic steps. 1) Identify the behaviors that have a significant impact on the employee's job performance. 2) Developing baseline performance information by observing the number of times the identified behavior is occurring under present conditions. 3) Perform a functional analysis to identify the behavioral contingencies or consequences of performance. 4) Develop and implement an intervention strategy to strengthen desirable performance behaviors and weaken undesirable behaviors. 5) The final step in OB Mod is to evaluate performance improvement.

4. Why might managers want to use employee involvement programs?
   Answer - Employee involvement is a participative process that uses the entire capacity of employees and is designed to encourage increased commitment to the organization's success. The underlying logic--involving workers in decisions that will affect them and increasing their autonomy and control will result in higher motivation, greater commitment, more productivity, and more satisfaction. Employee involvement draws on several motivation theories--Theory Y is consistent with participative management, Theory X aligns with the more traditional autocratic style of managing people, and two-factor theory relates to employee involvement programs that provide employees with intrinsic motivation by increasing opportunities for growth, responsibility, and involvement in the work itself.

5. If a manager decided to implement an employee involvement program what choices would she/he have? Why would he use one rather than another?
   Answer - Participative management--Characteristic of all participative management programs is joint decision making. Representative Participation--workers are represented by a small group of employees who actually participate. It is the most widely legislated form of employee involvement around the world. The goal of representative participation is to redistribute power within an organization. The two most common forms that representative participation takes are works councils and board representatives. Quality circles are the most widely discussed and undertaken formal style of employee involvement. It is a work group of eight to ten employees and supervisors who share an area of responsibility. Exhibit 5-3 describes a typical quality-circle process. Employee stock ownership plans are company-established benefit plans in which employees acquire stock as part of their benefits.

6. Explain how ESOPs can increase employee motivation.
Answer - Employee stock ownership plans are company-established benefit plans in which employees acquire stock as part of their benefits. In the typical ESOP, an employee stock ownership trust is created. Companies contribute either stock or cash to buy stock for the trust and allocate the stock to employees. Employees usually cannot take physical possession of their shares or sell them as long as they're still employed at the company. ESOPs increase employee satisfaction and frequently result in higher performance.

7. What is the relationship between skill-based pay plans and motivation theories?
Answer - Skill-based pay plans are consistent with several motivation theories. Because they encourage employees to learn, expand their skills, and grow, they are consistent with Maslow's hierarchy of needs theory. Paying people to expand their skill levels is also consistent with research on the achievement need. High achievers have a compelling drive to do things better or more efficiently. There is also a link between reinforcement theory and skill-based pay. Skill-based pay encourages employees to develop their flexibility, to continue to learn, to cross train, to be generalists rather than specialists, and to work cooperatively with others in the organization. Skill-based pay may also have equity implications. When employees make their input-outcome comparisons, skills may provide a fairer input criterion for determining pay.

EXERCISE

An application of motivation

Our goal here is to help students apply MBO as they will most likely have to deal with it in their first jobs. The emphasis should be on creating measurable realistic objectives. We will apply the MBO process to the classroom. Consider using this as an exercise to organize students' effort for the semester. You can use this as part of your grading for the course by holding the students accountable for their objectives at the end of the semester.

1. Review the principles of MBO with the class.
2. Assign them the task of individually creating five MBOs for themselves for this class for the semester.
   - By now the students have been in class long enough to have a sense of course content, your style, etc.
   - Students should have a clear idea of your objectives for the class.
   - Students should have a syllabus or an idea of the assignments or projects that will be due.
3. Have students write one MBO in class.
   - Ask volunteers to share their objective.
   - You will get a number of, "Get an A in the course." Be gentle as you point out why this is not an effective objective.
   - Critique the objective stressing both the principles of an effective objective and how well it relates to the course objectives.
4. Have students complete their assignment and bring written objectives into the next class.
5. Place students in pairs or small groups of five or less and have them share their objectives with each other.
6. Have each group share the 3-5 best objectives with the class either orally or by copying them on the board.
7. Discuss the objectives, collect the written copies.

CHAPTER 6 - INDIVIDUAL DECISION MAKING

CHAPTER OBJECTIVES

After reading this chapter, you should be able to:

1. Explain the six-step rational decision-making model and its assumptions.
2. Identify three methods for stimulating individual creativity.
3. Describe actions of the boundedly rational decision maker.
4. Define heuristics and explain how they bias decisions.
5. Explain escalation of commitment.
6. Identify four decision-making styles.
7. Explain the implications of stages of moral development to decision making.

LECTURE OUTLINE

I. INTRODUCTION

- A. Individuals in organizations make decisions.
  1. Top managers determine their organization's goals, what products or services to offer, how best to organize corporate headquarters, etc.
  2. Middle- and lower-level managers determine production schedules, select new employees, and decide how pay raises are to be allocated.
  3. Nonmanagerial employees also make decisions that affect their jobs and the organizations they work for.
  4. All individuals in every organization regularly engage in decision making--they make choices from among two or more alternatives.

II. HOW SHOULD DECISIONS BE MADE?

- A. The Rational Decision-Making Process
  1. The optimizing decision maker is rational.
     - a) He or she makes consistent, value-maximizing choices within specified constraints.
  2. The Rational Model
     - a) See Exhibit 6-1 for the six steps in the rational decision-making model.
  3. The model begins by defining the problem.
     - a) A problem exists when there is a discrepancy between an existing and a desired state of affairs.
  4. Next, the decision maker needs to identify the decision criteria that will be important in solving the problem.
     - a) Determining what is relevant to making the decision.
     - b) It engages the decision maker's interests, values, and personal preferences.
  5. The third step requires the decision maker to weight the previously identified criteria in order to give them correct priority in the decision.
  6. The fourth step requires the generation of possible alternatives that could succeed in resolving the problem.
     - a) Alternatives are not yet appraised.
  7. Once the alternatives have been generated, the decision maker must critically analyze and evaluate each one.
     - a) This is done by rating each alternative on each criterion.
  8. The final step in this model requires computing the optimal decision.
     - a) This is done by evaluating each alternative against the weighted criteria and selecting the alternative with the highest total score.

9. Assumptions of the Model
   a) Problem clarity--The problem is clear, unambiguous, and the decision maker has complete information.
   b) Known options--The decision maker can identify all the relevant criteria, can list all the viable alternatives, and is aware of all the possible consequences.
   c) Clear preferences--Rationality assumes that the criteria and alternatives can be ranked and weighted to reflect their importance.
   d) Constant preferences--Specific decision criteria are constant and that the weights assigned to them are stable over time.
   e) No time or cost constraints--The rational decision maker can obtain full information about criteria and alternatives because it is assumed that there are no time or cost constraints.
   f) Maximum payoff--The rational decision maker will choose the alternative that yields the highest perceived value.

B. Improving Creativity in Decision Making
   1. Creativity is the ability to combine ideas in a unique way or to make unusual associations between ideas.
   2. Creativity allows the decision maker to more fully appraise and understand the problem, including seeing problems others can not see.
   3. Creative Potential
      a) To tap creative potential most people have to climb out of their psychological ruts.
      b) Need to learn how to think about a problem in divergent ways.
   4. People differ in their inherent creativity.
      a) A study of lifetime creativity of 461 men and women found that fewer than 1 percent were exceptionally creative. But 10 percent were highly creative, and about 60 percent were somewhat creative.
   5. Methods for Stimulating Individual Creativity
      a) Evidence indicates that the mere action of instructing someone to "be creative" and to avoid obvious approaches to a problem results in unique ideas.
      b) Overtly telling yourself that you are going to seek out creative options should lead to an increase in unique alternatives.
      c) Another technique is attribute listing.
         (1) The decision maker isolates the major characteristics of traditional alternatives.
         (2) Each major attribute of each alternative is considered in turn and is changed in every conceivable way.
         (3) No ideas are rejected, no matter how ridiculous they may seem.
         (4) Once this extensive list is completed, the constraints of the problem are imposed in order to eliminate all but the viable alternatives.
      d) Creativity can also be stimulated by practicing zigzag, or lateral, thinking.
         (1) This is a replacement for the more traditional vertical, sequential thinking.
         (2) With lateral thinking, individuals emphasize thinking sideways: not developing a pattern but restructuring a pattern.
         (3) Lateral thinking does not have to be correct at each step.
         (4) Lateral thinking is not restricted to relevant information.

III. HOW DECISIONS ARE ACTUALLY MADE IN ORGANIZATIONS

A. Are decision makers in organizations rational?
   1. When decision makers are faced with a simple problem having few alternative courses of action and when the cost of searching out and evaluating alternatives is low, the rational model provides a fairly accurate description of the decision-making process.

2. But such situations are the exception. Most decisions in the real world do not follow the rational model.

B. Bounded Rationality
   1. College search example
   2. When faced with a complex problem, most people respond by reducing the problem to a level at which it can be readily understood.
      a) People satisfice. That is, they seek solutions that are satisfactory and sufficient.
   3. Because of the limitations of the human mind most individuals operate within the confines of bounded rationality.
      a) They construct simplified models that extract the essential features from problems without capturing all of their complexity.
   4. How does it work?
      a) A problem is identified, the search for criteria and alternatives begins.
      b) The decision maker limits alternatives to the more conspicuous choices.
         (1) Choices that are easy to find and that tend to be highly visible.
         (2) They represent familiar criteria and tried-and-true solutions.
      c) The limited set of alternatives is reviewed.
         (1) Review is limited.
         (2) It begins with alternatives that differ only in a relatively small degree from the choice currently in place.
         (3) The decision maker proceeds to review alternatives only until he or she identifies an alternative that is good enough--one that meets an acceptable level of performance.
      d) The first alternative that meets the "good enough" criterion ends the search.
      e) So the final solution represents a satisficing choice rather than an optimal one.
   5. The order in which alternatives are considered is critical in determining which alternative is selected because the satisficing choice will be the first acceptable one the decision maker encounters.
      a) Solutions that depart least from the status quo and meet the decision criteria are most likely to be selected.

C. Intuition
   1. Managers regularly use their intuition, and this may actually help improve decision making.
   2. Intuitive decision making is an unconscious process created out of distilled experience.
      a) It complements the rational approach.
      b) Research on chess playing provides an excellent illustration of how intuition works.
         (1) Experience allows the expert to recognize a situation and draw upon previously learned information associated with that situation in order to to quickly arrive at a decision.
         (2) The result is that the intuitive decision maker can decide rapidly with what appears to be very limited information.

D. Identifying Problems
   1. One person's problem is another person's acceptable status quo. So how do decision makers identify and select problems?
   2. Problems that are visible tend to have a higher probability of being selected than ones that are important.
      a) It is easier to recognize visible problems.

   b) Second, remember that we are concerned with decision making in organizations. Decision makers want to appear competent and "on top of problems." This desire motivates them to focus on problems that are visible to others.
3. If a decision maker faces a conflict between selecting a problem that is important to the organization and one that is important to the decision maker, self-interest tends to win out.

E. Developing Alternatives
   1. Since decision makers seek a satisficing one, they tend to show a minimal use of creativity.
   2. The search process is kept simple, largely confined to the neighborhood of the current alternative.
   3. The evidence indicates that decision making is incremental rather than comprehensive.
      a) Decision makers rarely formulate new and unique problem definitions and alternatives and rarely explore unfamiliar territory.
      b) This approach also makes it unnecessary for the decision maker to thoroughly examine an alternative and its consequences.
   4. The decision maker takes small steps toward an objective making successive comparisons.

F. Making Choices
   1. In order to avoid information overload, decision makers rely on heuristics, or judgmental shortcuts, in decision making.
   2. Availability Heuristic
      a) Example of peoples' fear of flying more than from fear of driving a car. The reason for the fear is that many people think flying is more dangerous. It isn't, of course.
   3. An availability heuristic is the tendency for people to base their judgments on information that is readily available to them.
      a) Events that evoke emotions, that are particularly vivid, or that have occurred recently tend to be most available in our memory.
   4. Representative Heuristic
      a) Example of inner-city African-American boys in the United States talk about playing basketball in the NBA. In reality, they have a better chance of becoming a medical doctor than they do of playing in the NBA.
      b) A representative heuristic--assesses the likelihood of an occurrence by trying to match it with a preexisting category.
   5. Escalation of Commitment
      a) It is an increased commitment to a previous decision, often in spite of negative information.
      b) It has been well documented that individuals escalate commitment to a failing course of action when they view themselves as responsible for the failure. They "throw good money after bad" to demonstrate that their initial decision was not wrong and to avoid having to admit they made a mistake.
      c) Implications for managerial decisions.
         (1) Many an organization has suffered large losses because a manager was determined to prove that his or her original decision was right by continuing to commit resources to what was a lost cause from the beginning.
         (2) Also, consistency is a characteristic often associated with effective leaders.

G. Individual Differences
   1. Two of these individual differences seem particularly relevant to decision making in organizations--decision-making styles and level of moral development.
   2. Decision-Making Styles
      a) The foundation of the model is the recognition that people differ along two dimensions.
         (1) The first is their way of thinking.
         (2) The other dimension addresses a person's tolerance for ambiguity.
      b) When these two dimensions are diagrammed, they form four styles of decision making.
         (1) See Exhibit 6-2. Four styles--directive, analytical, conceptual, and behavioral.
      c) Directive style
         (1) Low tolerance for ambiguity and seek rationality.
         (2) Efficient and logical. Decisions are based on minimal information after the consideration of few alternatives.
         (3) Directive types make decisions fast, and they focus on the short run.
      d) Analytical style
         (1) Greater tolerance for ambiguity than do directive decision makers.
         (2) They desire more information and consider more alternatives than do directives.
         (3) Characterized as careful decision makers with the ability to adapt or cope with new situations.
      e) Conceptual style
         (1) Very broad in their outlook and consider many alternatives.
         (2) Focus is long range, and they are very good at finding creative solutions to problems.
      f) Behavioral style
         (1) Characterizes decision makers who work well with others.
         (2) They are concerned with the achievement of peers and subordinates.
         (3) They are receptive to suggestions from others and rely heavily on meetings for communicating.
         (4) This type of manager tries to avoid conflict and seeks acceptance.
      g) Most managers have characteristics that fall into more than one.
         (1) But they have a dominant style and a backup style.
         (2) Business students, lower-level managers, and top executives tend to score highest in the analytic style.
      h) Focusing on decision styles can be useful for helping you understand how two equally intelligent people can differ in their decisions.
   3. Level of Moral Development
      a) Many decisions have an ethical dimension.
      b) Research confirms the existence of three levels of moral development, each comprising two stages.
         (1) See Exhibit 6-3.
         (2) At each successive stage, an individual's moral judgment grows less and less dependent on outside influences.
      c) Preconventional. Individuals respond to notions of right or wrong only when personal consequences are involved.
      d) Conventional. Reasoning at this level indicates that moral value resides in maintaining the conventional order and the expectations of others.
      e) Principled. Individuals make a clear effort to define moral principles apart from the authority of the groups to which they belong or society in general.
   4. Conclusions

a) First, people proceed through the six stages in a lock-step fashion. They gradually move up a ladder, stage by stage.
b) Second, there is no guarantee of continued development. Development can terminate at any stage.
c) Third, most adults are at stage 4. They are limited to obeying the rules and laws of society.
d) Finally, the higher the stage a manager reaches, the more he or she will be predisposed to make ethical decisions.

H. Organizational Constraints
1. The organization itself constrains decision makers.
2. Performance Evaluation
   a) Managers are strongly influenced by the criteria by which they are evaluated.
3. Reward Systems
   a) The organization's reward system influences decision makers by suggesting to them what choices are preferable in terms of personal payoff.
4. System-Imposed Time Constraints
   a) Organizations impose deadlines on decisions.
5. Historical Precedents
   a) Decisions have a context individual decisions are more accurately characterized as points in a stream of decisions.
   b) Decisions made in the past are ghosts that continually haunt current choices.

I. Cultural Differences
1. The rational model does not acknowledge cultural differences.
2. The cultural background of the decision maker can significantly influence his or her selection of problems, depth of analysis, the importance placed on logic and rationality, or whether organizational decisions should be made autocratically by an individual manager or collectively in groups.
3. Cultures, for example, differ in terms of time orientation, the importance of rationality, their belief in the ability of people to solve problems, and preference for collective decision making.

IV. ETHICS IN DECISION MAKING
A. Three different ways to frame decisions
1. Utilitarian criterion
   a) Decisions are made solely on the basis of their outcomes or consequences.
   b) The goal is to provide the greatest good for the greatest number.
   c) This view tends to dominate business decision making.
2. Focus on rights
   a) This calls on individuals to make decisions consistent with fundamental liberties and privileges as set forth in documents like the Bill of Rights.
   b) An emphasis on rights in decision making means respecting and protecting the basic rights of individuals, such as the right to privacy, to free speech, and to due process.
3. Focus on justice
   a) This requires individuals to impose and enforce rules fairly and impartially so there is an equitable distribution of benefits and costs.
   b) Union members typically favor this view.
4. Advantages and liabilities
   a) Utilitarianism

(1) Promotes efficiency and productivity, but it can result in ignoring the rights of some individuals, particularly those with minority representation in the organization.

b) Rights

(1) Protects individuals from injury, and is consistent with freedom and privacy, but it can create an overly legalistic workplace that hinders productivity and efficiency.

c) Justice

(1) Protects the interests of the underrepresented and less powerful, but it can encourage a sense of entitlement that reduces risk taking, innovation, and productivity.

5. Decision makers, particularly in for-profit organizations, tend to feel safe and comfortable when they use utilitarianism.
6. Increased concerns in society about individual rights and social justice suggest the need for managers to develop ethical standards based on nonutilitarian criteria.

V. IMPLICATIONS FOR MANAGERS

1. Individuals think and reason before they act. Thus an understanding of how people make decisions can be helpful if we are to explain and predict their behavior.
2. Under some decision situations, people follow the rational model. Most people and most nonroutine decisions do not use this model. Few important decisions are simple or unambiguous enough for the rational model's assumptions to apply. So individuals look for solutions that satisfice rather than optimize, inject biases and prejudices into the decision process, and rely on intuition.
3. Given the evidence we've described on how decisions are actually made in organizations, what can managers do to improve their decision making? We offer five suggestions.
4. First, analyze the situation. Adjust your decision-making style to the national culture in which you are operating and to criteria your organization evaluates and rewards. Similarly, organizations differ in terms of the importance they place on risk, the use of groups, and the like. Adjust your decision style to the organization's culture.
5. Second, be aware of biases. We all bring biases to the decisions we make. If you understand the biases influencing your judgment, you can begin to change the way you make decisions to reduce those biases.
6. Third, combine rational analysis with intuition. These are not conflicting approaches to decision making. By using both, you can actually improve your decision effectiveness.
7. Fourth, don't assume that your specific decision style is appropriate for every job. Just as organizations differ, so, too, do jobs within organizations. And your effectiveness as a decision maker will increase if you match your decision style to the requirements of the job. For instance, if you have a directive style of decision making, you'll be more effective working with people whose jobs require quick action. This style, for example, would match up well with managing stockbrokers. An analytic style, on the other hand, would work well managing accountants, market researchers, or financial analysts.
8. Finally, use creativity-stimulation techniques. You can improve your overall decision-making effectiveness by searching for new solutions to problems. Stimulating creativity can be as simple as telling yourself to think creatively and to specifically look for unique alternatives.

SUMMARY

1. Top managers determine their organization's goals, what products or services to offer, how best to organize corporate headquarters, etc. Middle- and lower-level managers determine production

schedules, select new employees, and decide how pay raises are to be allocated. Nonmanagerial employees also make decisions that affect their jobs and the organizations they work for.

2. The rational decision-making process uses six steps: It begins by defining the problem; then the decision maker needs to identify the decision criteria that will be important in solving the problem; third, the decision maker weights and prioritizes the criteria; fourth is the generation of possible alternatives; the alternatives must be critically analyzed and evaluated; the final step in this model requires computing the optimal decision.
3. Creativity is the ability to combine ideas in a unique way or to make unusual associations between ideas. Creativity allows the decision-maker to more fully appraise and understand the problem, including seeing problems others can not see. People differ in their inherent creativity but everyone can stimulate their individual creativity.
4. When decision makers are faced with a simple problem having few alternative courses of action and when the cost of searching out and evaluating alternatives is low, the rational model provides a fairly accurate description of the decision-making process. When faced with a complex problem, most people respond by reducing the problem to a level at which it can be readily understood. People satisfice, that is, they seek solutions that are satisfactory and sufficient.
5. Managers regularly use their intuition, and this may actually help improve decision making. Intuitive decision making is an unconscious process created out of distilled experience.
6. Decision makers identify and select problems based on their visibility and the decision makers self-interest. Since decision makers seek a satisficing one, they tend to show a minimal use of creativity.
7. In order to avoid information overload, decision makers rely on heuristics, or judgmental shortcuts, in decision making. An availability heuristic is the tendency for people to base their judgments on information that is readily available to them. A representative heuristic--assesses the likelihood of an occurrence by trying to match it with a preexisting category.
8. It has been well documented that individuals escalate commitment to a failing course of action when they view themselves as responsible for the failure. They "throw good money after bad" to demonstrate that their initial decision was not wrong and to avoid having to admit they made a mistake.
9. Two individual differences seem particularly relevant to decision making in organizations--decision-making styles and level of moral development. When these two dimensions are diagrammed, they form four styles of decision making--directive, analytical, conceptual, and behavioral.
10. The cultural background of the decision maker can significantly influence his or her selection of problems, depth of analysis, the importance placed on logic and rationality, or whether organizational decisions should be made autocratically by an individual manager or collectively in groups.
11. There are three different ways to frame decisions. Utilitarian criteria focuses decisions solely on the basis of their outcomes or consequences. A focus on rights calls on individuals to make decisions consistent with fundamental liberties and privileges as set forth in documents like the Bill of Rights.
12. A justice perspective requires individuals to impose and enforce rules fairly and impartially so there is an equitable distribution of benefits and costs.

DISCUSSION QUESTIONS

1. As a manager you need to decide between two different vendors for your computer needs. Use the six-step rational model to think through this decision.
   Answer - Students' answers will vary but they should clearly apply all six steps of the model. See Exhibit 6-1 for the six steps in the rational decision-making model.
   - The model begins by defining the problem. A problem exists when there is a discrepancy between an existing and a desired state of affairs.
   - Next, identify the decision criteria that will be important in solving the problem. Determining what is relevant to making the decision.
   - Third, weight the criteria, i.e., prioritize the criteria.

- The fourth step requires the generation of possible alternatives that could succeed in resolving the problem.
- Fifth, critically analyze each alternative by rating each alternative on each criterion.
- Finally, compute the optimal decision by evaluating each alternative against the weighted criteria and selecting the alternative with the highest total score.

2. How can you stimulate your creativity in decision making?
Answer - 1) Evidence indicates that the mere action of instructing someone to "be creative" and to avoid obvious approaches to a problem results in unique ideas. Overtly telling yourself that you are going to seek out creative options should lead to an increase in unique alternatives. 2) Attribute listing is when the decision maker isolates the major characteristics of traditional alternatives. Then each major attribute of each alternative is considered in turn and is changed in every conceivable way. No ideas are rejected, no matter how ridiculous they may seem. Once this extensive list is completed, the constraints of the problem are imposed in order to eliminate all but the viable alternatives. 3) Creativity can also be stimulated by practicing zigzag, or lateral, thinking. This is a replacement for the more traditional vertical, sequential thinking. With lateral thinking, individuals emphasize thinking sideways: not developing a pattern but restructuring a pattern. Lateral thinking does not have to be correct at each step. Lateral thinking is not restricted to relevant information.

3. The rational process may seem unrealistic. A more "real" way of making decisions is bounded rationality. Explain how this is different than the rational model.
Answer - When faced with a complex problem, most people respond by reducing the problem to a level at which it can be readily understood. People satisfice--they seek solutions that are satisfactory and sufficient. Because of the limitations of the human mind most individuals operate within the confines of <u>bounded rationality</u>. They construct simplified models that extract the essential features from problems without capturing all of their complexity. As with the rational model the process begins when a problem is identified and the search for criteria and alternatives is started. The difference is that the decision maker limits alternatives to the more conspicuous choices. Choices that are easy to find and that tend to be highly visible. The limited set of alternatives is reviewed. The review is limited--it begins with alternatives that differ only in a relatively small degree from the choice currently in place. The decision maker proceeds to review alternatives only until he or she identifies an alternative that is good enough--one that meets an acceptable level of performance. The order in which alternatives are considered is critical in determining which alternative is selected because the satisficing choice will be the first acceptable one the decision maker encounters. Solutions that depart least from the status quo and meet the decision criteria are most likely to be selected.

4. What is the mental process most managers use to handle the immense amount of information involved in decision making and how does the technique work?
Answer - In order to avoid information overload, decision makers rely on heuristics, or judgmental shortcuts, in decision making. An availability heuristic is the tendency for people to base their judgments on information that is readily available to them. A representative heuristic--assess the likelihood of an occurrence by trying to match it with a preexisting category.

5. What causes managers, CEOs, and other leaders to pursue a course of action that is failing rather than abandon it?
Answer - This is known as an escalation of commitment. It is an increased commitment to a previous decision, often in spite of negative information. It has been well documented that individuals escalate commitment to a failing course of action when they view themselves as responsible for the failure. They "throw good money after bad" to demonstrate that their initial decision was not wrong and to avoid having to admit they made a mistake. Many an organization has suffered large losses because a

manager was determined to prove that his or her original decision was right by continuing to commit resources to what was a lost cause from the beginning.

6. Identify four decision-making styles.
Answer - Two individual differences seem particularly relevant to decision making in organizations--decision-making styles and level of moral development. The foundation of the four-style model is the recognition that people differ along two dimensions. a) The first is their way of thinking. b) The other dimension addresses a person's tolerance for ambiguity. When these two dimensions are diagrammed, they form four styles of decision making. See Exhibit 6-2. Four styles--directive, analytical, conceptual, and behavioral.
   - Directive style
     - Low tolerance for ambiguity and seek rationality.
     - Efficient and logical. Decisions are based on minimal information after the consideration of few alternatives.
     - Directive types make decisions fast, and they focus on the short run.
   - Analytical style
     - Greater tolerance for ambiguity than do directive decision makers.
     - They desire more information and consider more alternatives than do directives.
     - Characterized as careful decision makers with the ability to adapt or cope with new situations.
   - Conceptual style
     - Very broad in their outlook and consider many alternatives.
     - Focus is long range, and they are very good at finding creative solutions to problems.
   - Behavioral style
     - Characterizes decision makers who work well with others.
     - They are concerned with the achievement of peers and subordinates.
     - They are receptive to suggestions from others and rely heavily on meetings for communicating.
     - This type of manager tries to avoid conflict and seeks acceptance.
   - Focusing on decision styles can be useful for helping you understand how two equally intelligent people can differ in their decisions.

7. Explain the implications of stages of moral development to decision making.
Answer - This is the second of the individual differences that are particularly relevant to decision making in organizations. Many decisions have an ethical dimension. Research confirms the existence of three levels of moral development, each comprising two stages. [See Exhibit 6-3.] At each successive stage, an individual's moral judgment grows less and less dependent on outside influences.
   - Preconventional. Individuals respond to notions of right or wrong only when personal consequences are involved.
   - Conventional. Reasoning at this level indicates that moral value resides in maintaining the conventional order and the expectations of others.
   - Principled. Individuals make a clear effort to define moral principles apart from the authority of the groups to which they belong or society in general.

   Conclusions. First, people proceed through the six stages in a lock-step fashion. They gradually move up a ladder, stage by stage. Second, there is no guarantee of continued development. Development can terminate at any stage. Third, most adults are at stage 4. They are limited to obeying the rules and laws of society. Finally, the higher the stage a manager reaches, the more he or she will be predisposed to make ethical decisions.

8. How do organizations shape both the alternatives considered and the final decisions made by managers?
Answer - The organization itself constrains decision makers. 1) Performance evaluation--Managers are strongly influenced by the criteria by which they are evaluated. 2) Reward systems--The organization's reward system influences decision makers by suggesting to them what choices are preferable in terms of personal payoff. 3) System-imposed time constraints--Organizations impose deadlines on decisions. 4) Historical precedent--Decisions have a context, individual decisions are more accurately characterized as points in a stream of decisions. Decisions made in the past are ghosts that continually haunt current choices.

9. How can dedicated, well-educated and trained, experienced managers have different ethical perspectives? What are the three primary approaches to framing an ethical issue?
Answer - Three different ways to frame decisions.
   - Utilitarian criterion
     - Decisions are made solely on the basis of their outcomes or consequences.
     - The goal is to provide the greatest good for the greatest number.
     - This view tends to dominate business decision making.
   - Focus on rights
     - This calls on individuals to make decisions consistent with fundamental liberties and privileges as set forth in documents like the Bill of Rights.
     - An emphasis on rights in decision making means respecting and protecting the basic rights of individuals, such as the right to privacy, to free speech, and to due process.
   - Focus on justice
     - This requires individuals to impose and enforce rules fairly and impartially so there is an equitable distribution of benefits and costs.
     - Union members typically favor this view.

   Advantages and liabilities. Utilitarianism--Promotes efficiency and productivity, but it can result in ignoring the rights of some individuals, particularly those with minority representation in the organization. Rights--Protects individuals from injury and is consistent with freedom and privacy, but it can create an overly legalistic workplace that hinders productivity and efficiency. Justice--Protects the interests of the underrepresented and less powerful, but it can encourage a sense of entitlement that reduces risk taking, innovation, and productivity.

EXERCISE

<u>You decide</u>

The following case can be used as an individual or group exercise. It is written in such a way a number of arguments can be made. The importance factor is that the students experience a decision-making process and see how different each strategy is in effort, process, and quality of decision. The "Scroggs" case on which the decision is to be made follows these instructions.

1. As an individual exercise: Give instructions in one class, have students report results in the next.
2. Prior to passing out the case, divide the class into three large groups without telling them how or why they are being divided.
   - Those who will use a rational model.
   - Those who will use bounded rationality.
   - Those who will make their decision intuitively.
3. Go to each group and quietly tell them the model they are to use to make their decision. Each large group should not know how the other groups are making their decisions.
   - Those using the rational model must be prepared to outline how they came to their decision.
   - Those using bounded rationality must be prepared to explain why they stopped where they did.

- Those using intuition are to read the case and make a decision based on their reaction without rereading the case or studying the details.
- Each group is to track how long it took them to come to their decision.
- Refer students to the appropriate section of their text for their process.

4. Next class, have students note on the board or orally present what their decisions were. Simply tabulate their decision, responsible or not.
   - Begin with those using the rational model, those using bounded rationality, and end with the intuitive.
   - Note if there is any pattern to the decisions. Did one style lead to a particular decision?
5. Now ask for volunteers to offer their reasons for their decision. Draw from each group and keep track of their reasons.
6. Now ask for times; how long did it take to make the decision?
7. Ask the students, after hearing the decisions and reasons, would anyone change their mind?
   - Who would change to guilty?
   - Who would change to not guilty?
   - Who wouldn't change.
8. Discuss the quality of the decisions, the influence of reasons, etc.

State vs. Scroggs

In the fall of 1875, Hiram Smith filed a claim on a very fertile piece of land in South Dakota with the land office. Before he could put any improvements on the land, he died. A young Swede, newly immigrated, filed a counterclaim to the land at once, and by late spring of the following year had built a home and had begun to cultivate the land.

In the meantime, the widow of the original claimant was on her way west with her two daughters and her son. She built a house on the land, across a ravine from the Swede's home, and cultivated that half of the claim. Both parties sent their claims to the Department of the Interior, but ten years went by without a decision. Both the Swede and Mrs. Smith built barns and cultivated the land intensively--on their own sides of the ravine.

A distant relative of Mrs. Smith, a minister named Scroggs lived in a small, town about two miles from the rival farms. He had been an advisor for the Swede on all matters of religion and politics since the fellow had first taken up farming in Dakota.

He had often complimented the Swede on his land and had expressed his opinion at the general store that it was the best land in the west.

Scroggs had acted as arbiter for the disputants and had corresponded with the Secretary of the Interior in regard to the land. One day at the general store he told the Swede that he thought the Swede's claim would be supported. The Swede swore that no one was going to put him off the land. The next day, Scroggs went to the Smith farm and showed Mrs. Smith a paper from Washington ratifying her claim to the land. He said it would be all right for them to take possession. Young Smith hitched a team to the plow and went over on to the Swede's side of the farm. Scroggs, Mrs. Smith, and the two daughters went along, Scroggs on his horse. Young Smith had just started plowing when the Swede ran out of his house with a gun and shot him.

Two more shots killed the horses on the plow. Scroggs galloped off and shouted that he was going after the marshal. When the marshal and a posse arrived, they found the Swede had killed the three women and had then committed suicide. Scroggs, being the only relative of the dead woman, inherited both pieces of land.

Question: Should Scroggs be held responsible for the killing?

CHAPTER 7 - FOUNDATIONS OF GROUP BEHAVIOR

CHAPTER OBJECTIVES

After reading this chapter students should be able to:

1 Differentiate between formal and informal groups.
2 Explain why people join groups.
3 Describe how role requirements change in different situations.
4 Explain the importance of the Hawthorne studies.
5 Describe the importance of the Asch studies.
6 Identify the implications of social loafing.
7 Outline the benefits and disadvantages of cohesive groups.
8 Explain the effect of diversity on group performance.
9 Contrast groupthink and groupshift.

LECTURE OUTLINE

I. DEFINING AND CLASSIFYING GROUPS

A. Definition

1. A group is defined as two or more individuals, interacting and interdependent, who come together to achieve particular objectives. Groups can be either formal or informal.
   a) By formal, we mean a group that is defined by the organization's structure, with designated work assignments establishing tasks and work groups.
   b) In formal groups, the behaviors that one should engage in are stipulated by and directed toward organizational goals.
   c) In contrast, informal groups are alliances that are neither structured nor organizationally determined. In the work environment, these groups form naturally as responses to the need for social contact.
2. Subclassify groups into command, task, interest, or friendship categories.
   a) Command and task groups are dictated by the formal organization, whereas interest and friendship groups are informal alliances.
   b) The command group is determined by the organizational chart.
   c) Task groups, also organizationally determined, represent persons working together to complete a job.
      (1) A task group's boundaries are not limited to its immediate hierarchical superior.
      (2) All command groups are also task groups, but the reverse need not be true.
   d) Groups may affiliate to attain a specific objective. This is an interest group.
   e) Friendship groups often develop because the individual members have one or more common characteristics or social allegiances.
3. Informal groups provide a very important function by satisfying their members' social needs.
4. Exhibit 7-1 summarizes the most popular reasons why people join a group.

II. BASIC GROUP CONCEPTS

A. Groups have a structure that shapes the behavior of their members.

B. Roles

1. Laura Campbell is a buyer with Marks & Spencer, the large British retailer. Her job requires her to play a number of roles: that is, to engage in a set of expected behavior patterns that are attributed to occupying a given position in a social unit.
2. Like Laura Campbell, we all are required to play a number of roles, and our behavior varies with the role we're playing.

3. The understanding of role behavior would be dramatically simplified if each of us chose one role and played it regularly and consistently.
    a) We are required to play diverse roles, both on and off our jobs.
    b) Different groups impose different role requirements on people.
4. Role research conclusions:
    a) People play multiple roles.
    b) People learn roles from the stimuli around them friends, books, movies, television.
    c) People have the ability to shift roles rapidly when they recognize that the situation and its demands clearly require major changes.
    d) People often experience role conflict when compliance with one role requirement is at odds with another.
5. What is the value of a knowledge of roles?
    a) It helps to think in terms of what group they're predominantly identifying with at the time and what behaviors would be expected of them in that role.
    b) It allows the manager to more accurately predict the employee's behavior.

C. Norms

1. Norms are acceptable standards of behavior within a group that are shared by the group's members.
2. Each group will establish its own set of norms.
3. Probably the most widespread norms--and the ones with which managers tend to be most concerned---deal with performance-related processes.
    a) Work groups typically provide their members with explicit cues on how hard they should work, how to get the job done, their level of output, appropriate communication channels, and the like.
    b) These norms are extremely powerful in affecting an individual employee's performance.
4. A key about norms--groups exert pressure to bring members' behavior into conformity with the group's standards.
5. The Hawthorne Studies
    a) Full-scale appreciation of the importance norms play in influencing worker behavior did not occur until the early 1930s.
    b) This enlightenment grew out of a series of studies undertaken at Western Electric Company's Hawthorne Works in Chicago between 1924 and 1932.
        (1) Initiated by Western Electric officials.
        (2) Later overseen by Harvard professor Elton Mayo.
    c) The Hawthorne studies concluded that a worker's behavior and sentiments were closely related, that group influences were significant in affecting individual behavior, that group standards were highly effective in establishing individual worker output, and that money was less of a factor in determining worker output than were group standards, sentiments, and security.
6. The Hawthorne researchers began by examining the relation between the physical environment and productivity.
    a) Illumination and other aspects of working conditions were manipulated.
    b) Initial findings contradicted anticipated results.
7. Results varied but in no case was the increase or decrease in output in proportion to the increase or decrease in illumination.
    a) Researchers introduced a control group--an experimental group was presented with varying intensity of illumination, while the controlled unit worked under a constant illumination intensity.

8. Again, the results were bewildering. Output rose for both the control and the experimental groups whether light was raised or lowered.
   a) The Hawthorne researchers concluded that illumination intensity was only a minor influence among the many influences on an employee's productivity.
9. A second set of experiments in the relay assembly test room at Western Electric.
   a) A small group of women was isolated from the main work group so that their behavior could be more carefully observed.
   b) They went about their job of assembling telephones, the only significant difference was the placement in the room of a research assistant who acted as an observer keeping records of output, rejects, working conditions, and describing everything that happened in a daily log.
   c) Observations over a multiyear period found that this small group's output increased steadily.
   d) The number of personal absences and those lost to sickness were approximately one third of those recorded by women in the regular production department.
   e) What became evident was that this group's performance was significantly influenced by its status of being a "special" group.
10. A third study in the bank wiring observation room was introduced to ascertain the effect of a sophisticated wage incentive plan.
    a) The assumption was that individual workers would maximize their productivity when they saw that it was directly related to economic rewards.
    b) The most important finding of this study was that employees did not individually maximize their outputs.
    c) Output became controlled by a group norm that determined what was a proper day's work.
       (1) Output was not only restricted, but individual workers gave erroneous reports.
11. The group was operating well below its capability.
    a) Members were afraid that if they significantly increased their output, the unit incentive rate would be cut, the expected daily output would be increased, layoffs might occur, or slower workers would be reprimanded.
    b) The group established its idea of a fair output--neither too much nor too little.
12. The norms the group established included a number of "don'ts."
    a) Don't be a rate-buster, turning out too much work.
    b) Don't be a chiseler, turning out too little work.
    c) Don't be a squealer on any of your peers.
13. How did the group enforce these norms? Their methods were neither gentle nor subtle.
    a) They included sarcasm, name-calling, ridicule, and even physical punches on the upper arms of members who violated the group's norms.
    b) Members would also ostracize individuals whose behavior was against the group's interest.

D. Conformity and the Asch Studies.
   1. Group members want acceptance by the group.
      a) Evidence from the now-classic studies undertaken by Solomon Asch, shows that groups can place strong pressures on individual members to change their attitudes and behaviors to conform to the group's standard.
   2. Study design
      a) Asch made up groups of seven or eight people who sat in a classroom and were asked to compare two cards held by the experimenter.
      b) One card had one line, the other had three lines of varying length.
         (1) See Exhibit 7-2.

c) The object was to announce aloud which of the three lines matched the single line.
(1) The difference in line length was quite obvious; under ordinary conditions, subjects made less than one percent errors.
d) But what happens if all the members in the group begin to give incorrect answers?
e) The experiment began with several sets of matching exercises. All the subjects gave the right answers. On the third set, however, the first subject gave an obviously wrong answer.
f) Asch demonstrated that over many experiments and many trials, subjects conformed in about 35 percent of the trials; that is, the subjects gave answers they knew were wrong but were consistent with the replies of other group members.
g) The results suggest that there are group norms that press us toward conformity.

E. Cohesiveness
1. Groups differ in their cohesiveness; that is, the degree to which members are attracted to each other and are motivated to stay in the group.
a) Cohesiveness is important because it's been found to be related to the group's productivity.
2. The relationship of cohesiveness and productivity depends on the performance-related norms established by the group.
a) The more cohesive the group, the more its members will follow its goals.
b) See summary of results in Exhibit 7-3.
3. What can you do as a manager if you want to encourage group cohesiveness?
a) Make the group smaller.
b) Encourage agreement with group goals.
c) Increase the time members spend together.
d) Increase the status of the group and the perceived difficulty of attaining membership in the group.
e) Stimulate competition with other groups.
f) Give rewards to the group rather than to members.
g) Physically isolate the group.

F. Size
1. Size affects group behavior.
a) Smaller groups complete tasks faster than larger ones.
b) If the group is engaged in problem solving, however, large groups consistently get better marks than their smaller counterparts.
c) Large groups--with a dozen or more members--are good for gaining diverse input.
(1) If the goal of the group is fact finding, larger groups should be more effective.
d) Smaller groups are better at doing something productive with that input.
(1) Groups of approximately seven members tend to be more effective for taking action.
2. Social loafing is the tendency for individuals to expend less effort when working collectively than when working individually.
3. A common stereotype about groups is that the sense of team spirit spurs individual effort and enhances the group's overall productivity.
4. But in the late 1920s, a German psychologist named Ringelmann discovered that groups of three people exerted a force only two-and-a-half times the average individual performance.
a) Groups of eight collectively achieved less than four times the solo rate.
5. Social loafing may be due to a belief that others in the group are not carrying their fair share.

G. Composition
1. Most group activities require a variety of skills and knowledge.
2. Heterogeneous groups--those composed of dissimilar individuals---are more likely to have diverse abilities and information and are more effective than homogeneous groups.
3. When a group is heterogeneous in terms of gender, personalities, opinions, abilities, skills, and perspectives, there is an increased probability that the group will possess the needed characteristics to complete its tasks effectively.
   a) There may be more conflict.
4. The evidence indicates that racial or national differences interfere with group processes, at least in the short term.
   a) These difficulties seem to dissipate with time.
   b) The differences disappear after about three months.

H. Status
1. Status is a prestige grading, position, or rank within a group.
   a) It may be formally imposed by a group.
   b) More often, we deal with status in an informal sense.
   c) Informal status is not necessarily less important than the formal variety.
2. William F. Whyte, classic restaurant study.
   a) Whyte proposed that people work more smoothly if high-status personnel customarily originate action for lower-status personnel.
   b) He found instances in which, when those of lower status were initiating action, a conflict arose between formal and informal status systems.
   c) Whyte also noted that in the kitchen, supply men secured food supplies from the chefs. This was, in effect, a case of low-skilled employees initiating action upon the highly skilled.
      (1) Conflict was stimulated when several supply men explicitly and implicitly urged the chefs to "get a move on."
      (2) Whyte observed, however, that one supply man had little trouble.
      (3) He gave the chef the order and asked the chef to call him when it was ready, thus reversing the initiating process.
3. In Whyte's analysis, he suggested several changes in procedures that aligned interactions more closely with the accepted status hierarchy and resulted in substantial improvements in worker relations and effectiveness.
4. It's important for group members to believe that the status hierarchy is equitable.
   a) Any perceived inequity creates disequilibrium resulting in various types of corrective behavior.
5. The trappings that go with formal positions are also important elements in maintaining equity.
   a) Inequity between the perceived ranking of an individual and the status accouterments generates status incongruence.
6. Even though members of groups generally agree among themselves on status criteria and hence tend to rank individuals fairly closely, conflict can arise when individuals move between groups whose status criteria are different or when groups are formed of individuals with heterogeneous backgrounds.

III. GROUP DECISION MAKING
A. The belief
1. That two heads are better than one has long been accepted as a basic component of North American and many other countries' legal systems.

2. It has expanded to the point that today many decisions in organizations are made by groups, teams, or committees.

B. The Individual versus the Group
   1. A major plus of individual decision making is speed.
   2. Individual decisions have clear accountability.
   3. Individual decisions tend to convey consistent values.
      a) Although individuals are not perfectly consistent in their decision making, they do tend to be more consistent than groups.
   4. Groups generate more complete information and knowledge.
   5. Groups can bring heterogeneity to the decision process.
   6. A group will almost always outperform even the best individual--higher--quality decisions.
   7. Finally, groups lead to increased acceptance of a solution.
      a) Many decisions fail after the final choice is made because people don't accept the solution.
   8. Which is better? "It depends."
      a) Individuals are preferred when the decision is relatively unimportant and doesn't require subordinate commitment to its success.
      b) Similarly, individuals should make the decision when they have sufficient information and when subordinates will be committed to the outcome.
   9. The choice comes down to weighing effectiveness against efficiency.
      a) In terms of effectiveness, groups are superior.
      b) Individuals are more efficient than groups.

C. Groupthink and Groupshift
   1. Groupthink
      a) Groupthink is the phenomenon that occurs when group members become so enamored of concurrence that the norm for consensus overrides the realistic appraisal of alternative courses of action and the full expression of deviant, minority, or unpopular views.
      b) It describes a deterioration in an individual's mental efficiency, reality testing, and moral judgment as a result of group pressures.
   2. Symptoms of groupthink
      a) Group members rationalize any resistance to the assumptions they've made.
      b) Members pressure any doubters to support the alternative favored by the majority.
      c) To give the appearance of group consensus, doubters keep silent about misgivings and even minimize to themselves the importance of their doubts.
      d) The group interprets members' silence as a "yes" vote for the majority.
   3. The above symptoms lead to a number of decision-making deficiencies.
      a) Incomplete assessment of the problem.
      b) Poor information search.
      c) Selective bias in processing information.
      d) Limited development of alternatives.
      e) Incomplete assessment of alternatives.
      f) Failure to examine risks of preferred choice.
      g) Failure to reappraise initially rejected alternatives.
   4. Studies of decision making in U.S. government agencies have found deficient outcomes were frequently preceded by symptoms of groupthink.
   5. Evidence suggests that not all groups are equally vulnerable to groupthink.

a) Researchers have focused on five variables:
 (1) The group's cohesiveness.
 (2) Its leader's behavior.
 (3) Its insulation from outsiders.
 (4) Time pressures.
 (5) Failure to follow methodical decision-making procedures.

6. To minimize the influence of groupthink.
 a) Highly cohesive groups have more discussion and bring out more information than do loose groups but also discourage dissent.
 b) An open leadership style--including encouraging member participation, refraining from stating one's opinion at the beginning of the meeting, encouraging divergent opinions from all group members, and emphasizing the importance of reaching a wise decision.
 c) Do not allow the group to detach itself from external sources.
 d) Downplay time constraints.
 e) Encourage the use of methodical decision-making procedures.
7. Groupshift
 a) A shift is toward an extreme position.
  (1) In the direction of a predisposition of a team member.
  (2) Most frequently toward greater risk.
 b) Discussion leads to a significant shift in the positions of members toward a more extreme position in the direction toward which they were already leaning before the discussion.
 c) The groupshift can be viewed as a special case of groupthink.
  (1) The decision of the group reflects the dominant decision-making norm.
8. Explanations for the phenomenon.
 a) Discussion creates familiarization among the members, increasing boldness and daring.
 b) The group diffuses responsibility--freeing any single member from accountability.
9. How to use the findings on groupshift?
 a) Recognize that group decisions exaggerate the initial position of the individual members.
 b) The shift is more often to be toward greater risk.
 c) The shift is a function of the members' prediscussion inclinations.

D. Selecting the Best Group Decision-Making Technique
1. The most common form of group decision making takes place in face-to-face interacting groups.
2. Brainstorming, the nominal group technique, and electronic meetings have been proposed as ways to reduce many of the problems inherent in the traditional interacting group.
3. Brainstorming
 a) Brainstorming is meant to overcome pressures for conformity.
 b) It does so by utilizing an idea-generation process that specifically encourages any and all alternatives while withholding any criticism of those alternatives.
4. Typical brainstorming session
 a) A half-dozen to a dozen people sit around a table.
 b) The group leader states the problem clearly.
 c) Members then "freewheel" as many alternatives as they can in a given length of time.
 d) No criticism is allowed, and all the alternatives are recorded for later discussion and analysis.
 e) Group members are encouraged to "think the unusual."

f) Brainstorming, however, is merely a process for generating ideas.

5. Nominal Group Technique
   a) The nominal group restricts discussion or interpersonal communication during the decision-making process.
   b) Group members are all physically present, but operate independently.
   c) Members meet as a group, but, before any discussion takes place, each member independently writes down his or her ideas on the problem.
   d) This silent period is followed by each member's presenting one idea to the group.
      (1) No discussion takes place until all ideas have been recorded.
   e) The group then discusses the ideas for clarity and evaluates them.
      (1) Each group member silently and independently ranks the ideas. The final decision is determined by the idea with the highest aggregate ranking.
   f) Chief advantage--permits the group to meet formally but does not restrict independent thinking
6. Electronic Meetings.
   a) The most recent approach to group decision making.
      (1) Blends the nominal group technique with sophisticated computer technology.
   b) Up to fifty people sit around a horseshoe-shaped table, empty except for a series of computer terminals.
   c) Issues are presented to participants, and they type their responses onto their computer screen.
   d) Individual comments, as well as aggregate votes, are displayed on a projection screen in the room.
   e) The major advantages of electronic meetings are anonymity, honesty, and speed.
      (1) Participants can anonymously type any message they want, and it flashes on the screen for all to see.
      (2) It also allows people to be brutally honest without penalty.
      (3) It's fast.

IV. IMPLICATIONS FOR MANAGERS

1. In order to accomplish work tasks, the individuals who make up an organization are typically united into various work groups.
   a) Group behavior is not merely the summation of the individual behavior of its members. The group itself adds an additional dimension to its members' behavior.
2. Knowledge of the role that a person is attempting to enact can make it easier for us to deal with the person, for we have insight into her expected behavior patterns.
   a) Knowledge of a job incumbent's role makes it easier for others to work with her, for she should behave in ways consistent with others' expectations.
3. Norms control group member behavior by establishing standards of right or wrong.
   a) Knowing the norms of a given group can help us explain the attitudes and behaviors of its members.
4. Should managers seek cohesive groups? Our answer is a qualified "Yes."
   a) The qualification lies in the degree of alignment between the group and the organization's goals.
5. The implications of the social.
   a) When managers use collective work situations to enhance morale and teamwork, managers must also provide means by which individual efforts can be identified.
   b) This conclusion is consistent with individualistic cultures, such as the United States and Canada, that are dominated by self-interest.
      (1) It is not consistent with collective societies in which individuals are motivated by in-group goals.

6. To increase the performance of work groups, you should try to choose individuals as members who can bring a diverse perspective to problems and issues.
   a) This may cause conflict in the short term.
   b) As members learn to work with their differences, group performance will improve.
7. Status inequities within a group divert activity away from goal accomplishment and direct it toward resolving the inequities.
   a) When inequities exist, group members reduce their work effort, attempt to undermine the activities of those members with higher status, or pursue similar dysfunctional behaviors.
8. Finally, if managers use group decision making, they should particularly try to minimize groupthink.

SUMMARY

1 A group is defined as two or more individuals, interacting and interdependent, who come together to achieve particular objectives. Groups can be either formal or informal. By formal, we mean a group that is defined by the organization's structure, with designated work assignments establishing tasks and work groups. In contrast, informal groups are alliances that are neither structured nor organizationally determined. In the work environment, these groups form naturally as a response to the need for social contact. Groups can also be subclassifed into command, task, interest, or friendship categories.

2 The reasons people join groups is summarized in Exhibit 7-1.

3 We all play different roles in groups and those role requirements change in different situations. Research shows that people play multiple roles, people learn roles from the stimuli around them, and that people have the ability to shift roles rapidly when they recognize that the situation and its demands clearly require major changes.

4 The Hawthorne studies revealed the importance of norms. Norms are acceptable standards of behavior within a group that are shared by the group's members. Each group will establish its own set of norms. A key about norms--groups exert pressure to bring members' behavior into conformity with the group's standards. Full-scale appreciation of the importance norms play in influencing worker behavior did not occur until the early 1930s. This enlightenment grew out of a series of studies undertaken at Western Electric Company's Hawthorne Works in Chicago between 1924 and 1932.

5 Studies by Asch showed that group members want acceptance by the group, and just how powerful that need is. Evidence from the now-classic studies undertaken by Solomon Asch, shows that groups can place strong pressures on individual members to change their attitudes and behaviors to conform to the group's standard.

6 Social loafing is the tendency for individuals to expend less effort when working collectively than when working individually. A common stereotype about groups is that the sense of team spirit spurs individual effort and enhances the group's overall productivity. But in the late 1920s, a German psychologist named Ringelmann discovered that groups of three people exerted a force only two-and-a-half times the average individual performance. Groups of eight collectively achieved less than four times the solo rate.

7 Groups differ in their cohesiveness; that is, the degree to which members are attracted to each other and are motivated to stay in the group. The relationship of cohesiveness and productivity depends on the performance-related norms established by the group. The more cohesive the group, the more its members will follow its goals. See summary of results in Exhibit 7-3.

8 The composition of the group has an effect on its performance, specifically the diversity of the group. Heterogeneous groups are more likely to have diverse abilities and information and are more effective than homogeneous groups. When a group is heterogeneous in terms of gender, personalities, opinions, abilities, skills, and perspectives, there is an increased probability that the group will possess the needed characteristics to complete its tasks effectively.

9 Groupthink occurs when group members become so enamored of concurrence that the norm for consensus overrides the realistic appraisal of alternative courses of action and the full expression of deviant, minority, or unpopular views. The groupshift can be viewed as a special case of groupthink. The decision of the group reflects the dominant decision-making norm. It is often a shift toward an extreme position.

10 Managers have a variety of group decision-making techniques at their disposal. The most common form of group decision making takes place in face-to-face interacting groups. Brainstorming, the nominal group technique, and electronic meetings have been proposed as ways to reduce many of the problems inherent in the traditional interacting group. The nominal group technique is similar to brainstorming but it restricts discussion or interpersonal communication during the decision-making process. Electronic meetings are a recent approach to group decision making and is a nonface-to-face technique. It blends the nominal group technique with sophisticated computer technology.

DISCUSSION QUESTIONS

1 Organizations are made up of different types of groups. Explain what these are and why they are formed.
Answer - A group is defined as two or more individuals, interacting and interdependent, who come together to achieve particular objectives. Groups can be either formal or informal. By formal, we mean a group that is defined by the organization's structure, with designated work assignments establishing tasks and work groups. Informal groups are alliances that are neither structured nor organizationally determined. In the work environment, these groups form naturally as responses to the need for social contact. Groups may also be classified by the purpose: command, task, interest, or friendship categories. Command and task groups are dictated by the formal organization, whereas interest and friendship groups are informal alliances. Task groups, also organizationally determined, represent persons working together to complete a job. An interest group is composed of people who affiliate to attain a specific objective. Friendship groups often develop because the individual members have one or more common characteristics or social allegiances.

2 Why do people join groups?
Answer - Exhibit 7-1 summarizes the most popular reasons why people join a group.

3 What are group roles and why is it important for a manager to understand them?
Answer - We all play different roles in groups and those role requirements change in different situations. Research shows that people play multiple roles, people learn roles from the stimuli around them, and that people have the ability to shift roles rapidly when they recognize that the situation and its demands clearly require major changes. People often experience role conflict when compliance with one role requirement is at odds with another. The knowledge of roles helps managers to think in terms of what group they're predominantly identifying with at the time and what behaviors would be expected of them in that role. It allows the manager to more accurately predict the employee's behavior.

4 The Hawthorne studies were pivotal both in organizational behavior research and for their impact on future management practices. What were they, how were they conducted, and what were the results?
Answer - Full-scale appreciation of the importance norms play in influencing worker behavior came from a series of studies undertaken at Western Electric Company's Hawthorne Works in Chicago between 1924 and 1932. They were initiated by Western Electric officials and later overseen by Harvard professor Elton Mayo. The Hawthorne studies concluded that a worker's behavior and sentiments were closely related, that group influences were significant in affecting individual behavior, that group standards were highly effective in establishing individual worker output, and that money was less of a factor in determining worker output than were group standards, sentiments, and security. The Hawthorne researchers began by examining the relation between the physical

environment and productivity. Results varied but in no case was the increase or decrease in output in proportion to the increase or decrease in illumination. Researchers introduced a control group--an experimental group was presented with varying intensity of illumination, while the controlled unit worked under a constant illumination intensity. Again, the results were bewildering. Output rose for both the control and the experimental groups whether light was raised or lowered. A second set of experiments in the relay assembly test room at Western Electric. A small group of women was isolated from the main work group so that their behavior could be more carefully observed. What became evident was that this group's performance was significantly influenced by its status of being a "special" group. A third study in the bank wiring observation room was introduced to ascertain the effect of a sophisticated wage incentive plan. The assumption was that individual workers would maximize their productivity when they saw that it was directly related to economic rewards. The most important finding of this study was that employees did not individually maximize their outputs. The norms the group established included a number of "don'ts."

5 What is the importance of the Asch studies to understanding the power of a group to shape individual behavior?
Answer - Evidence from the now-classic studies undertaken by Solomon Asch, shows that groups can place strong pressures on individual members to change their attitudes and behaviors to conform to the group's standard. Asch demonstrated that over many experiments and many trials, subjects conformed in about 35 percent of the trials; that is, the subjects gave answers they knew were wrong but were consistent with the replies of other group members. The results suggest that there are group norms that press us toward conformity.

6 What are the implications of social loafing for group productivity?
Answer - Social loafing is the tendency for individuals to expend less effort when working collectively than when working individually. In the late 1920s, a German psychologist named Ringelmann discovered that groups of three people exerted a force only two-and-a-half times the average individual performance. Groups of eight collectively achieved less than four times the solo rate. Increases in group size are inversely related to individual performance. Social loafing may be due to a belief that others in the group are not carrying their fair share. Another explanation is the dispersion of responsibility in that the relationship between an individual's input and the group's output is clouded.

7 As a manager you want your work teams to work together more effectively and you've decided to help them increase their cohesiveness to that end. What practical steps can you take to increase your work teams' group cohesion?
Answer -

- Make the group smaller.
- Encourage agreement with group goals.
- Increase the time members spend together.
- Increase the status of the group and the perceived difficulty of attaining membership in the group.
- Stimulate competition with other groups.
- Give rewards to the group rather than to members.
- Physically isolate the group.

8 How does the diversity of a group effect its performance?
Answer - Most group activities require a variety of skills and knowledge so the more diversity the better. Heterogeneous groups--those composed of dissimilar individuals---are be more likely to have diverse abilities and information and are more effective than homogeneous groups. But they also experience more conflict. The evidence indicates that racial or national differences interfere with

group processes, at least in the short term. These difficulties seem to dissipate with time and the differences disappear after about three months.

9 You need a quick decision that is consistent with past decisions and you are willing to sacrifice the variety of alternatives considered in order to meet these parameters. Which would be better for making this decision, an individual or group and why?
Answer - The Individual. A major plus of individual decision making is speed. Individual decisions have clear accountability. Individual decisions tend to convey consistent values. Individuals are preferred when the decision is relatively unimportant and doesn't require subordinate commitment to its success. While a group would generate more complete information and knowledge it will take longer. The choice comes down to weighing effectiveness against efficiency.

10 As a manager what should you know about groupthink and groupshift?
Answer - Groupthink, the phenomenon that occurs when group members become so enamored of concurrence that the norm for consensus overrides the realistic appraisal of alternative courses of action and the full expression of deviant, minority, or unpopular views. The symptoms of groupthink are:

- Group members rationalize any resistance to the assumptions they've made.
- Members pressure any doubters to support the alternative favored by the majority.
- To give the appearance of group consensus, doubters keep silent about misgivings and even minimize to themselves the importance of their doubts.
- The group interprets members' silence as a "yes" vote for the majority.

These symptoms lead to a number of decision-making deficiencies.

- Incomplete assessment of the problem.
- Poor information search.
- Selective bias in processing information.
- Limited development of alternatives.
- Incomplete assessment of alternatives.
- Failure to examine risks of preferred choice.
- Failure to reappraise initially rejected alternatives.

Managers can minimize the influence of groupthink by:

- Highly cohesive groups have more discussion and bring out more information than do loose groups but also discourage dissent.
- An open leadership style--including encouraging member participation, refraining from stating one's opinion at the beginning of the meeting, encouraging divergent opinions from all group members, and emphasizing the importance of reaching a wise decision.
- Do not allow the group to detach itself from external sources.
- Downplay time constraints.
- Encourage the use of methodical decision-making procedures.

Groupshift is a shift toward an extreme position generally in the direction of a predisposition of a team member and most frequently toward greater risk. The groupshift can be viewed as a special case of groupthink. This happens for several reasons. Discussion creates familiarization among the members, increasing boldness and daring. The group diffuses responsibility--freeing any single member from accountability. Managers need to recognize that group decisions exaggerate the initial position of the individual members.

11 You need a group to make a decision that is creative, looks at a number of alternatives, but you have some members who are intimidated by other members and therefore do not tend to speak up in meetings. What technique will work best?
Answer - Students' choices will vary but the best choice is a nominal group technique. The nominal group restricts discussion or interpersonal communication during the decision-making process. Group

members are all physically present, but operate independently. Members meet as a group, but, before any discussion takes place, each member independently writes down his or her ideas on the problem. This silent period is followed by each member's presenting one idea to the group. Chief advantage--permits the group to meet formally but does not restrict independent thinking.

EXERCISE

Win as Much as You Can

This exercise shows the power of cooperation and the damage of competition within a group. You may have seen this exercise as the "Red/Green" matrix or under any of a number of names. It is a forced choice exercise where cooperation leads to rewards, competition to disaster.

1. You will need a helper to record the decisions, and you will need a set of 3x5 cards marked X and Y for each team. Add a 1, 2, 3, etc., to correspond to the number of the team.
2. Divide the class in half and move them to opposite sides of the room.
3. On each side form small groups of 3-5 students and have them choose a captain and recorder. (A variation is to form same gender groups, mix gender equally, divide athletes from nonathletes, etc.)
4. Number the teams so there are two team 1, two team 2, etc., one on each side of the room.
5. Refer to the pair of teams as being "counterparts." Be careful to use this term.
6. Pass out the X and Y cards to the correspondingly numbered team.
7. Pass out the instructions. [Copy follows.]
8. Read through the instructions. Always answer any questions with "The goal is to Win as Much as you Can," without elaboration.
9. Begin the round.
   - Keep time, do not let them have more than two minutes.
   - Be sure to have all teams show their decision cards at the same time.
   - Teams should use the form to track their choices.
   - Only the captain reveals the choice and only when asked.
10. Keep the exercise moving, count and record decisions quickly, score them, and move on.
11. Have your helper count the number of Xs and Ys and then calculate the score as the teams are making their next decision, it keeps the process moving.

Payoff Schedule

4Xs	-$1 each
3Xs	+$1 each
1Y	-$3 each
2Xs	+$2 each
2Ys	-$2 each
1X	+$3 each
3Ys	-$1 each
4Ys	+$1 each

12. At the beginning of rounds 5, 8, and 10 let the team captains meet with their "counterpart team captains." [You need a separate room so they meet out of sight and hearing of the teams.] Give them up to five minutes.
13. When they return the teams have one minute to confer and show their answer.
14. Teams can refuse to meet with their "counterparts."
15. At the end of all 10 rounds you will have some teams with very large negative scores.
16. Occasionally one or two teams will catch on and begin cooperating.

Discuss the exercise and the students' interpretation of "Win as Much as You Can," and their strategy. Note that they tend to see it competitively--they win more if someone loses. In reality they can only win if they let their "counterpart team" win as well. Note that if teams cooperated from the beginning their scores could have been a +100. Discuss if they trusted each other, why or why not. What effort did they make to build trust?

Win as Much As You Can

Instructions

Payoff Schedule	
4Xs	-$1 each
3Xs	+$1 each
1Y	-$3 each
2Xs	+$2 each
2Ys	-$2 each
1X	+$3 each
3Ys	-$1 each
4Ys	+$1 each

Scorecard

Round	Choice	Pattern	Payoff	Balance
1	X Y	___X___Y	______	_____
2	X Y	___X___Y	______	_____
3	X Y	___X___Y	______	_____
4	X Y	___X___Y	______	_____
5	X Y	___X___Y x 3	______	_____
6	X Y	___X___Y	______	_____
7	X Y	___X___Y	______	_____
8	X Y	___X___Y x 5	______	_____
9	X Y	___X___Y	______	_____
10	X Y	___X___Y x 10	______	_____

Rules:

1. Win as much as you can.
2. Pick a captain who will count and report your vote.
3. Pick a recorder who will track your vote on this form.
4. Confer only with your group. Group must decide on a single choice. Captain breaks ties.
   - You will have two minutes to confer.
5. Only the captain reveals the choice and only when asked.
6. Rounds 5, 8, and 10 your captain may meet with other team captains for a negotiation session.
   - Your captain will have five minutes to confer.
   - Your team will have one minute to confer from round 5 on.

CHAPTER 8 - UNDERSTANDING WORK TEAMS

CHAPTER OBJECTIVES

After reading this chapter, you should be able to:

1. Explain the growing popularity of teams in organizations.
2. Contrast teams with groups.
3. Identify three types of teams.
4. Demonstrate the linkage between group concepts and high performing teams.
5. Explain how organizations can create team players.

LECTURE OUTLINE

I. WHY HAVE TEAMS BECOME SO POPULAR?

A. Introduction

1. Twenty-five years ago the introduction of teams into production processes made news because no one was doing it.
2. How do we explain the current popularity of teams?
    a) Teams typically out-perform individuals when the tasks being done require multiple skills, judgment, and experience.
    b) Restructuring to compete more effectively and efficiently, companies have turned to teams as a way to better utilize employee talents.
    c) Teams have the capability to quickly assemble, deploy, refocus, and disband.
    d) Teams facilitate employee participation in operating decisions.
    e) Teams are an effective means for management to democratize their organizations and increase employee motivation.

II. TEAMS VERSUS GROUPS: WHAT'S THE DIFFERENCE?

A. Definitions

1. A work group is a group that interacts primarily to share information and to make decisions to help one another perform within each member's area of responsibility.
    a) Work groups have no need or opportunity to engage in collective work that requires joint effort.
    b) Their performance is merely the summation of all the group members' individual contributions.
2. A work team generates positive synergy through coordinated effort.
    a) The individual efforts result in a level of performance that is greater than the sum of those individual inputs.
3. See Exhibit 8-1.
4. Many organizations have recently restructured work processes around teams looking for that positive synergy that will increase performance.
5. There is potential but nothing inherently magical in the creation of teams that assures the achievement of this positive synergy.

III. TYPES OF TEAMS

A. Classified According to Their Objective

1. The four most common forms are problem--solving teams, self-managed teams, cross-functional teams, and virtual teams.
2. See Exhibit 8-2.

B. Problem-Solving Teams
1. 20 years ago teams were typically were composed of 5 to 12 hourly employees from the same department who met for a few hours each week to discuss ways of improving quality, efficiency, and the work environment.
    a) Problem-solving teams
    b) Members share ideas or offer suggestions on how work processes and methods can be improved.
    c) The teams weren't given the authority to unilaterally implement their ideas.
2. One of the most widely practiced applications of problem-solving teams during the 1980s was the quality circle.
    a) Work teams of eight to ten employees and supervisors who have a shared area of responsibility and meet regularly to discuss their quality problems, investigate causes of the problems, recommend solutions, and take corrective actions.

C. Self-Managed Teams
1. Problem-solving teams didn't go far enough in getting employees involved in work-related decisions and processes.
2. This led to experimentation with truly autonomous teams that could not only solve problems but also could implement solutions and take full responsibility for outcomes.
    a) Self-managed teams
    b) 10 to 15 people who take on the responsibilities of their former supervisors.
    c) Responsibilities include collective control over the pace of work, determination of work assignments, organization of breaks, and collective choice of inspection procedures.
    d) Fully self-managed teams select their own members, and the members evaluate each other's performance.
3. GE's locomotive-engine plant in Grove City, Pennsylvania example.
4. At the L-S Electrogalvanizing Co. in Cleveland, self-managed teams run the entire plant.
5. Xerox, General Motors, Coors Brewing, PepsiCo, Hewlett-Packard, Honeywell, M&M/Mars, and Aetna Life have implemented self-managed teams.
6. About 30 percent of U.S. employers now use this form of team.
7. A caution
    a) Research on the effectiveness of self-managed teams has not been uniformly positive.
        (1) Employees on self-managed teams seem to have higher absenteeism and turnover rates than do employees in traditional work structures.

D. Cross-Functional Teams
1. Custom Research's reorganization illustrates the latest application of the team concept--cross-functional teams made up of employees at about the same hierarchical level, but from different work areas, who come together to accomplish a task.
2. Many organizations have used horizontal, boundary-spanning groups for decades.
    a) A task force is really nothing other than a temporary cross-functional team. Similarly, committees composed of members from across departmental lines are another example of cross-functional teams.
3. The popularity of cross-discipline work teams exploded in the late 1980s.
    a) All the major automobile companies went to using this form of team to coordinate complex projects.
        (1) Example, the Chrysler Neon subcompact was completely developed by a cross-functional team.
        (2) Chrysler delivered the Neon in a speedy 42 months and for a fraction of what any other manufacturer's small car had cost.

4. Motorola's Iridium Project illustrates why so many companies have turned to cross-functional teams.
   a) This project is developing a huge network that will contain 66 satellites.
   b) For the first year and a half of the project, a cross-functional team of 20 Motorola people met every morning.
5. Cross-functional teams are an effective means of allowing people from diverse areas within an organization (or even between organizations) to exchange information, develop new ideas and solve problems, and coordinate complex projects.
6. They are difficult to manage.
   a) It takes time to build trust and teamwork, especially among people from different backgrounds, with different experiences and perspectives.

E. Virtual Teams

1. Virtual teams use computer technology to tie together physically dispersed members in order to achieve a common goal. They allow people to collaborate online, whether they're only a room apart or separated by continents.
   a) Virtual teams can do all the things that other teams do---share information, make decisions, and complete tasks.
   b) They can include all members from the same organization or link an organization's members with employees from other organizations (i.e., suppliers and joint partners).
2. The three primary differentiating factors:
   a) the absence of paraverbal and nonverbal cues.
   b) limited social context.
   c) the ability to overcome time and space constraints.
3. In face-to-face conversation, people use paraverbal (tone of voice, inflection, voice volume) and nonverbal (eye movement, facial expression, hand gestures, and other body language) cues. These help clarify communication, but they aren't available in online interactions.
4. Virtual teams often suffer from less social rapport and less direct interaction among members.
   a) They aren't able to duplicate the normal give-and-take of face-to-face discussion.
   b) Virtual team members report less satisfaction with the group interaction process than face-to-face teams.
   c) But virtual teams allow people to work together who might otherwise never be able to collaborate.
5. Companies like Texas Instruments and Boeing have become heavy users of virtual teams.

IV. LINKING TEAMS AND GROUP CONCEPTS: TOWARD CREATING HIGH-PERFORMANCE TEAMS

A. Size of Work Teams

1. The best work teams tend to be small.
2. When larger than about 10 to 12 members, it becomes difficult to get much done; they will have trouble interacting constructively and agreeing on much.
3. Designing effective teams, managers should keep them to under a dozen.

B. Abilities of Members

1. To perform effectively, a team requires three different types of skills.
   a) Technical expertise.
   b) Problem-solving and decision-making skills to be able to identify problems, generate alternatives, evaluate those alternatives, and make competent choices.
   c) Good listening, feedback, conflict-resolution, and other interpersonal skills.

2. The right mix is crucial.
    a) It's not uncommon for one or more members to learn the skills in which the group is deficient, thereby allowing the team to reach its full potential.

C. Allocating Roles and Promoting Diversity
1. People differ in terms of personality traits and employee performance is enhanced when individuals are put into jobs that are compatible with their personalities.
2. Teams have different needs, and people should be selected for a team on the basis of their personalities and preferences.
3. High-performing teams properly match people to various roles.
    a) Successful teams have selected people to fill all the key roles and play those roles on the basis of their skills and preferences.
4. Nine potential team roles that people prefer to play.
    a) See Exhibit 8-3.
    b) Creator-Innovators--are imaginative and good at initiating ideas or concepts. They are typically very independent and prefer to work at their own pace.
    c) Explorer-Promoters--like to take new ideas and "champion" their cause. They are good at picking up ideas from creator-innovators and finding the resources to promote those ideas. Their primary weakness is that they may not always have the patience and control skills to ensure that the ideas are followed through in detail.
    d) Assessor-Developers--have strong analytical skills. They're at their best when given several different options to evaluate and analyze before a decision is made.
    e) Thruster-Organizers--like to set up operating procedures to turn ideas into reality and get things done. They set goals, establish plans, organize people, and establish systems to ensure that deadlines are met.
    f) Concluder-Producers--like Thruster-organizers, they are also concerned with results, but they insist that deadlines are kept and commitments are followed through.
    g) Controller-Inspectors--people with a high concern for establishing and enforcing rules and regulations. They are good at examining details and making sure that inaccuracies are avoided. They want to check all the facts and figures; they want to make sure that the "i"s are dotted and the "t"s are crossed.
    h) Upholders-Maintainers--hold strong convictions about the way things should be done. They'll defend and fight the team's battles with outsiders while strongly supporting internal team members. Upholder-maintainers provide team stability.
    i) Reporter-Advisers--good listeners who don't tend to press their point of view on others. They encourage the team to seek additional information before making decisions.
    j) Linkers--try to understand all views. They are coordinators and integrators. They dislike extremism and try to build cooperation among all team members. They recognize the various contributions that other team members can make and try to integrate people and activities despite the differences that may exist.
5. If forced to, most people can perform any of these roles, but most have two or three roles they strongly prefer.
6. By matching individual preferences with team role demands, managers increase the likelihood that the team members will work well together.

D. Having a Commitment to a Common Purpose
1. Effective teams have a common vision that provides direction, momentum, and commitment for members.

a) The development team at Apple Computer that designed the Macintosh, for example, was almost religiously committed to creating a user-friendly machine that would revolutionize the way people used computers.
b) Production teams at Saturn Corp. are driven and united by the common purpose of building an American automobile that can successfully compete in terms of quality and price with the best Japanese cars.

2. Members of successful teams put a tremendous amount of time and effort into discussing, shaping, and agreeing upon a purpose that belongs to them both collectively and individually.
3. This common purpose, when accepted by the team, becomes the equivalent of what celestial navigation is to a ship captain--it provides direction and guidance under any and all conditions.

E. Establishing Specific Goals
1. Successful teams translate their common purpose into specific, measurable, and realistic performance goals.
2. These specific goals facilitate clear communication.
3. They also help teams maintain their focus on results.
4. Thermos Corp., example.

F. Leadership and Structure
1. Goals define the team's end targets.
2. But high-performance teams also need leadership and structure to provide focus and direction.
3. Team members must agree on who is to do what and must ensure that all members share equally in the work load.

G. Social Loafing and Accountability
1. Individuals can engage in "social loafing" and coast on the group's effort because their individual contributions can't be identified.
2. High-performing teams undermine this tendency by holding themselves accountable at both the individual and team level.
3. Successful teams' members are clear on both their individual and joint responsibilities.

H. Appropriate Performance Evaluation and Reward Systems
1. How do you get team members to be both individually and jointly accountable?
2. The traditional individually oriented evaluation and reward system must be modified.
3. In addition to evaluating and rewarding employees for their individual contribution, management should consider group-based appraisals, profit sharing, gainsharing, small-group incentives, and other system modifications that will reinforce team effort and commitment.

V. TURNING INDIVIDUALS INTO TEAM PLAYERS

A. The Challenge
1. One substantial barrier to using work teams is individual resistance.
2. To perform well as team members, individuals must be able to communicate openly and honestly, confront differences and resolve conflicts, and sublimate personal goals for the good of the team.
3. The challenge is greatest where:
a) the national culture is highly individualistic.

b) the teams are being introduced into an established organization that has historically valued individual achievement.
c) Examples: AT&T, Ford, Motorola, and other large U.S.-based companies.

4. On the other hand, the challenge for management is less demanding when teams are introduced:
   a) where employees have strong collectivist values--such as in Japan or Mexico.
   b) Or in new organizations that use teams as their initial form for structuring work. Saturn Corp.

B. Shaping Team Players

1. The primary options for turning individuals into team players.
2. Selection
   a) Some people already possess the interpersonal skills to be effective team players.
   b) When faced with candidates lacking team skills/orientation there are three options.
      (1) Train the candidate.
      (2) Place the candidate in a unit within the organization that doesn't have teams.
      (3) Don't hire the candidate.
3. Training
   a) People raised on the importance of individual accomplishment can be trained to become team players.
   b) Training improves problem-solving, communication, negotiation, conflict-management, coaching, and group-development skills.
4. Rewards
   a) The reward system needs to be reworked to encourage cooperative efforts rather than competitive ones.
   b) Promotions, pay raises, and other forms of recognition should be given to individuals depending upon how effective they are as collaborative team members.
   c) Behaviors that should be rewarded include training new colleagues, sharing information with teammates, helping resolve team conflicts, and mastering new skills that your team needs.
   d) Don't forget the intrinsic rewards that employees can receive from teamwork. Teams provide camaraderie. It's exciting and satisfying to be an integral part of a successful team.

VI. IMPLICATIONS FOR MANAGERS

1. Few trends have influenced jobs as much as the introduction of teams into the workplace. Teams require employees to cooperate with others, share information, confront differences, and sublimate personal interests for the greater good of the team.
2. High-performing teams have common characteristics. They tend to be small. They contain people with three different types of skills: technical, problem-solving and decision-making, and interpersonal. They properly match people to various roles. These teams have a commitment to a common purpose, establish specific goals, and have the leadership and structure to provide focus and direction. They also hold themselves accountable at both the individual and team level.
3. Because individualistic organizations and societies attract and reward individual accomplishment, it is more difficult to create team players in these environments. To change, management should select individuals with effective interpersonal skills, provide training to develop teamwork skills, and reward individuals for cooperative efforts.

SUMMARY

1. Teams are growing in popularity because they typically outperform individuals when the tasks being done require multiple skills, judgment, and experience. When restructuring to compete more effectively and efficiently, companies have turned to teams as a way to better utilize employee talents. Teams also facilitate employee participation in operating decisions and help managers democratize their organizations and increase employee motivation.
2. A work group is a group that interacts primarily to share information and to make decisions to help one another perform within each member's area of responsibility. Work groups have no need or opportunity to engage in collective work that requires joint effort. A work team generates positive synergy through coordinated effort. The individual efforts result in a level of performance that is greater than the sum of those individual inputs.
3. The four most common forms are problem--solving teams, self-managed teams, cross-functional teams, and virtual teams.
4. There are a number of group concepts that link directly to high performance in teams. The best work teams tend to be small. To perform effectively, a team requires four different types of skills--technical expertise, problem-solving and decision-making skills, and good interpersonal skills. Teams have different needs, and people should be selected for a team on the basis of their personalities and preferences. High-performing teams properly match people to various roles. Effective teams have a common vision that provides direction, momentum, and commitment for members. Successful teams translate their common purpose into specific, measurable, and realistic performance goals. High-performance teams also need leadership and structure to provide focus and direction. High-performing teams undermine the tendency toward social loafing by holding themselves accountable at both the individual and team level. Finally, high performing teams have appropriate performance evaluation and reward systems.
5. Organizations have a number of options when creating team players; selection, training, and through rewarding cooperative effort.

DISCUSSION QUESTIONS

1. Why have teams become a popular organizational tool for productivity improvement and empowerment of employees?
   Answer - Teams typically outperform individuals when the tasks being done require multiple skills, judgment, and experience. In their restructuring to compete more effectively and efficiently, companies have turned to teams as a way to better utilize employee talents. Teams have the capability to quickly assemble, deploy, refocus, and disband. Teams facilitate employee participation in operating decisions. Teams are an effective means for management to democratize their organizations and increase employee motivation.

2. Why is it important for managers to understand the difference between teams and groups?
   Answer - A <u>work group</u> is a group that interacts primarily to share information and to make decisions to help one another perform within each member's area of responsibility. Work groups have no need or opportunity to engage in collective work that requires joint effort. Their performance is merely the summation of all the group members' individual contributions. A <u>work team</u> generates positive synergy through coordinated effort. The individual efforts result in a level of performance that is greater than the sum of those individual inputs. Exhibit 8-1 outlines the differences.

3. As a manager you are assigned a short-term project, 3-4 months, to study your small company's computer and information needs and then recommend a course of action. You need someone who has expertise in computers, someone with a knowledge of information systems, a couple of users within your organization, and a software specialist but your company only has the users. What type of team would be most effective? Why?

Answer - Students can make an argument for a problem-solving team using some consultants or a virtual team. They might argue for a cross-functional team, seeing the content experts as functional experts even though they aren't employees of the company. A self-managed team clearly won't work. Problem-solving team--members share ideas or offer suggestions on how work processes and methods can be improved. Cross-functional team--is made up of employees at about the same hierarchical level, but from different work areas, who come together to accomplish a task. Many organizations have used horizontal, boundary-spanning groups for decades. A task force is really nothing other than a temporary cross-functional team. Similarly, committees composed of members from across departmental lines are another example of cross-functional teams. Cross-functional teams are an effective means of allowing people from diverse areas within an organization (or even between organizations) to exchange information, develop new ideas and solve problems, and coordinate complex projects. Virtual team--use computer technology to tie together physically dispersed members in order to achieve a common goal. They allow people to collaborate online, whether they're only a room apart or separated by continents. Virtual teams can do all the things that other teams do---share information, make decisions, and complete tasks. They can include all members from the same organization or link an organization's members with employees from other organizations (i.e., suppliers and joint partners).

4. As a manager what basic group concepts do you need to consider in forming high performing teams?
Answer - Size--the best work teams tend to be small. When larger than about 10 to 12 members, it becomes difficult to get much done; they will have trouble interacting constructively and agreeing on much. Abilities of members--to perform effectively, a team requires three different types of skills; technical expertise, problem-solving and decision-making skills, and interpersonal skills. Allocating roles and promoting diversity--teams have different needs, and people should be selected for a team on the basis of their personalities and preferences. High-performing teams select people to fill all the key roles and play those roles on the basis of their skills and preferences. Commitment to a common purpose--effective teams have a common vision that provides direction, momentum, and commitment for members. Establishing specific goals--successful teams translate their common purpose into specific, measurable, and realistic performance goals. Leadership and structure--High-performance teams also need leadership and structure to provide focus and direction. Social loafing and accountability--High-performing teams undermine this tendency by holding themselves accountable at both the individual and team level. Successful teams' members are clear on both their individual and joint responsibilities. Appropriate performance evaluation and reward systems--The traditional individually oriented evaluation and reward system must be modified.

5. Your company has always rewarded individual effort. Now top management wants to implement teams as part of a reengineering process. As a manager how can you prepare your people to be team players?
Answer - You face a challenge because the teams are being introduced into an established organization that has historically valued individual achievement. To perform well as team members, individuals must be able to communicate openly and honestly, confront differences and resolve conflicts, and sublimate personal goals for the good of the team. The primary options for turning individuals into team players are: Selection--some people already possess the interpersonal skills to be effective team players. Training--people raised on the importance of individual accomplishment can be trained to become team players. Training improves problem-solving, communication, negotiation, conflict-management, coaching, and group-development skills. Rewards.--The reward system needs to be reworked to encourage cooperative efforts rather than competitive ones. Behaviors that should be rewarded include training new colleagues, sharing information with teammates, helping resolve team conflicts, and mastering new skills that your team needs. Don't forget the intrinsic rewards that employees can receive from teamwork. Teams provide camaraderie. It's exciting and satisfying to be an integral part of a successful team.

EXERCISE

International Office Building

Students will learn not only the power of cooperation but also the importance of planning group work prior to begining a project.

1. You will need sufficient "Legos" to make a parts bag for each team.
   - You will need a second room and a helper.
   - You need to build a "model." I suggest gluing it together once you build it so it doesn't come apart.
   - A suggested model design.

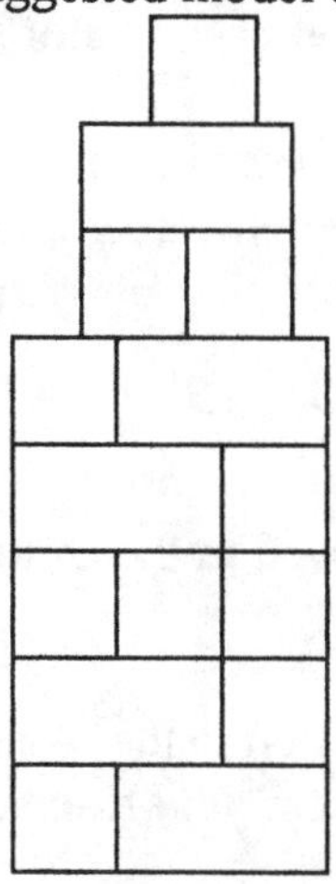

4-prong white

8-prong red

4-prong blue/4-prong yellow

4-prong white/8-prong blue
8-prong yellow/4-prong yellow

4-prong yellow/4-prong red/4-prong black

8-prong blue/4-prong white

4-prong blue/8-prong yellow

Once you build the model, map each side by color. Students can sometimes make a model that looks correct on one side but isn't on one or more of the other sides.

2. Divide students into teams of 6 or fewer students.
3. Pass out the instructions and read through them.
   - At this point read the student instructions yourself, it explains the details.
4. Pass out the bags of "Legos." Let students count them to make sure they have the right number of each color. As soon as they do that they must put them on a desk between them and not touch them again until you start the game.
5. At this point pass out the "International Visas," one to a team, and send your helper with the unseen model into another room.
   - The assistant is to collect the visa when students enter and return it when they leave, to control for no more than one student at a time from each team.
   - The assistant is to keep students from touching the model. The students may move around but they may not touch the model.
6. You made need another assistant in the room with you to keep track of the time when teams report they are moving to construction or when they want to be certified.
   - When a team moves to construction, record the amount of time they spent planning.
   - When a team asks for certification, record the time. If they are certifiable, keep the time. If not, return the model with only the comment, "Not certified," and erase their time, which keeps running.
7. The first team done wins. You should continue the exercise until at least half of your teams complete their models.
8. Discuss the results.
   - Ask teams to explain how they decided to go about the task.
   - Ask about leadership and participation.
   - Frequently there is a direct relationship between planning time and construction time. The more time planning the less time constructing.

Student handout

This is a team work exercise. You are to build an overseas headquarters for a multinational America-based corporation. They want their international headquarters to look like their American headquarters. Unfortunately the blueprints for the building have been lost. You must study the American headquarters building and then replicate it. Yours is a competitive company and other project teams have been given the same assignment. The team that accomplishes the task first receives a bonus.

Process:

1. You have 45 minutes to build your international office building. Your time is divided into two parts: planning time and building time. You may use as much planning time as you desire before you build but once you begin to build you MAY NOT return to planning time.
2. Study the American model. Your model American building is located in another room.
   - Only one member of your team may study the model at a time. That team member must return to your circle before the next team member leaves. The "studying" team member must carry his/her international Visa to be permitted entry back into the U.S.
   - You may take notes, sketches, etc., but you cannot touch the building.
   - You may send as many or as few of your team as you please.
   - Anyone may visit the site as many times as they please. Each visit, as well as the entire planning process, may take as long as you please.

3. When you finish planning and start to build, you must announce your intention to the "Master Builder" so he/she may record the transition. Be sure to announce the name of your team and be certain the "Master Builder" hears you.

4. When you complete your building, call to the "Master Builder" to certify your construction. Your time stops when you call him/her. If you are certified, you are done. If you are not certified, you may try again but your time begins again from when you first called to the "Master Builder."

5. The team with a "certified" building in the least total time wins. There are significant awards for winning and placing.

Materials

a. Do not open your bag of "construction materials" until told to do so.
b. When told to open your bag and count your "materials" make sure that you have the following: (#'s refer to the number of male fittings on the top of the Lego)

5 - Blue 8s	1 - Red 6s	1 - Red 4s
4 - Yellow 8s	1 - White 6s	1 - White 4s
3 - White 8s	3 - Yellow 4s	
2 - Red 8s	1 - Black 4s	

c. Once counted you may not handle your materials any further until we begin.
d. Take the next few minutes and plan your strategy. Remember the restrictions of #1-5 above.
e. Any questions?

CHAPTER 9 - COMMUNICATION

CHAPTER OBJECTIVES

After reading this chapter, you should be able to:

1. Define communication and list its four functions.
2. Describe the communication process.
3. Contrast the three common types of small-group networks.
4. Identify factors affecting the use of the grapevine.
5. Describe common barriers to effective communication.
6. List four rules for improving cross-cultural communication.
7. Outline behaviors associated with providing effective feedback.
8. Identify the behaviors related to effective active listening.

LECTURE OUTLINE

I. FUNCTIONS OF COMMUNICATION

   A. Communication's Four Major Functions

      1. Control. Communication controls member behavior in several ways.
         a) Employees are required to follow authority hierarchies and formal guidelines.
         b) Informal communication also controls behavior.
            (1) When work groups tease or harass a member who produces too much, they are informally communicating with, and controlling, the member's behavior.
      2. Motivation. Communication fosters motivation by clarifying for employees what is to be done, how well they are doing, and what can be done to improve performance.
         a) The formation of specific goals, feedback on progress toward the goals, and reinforcement of desired behavior all stimulate motivation and require communication.
      3. Emotional expression. For many employees, their work group is a primary source for social interaction.
         a) Communication within the group is a fundamental mechanism by which members show their frustrations and feelings of satisfaction.
         b) Communication provides an avenue for expression of emotions and fulfillment of social needs.
      4. Information. The final function that communication performs is related to its role in facilitating decision making.
         a) It provides the needed information.
      5. No one of these four functions should be seen as more important than the others.

II. THE COMMUNICATION PROCESS

   A. The Model

      1. A purpose, expressed as a message to be conveyed, is needed to begin the process.
      2. It passes between a source (the sender) and a receiver.
      3. The message is encoded (converted to a symbolic form).
      4. It is passed by way of some medium (channel) to the receiver.
      5. The receiver retranslates (decodes) the message initiated by the sender.
      6. The result is a transference of meaning from one person to another.
      7. See Exhibit 9-1, the communication process.
         a) The source encodes the message.
         b) The message is the actual physical product from the source encoding.
         c) The channel is the medium through which the message travels.

(1) Formal channels are established by the organization and transmit messages that are related to the professional activities of members.
(2) Other forms of messages, such as personal or social, follow the informal channels in the organization.

d) The receiver is the object to whom the message is directed.
e) Before the message can be received, the symbols in it must be translated into a form that can be understood by the receiver--decoding of the message.
f) The final link is a feedback loop--the check on how successful we have been in transferring our messages as originally intended.

III. DIRECTION OF COMMUNICATION

A. Direction

1. Communication can flow vertically or laterally.
2. The vertical dimension can be further divided into downward and upward directions.

B. Downward

1. Communication that flows from one level of a group or organization to a lower level.
   a) Managers communicating with subordinates.
2. Used by group leaders and managers to assign goals, provide job instructions, and inform underlings of policies and procedures, point out problems that need attention, and offer feedback about performance.

C. Upward

1. Communication that flows to a higher level in the group or organization.
2. Used to provide feedback to higher-ups, inform them of progress toward goals, and relay current problems.
3. Upward communication keeps managers aware.
4. Examples of upward communication are performance reports prepared by lower management for review by middle and top management, suggestion boxes, employee attitude surveys, grievance procedures, superior-subordinate discussions, and informal "gripe" sessions in which employees have the opportunity to identify and discuss problems with their boss or representatives of higher management.

D. Lateral

1. Communication among members of the same work group, among members of work groups at the same level, among managers at the same level, or among any horizontally equivalent personnel.
   a) Horizontal communications are often necessary to save time and facilitate coordination.
   b) Lateral relationships are formally sanctioned.
   c) Often, they are informally created to short-circuit the vertical hierarchy and expedite action.
   d) Lateral communications can, from management's viewpoint, be good or bad.

IV. POPULAR WAYS TO COMMUNICATE

A. The Obvious: Oral and Written Communication

1. The chief means of conveying messages is oral communication.
   a) Speeches, formal one-on-one and group discussions, and the informal rumor mill or grapevine.
2. The advantages-- speed and feedback.

3. The major disadvantage-- whenever the message has to be passed through a number of people there is a potential for distortion.
4. Written communications include memos, letters, electronic mail, fax transmissions, organizational periodicals, notices placed on bulletin boards, or any other device that is transmitted via written words or symbols.
5. Advantages
   a) They're tangible and verifiable.
   b) Both the sender and receiver have a record of the communication.
   c) The message can be stored for an indefinite period of time.
   d) Written communications are more likely to be well thought out, logical, and clear.
6. Drawbacks
   a) Time consuming because it is more precise.
   b) The lack of feedback.

B. The Not-So-Obvious: Nonverbal Communication
1. Verbal messages also impart a nonverbal message.
2. In some instances, the nonverbal component may stand alone.
3. Nonverbal communication includes body movements, the intonations or emphasis we give to words, facial expressions, and the physical distance between the sender and receiver.
4. Kinesics is the academic study of body motions. It refers to gestures, facial configurations, and other movements of the body.
   a) Much of the research findings are debatable therefore consideration of the ways body motions convey meaning must be qualified.
5. It can be argued that every body movement has a meaning and no movement is accidental.
   a) We act out our state of being with nonverbal body language.
6. We may disagree with the specific meanings of the movements, but we cannot deny that body language adds to, and often complicates, verbal communication.
   a) A body position or movement does not by itself have a precise or universal meaning but when it is linked with spoken language, it gives fuller meaning to a sender's message.
   b) Intonations can change the meaning of a message.
   c) Facial expression conveys meaning.
   d) Space in terms of physical distance also has meaning.
7. Look for nonverbal cues as well as listen to the literal meaning of a sender's words.
8. Particularly be aware of contradictions between the messages.
9. We misinform others when we express one emotion verbally, such as trust, but nonverbally communicate a contradictory message that reads, "I don't have confidence in you."

V. COMMUNICATION NETWORKS

A. Formal Small-Group Networks
1. Most studies of communication networks have taken place in groups created in a laboratory setting. As a result, the research conclusions tend to be constrained by the artificial setting and limited to small groups.
2. Three common types of small-group networks.
   a) See Exhibit 9-2.
   b) The chain rigidly follows the formal chain of command.
   c) The wheel relies on the leader to act as the central conduit for all the group's communication.

d) The all-channel permits all group members to actively communicate with each other and is most often characterized in practice by the problem-solving task force.

3. The effectiveness of each type of network depends on the goals of the group.
   a) If speed is important, the wheel and all-channel networks are most effective.
   b) For accuracy use the chain or wheel.
   c) The wheel is best for allowing leaders to emerge.
   d) If member satisfaction is important, the all-channel network is best and the wheel worst.

B. The Informal Group Communication Network
1. An informal system--information flows along the well-known grapevine and rumors can flourish.
2. A classic study of the grapevine was reported more than 40 years ago. The researcher investigated the communication pattern among 67 managerial personnel in a small manufacturing firm.
   a) The grapevine was an important source of information, only 10 percent of the executives acted as liaison individuals.
   b) Information on events of general interest tended to flow between the major functional groups.
   c) No evidence surfaced to suggest that any one group consistently acted as liaisons; rather, different types of information passed through different liaison persons.
3. Replication found that only 10 percent act as liaison individuals.
4. Grapevine accuracy.
   a) 75 percent of what is carried is accurate.
5. Rumors emerge as a response to situations that are important to us, where there is ambiguity, and under conditions that arouse anxiety.
6. A rumor will persist either until the wants and expectations creating the uncertainty underlying the rumor are fulfilled or until the anxiety is reduced.
   a) The grapevine is an important part of any group or organization's communication network.
   b) It identifies for managers those confusing issues that employees consider important and that create anxiety.
   c) It acts as both a filter and a feedback mechanism, picking up the issues that employees consider relevant.
   d) For employees, the grapevine is particularly valuable for translating formal communications into their group's own jargon.

VI. BARRIERS TO EFFECTIVE COMMUNICATION

A. Filtering
1. Filtering refers to a sender's purposely manipulating information so that the receiver will see it more favorably.
2. The major determinant of filtering is the number of levels in an organization's structure.
   a) The more vertical levels the more filtering.
   b) Filtering occurs wherever there are status differences.

B. Selective Perception
1. Selective perception-- the receiver, in the communication process, sees and hears things in a selective way based on his needs, motivations, experience/background, and other personal characteristics.
2. The receiver also projects his interests and expectations into communications as he decodes them.

C. Gender Styles
1. Men and women use oral communication for different reasons.
2. Men use talk to emphasize status, women use it to create connection.
    a) For many men, conversations are primarily a means to preserve independence and maintain status in a hierarchical social order.
    b) For many women, conversations are negotiations for closeness in which people try to seek and give confirmation and support.
    c) When men hear a problem, they want to assert their desire for independence and control by providing solutions.
    d) The women present the problem to gain support and connection, not to get the male's advice.

D. Emotions
1. How the receiver feels at the time of receipt of a communication message will influence how he or she interprets it.
2. Extreme emotions are most likely to hinder effective communication.

E. Language
1. Age, education, and cultural background are variables that influence the language a person uses and the definitions he gives to words.
2. In an organization, employees usually come from diverse backgrounds.
3. Grouping of employees into departments creates specialists who develop their own jargon or technical language.
4. In large organizations, members are also frequently widely dispersed geographically.
5. The existence of vertical levels can also cause language problems.
6. Speaking a common language--English--does not prevent differences in usage of that language.
7. The problem is that members in an organization usually don't know how those with whom they interact have modified the language.

F. Nonverbal Cues
1. Nonverbal communication is almost always accompanied by oral communication.
2. When nonverbal cues are inconsistent with the oral message the receiver becomes confused, and the clarity of the message suffers.

VII. CROSS-CULTURAL COMMUNICATION
A. Cross-cultural Factors
1. The greater the differences in backgrounds between sender and receiver, the greater the differences in meanings attached to particular words or behaviors.
2. Four rules to reduce misperceptions, misinterpretations, and misevaluation.
    a) Assume differences until similarity is proved.
    b) Emphasize description rather than interpretation or evaluation.
        (1) Description is less based on the observer's culture and background than on the interpretation or evaluation.
    c) Practice empathy.
        (1) Before sending a message, put yourself in the receiver's shoes.
    d) Treat your interpretation as a working hypothesis.
        (1) Once you've developed an explanation for a new situation treat your interpretation as a hypothesis that needs further testing.

VIII. IMPLICATIONS FOR MANAGERS

A. Suggestions for Making Communication More Effective

B. Use Feedback

1. Many communication problems can be attributed directly to misunderstandings and inaccuracies.
2. These are less likely to occur with effective feedback.
   a) See Exhibit 9-3.
   b) The manager can ask a set of questions relating to a message in order to determine whether the message was received as intended.
   c) Performance appraisals, salary reviews, and promotion decisions represent important but more subtle forms of feedback.
3. Feedback does not have to be conveyed in words.
   a) Actions can speak louder than words.

C. Simplify Language

1. Structure messages in ways that will make them clear and understandable.
2. Words should be chosen carefully.
3. Jargon can facilitate understanding when it is used with other group members who speak that language, but it can cause innumerable problems when used outside that group.

D. Listen Actively

1. See Exhibit 9-4.
2. Many of us are poor listeners because it's difficult and because it's usually more satisfying to talk.
3. Listening, in fact, is often more tiring than talking. It demands intellectual effort.
   a) The average person speaks at a rate of about 150 words per minute, whereas we have the capacity to listen at the rate of over 1,000 words per minute.
4. Active listening is enhanced when the receiver develops empathy with the sender, that is, when the receiver tries to place himself in the sender's position.
5. Because senders differ in attitudes, interests, needs, and expectations, empathy makes it easier to understand the actual content of a message.
6. An empathetic listener reserves judgment on the message's content and carefully listens to what is being said.

E. Constrain Emotions

1. If we're emotionally upset over an issue, we're likely to misconstrue incoming messages.
2. The best approach is to defer further communication until composure is regained.

F. Watch Your Nonverbal Cues

1. Assume that actions speak louder than words.
2. Nonverbal messages carry a great deal of weight.

G. Use the Grapevine

1. You can't eliminate the grapevine, therefore use it and make it work for you.
2. The grapevine is a valuable source of feedback.
3. The grapevine can carry damaging rumors that reduce the effectiveness of formal communication.
   a) To lessen this destructive force, make good use of formal channels.

SUMMARY

1. Organizations use communication for four primary purposes or functions; control, motivation, emotional expression, and for exchanging information.
2. The communication process model consists of a purpose, expressed as a message that passes between a source (the sender) and a receiver. The message is encoded (converted to a symbolic form). It is passed by way of some medium (channel) to the receiver. The receiver retranslates (decodes) the message initiated by the sender. The result is a transference of meaning from one person to another.
3. Communication can flow in two primary directions in an organization--vertically or laterally. The vertical dimension can be further divided into downward and upward directions.
4. Managers have a number of channels of communication available to them, but each has its own unique strengths and weaknesses. The chief means of conveying messages is oral communication. It is fast and provides feedback. The major disadvantage-- whenever the message has to be passed through a number of people there is a potential for distortion. Written communications are tangible and verifiable. But they are time consuming and often lack in feedback. Verbal messages also impart a nonverbal message.
5. Organizations have both formal small group networks; the chain, wheel, and all-channel networks but also information networks like the grapevine.
6. There are five common barriers to effective communication. Filtering refers to a sender's purposely manipulating information so that the receiver will see it more favorably. Filtering occurs wherever there are status differences. Selective perception--the receiver, in the communication process, sees and hears things in a selective way based on his needs, motivations, experience/background, and other personal characteristics. Gender styles--Men use talk to emphasize status women use it to create connection. Emotions--how the receiver feels at the time of receipt of a communication message will influence how he or she interprets it. Language--age, education, and cultural background are variables that influence the language a person uses and the definitions he gives to words. Nonverbal cues--When nonverbal cues are inconsistent with the oral message the receiver becomes confused, and the clarity of the message suffers.
7. There are four rules for improving cross-cultural communication. 1) Assume differences until similarity is proved. 2) Emphasize description rather than interpretation or evaluation. 3) Practice empathy. 4) Treat your interpretation as a working hypothesis.
8. Many communication problems can be attributed directly to misunderstandings and inaccuracies. These are less likely to occur with effective feedback. The steps for effective feedback are listed in Exhibit 9-3. The manager can ask a set of questions relating to a message in order to determine whether the message was received as intended.
9. Many of us are poor listeners because it's difficult and because it's usually more satisfying to talk. Listening, in fact, is often more tiring than talking. It demands intellectual effort. Active listening is enhanced when the receiver develops empathy with the sender, that is, when the receiver tries to place himself in the sender's position.

DISCUSSION QUESTIONS

1. How do managers use communication in an organization?
   Answer - Communication controls member behavior by requiring employees to follow authority hierarchies and formal guidelines. Informal communication also controls behavior. Communication fosters motivation by clarifying for employees what is to be done, how well they are doing, and what can be done to improve performance. Emotional expression as communication within the group is a fundamental mechanism by which members show their frustrations and feelings of satisfaction. Communication provides an avenue for expression of emotions and fulfillment of social needs. The final function that communication performs is related to its role in facilitating decision making. No one of these four functions should be seen as more important than the others.

2. Describe the communication process in terms of a student asking a professor for permission to take an examination later than the rest of his/her class.
Answer - In their answers have students give special thought to encoding and decoding. What encoding would be especially persuasive, what is the likely decoding of the professor? The student begins with a purpose, expressed as a message to be conveyed, that is needed to begin the process--"I need to take the exam late because I've been ill and unable to keep up on my studies." The message passes between a source (the student) and a receiver (the professor). The message is encoded--converted to a symbolic form (this is the wording chosen by the student). The message then is passed by way of some medium--channel--a note, a face-to-face meeting, to the receiver (the professor). The receiver (professor) retranslates--decodes, phrases into words he/she understands, the message initiated by the sender (student). The result is a transference of meaning from one person to another. The question is did the encoding and decoding match?

3. Describe the three types of communication flows that exist within organizations.
Answer - Communication can flow vertically or laterally. The vertical dimension can be further divided into downward and upward directions. Downward--communication that flows from one level of a group or organization to a lower level. Managers communicating with subordinates. Used by group leaders and managers to assign goals, provide job instructions, and inform underlings of policies and procedures, point out problems that need attention, and offer feedback about performance. Upward--communication that flows to a higher level in the group or organization. Used to provide feedback to higher-ups, inform them of progress toward goals, and relay current problems. Upward communication keeps managers aware. Lateral--communication among members of the same work group, among members of work groups at the same level, among managers at the same level, or among any horizontally equivalent personnel, we describe it as lateral communications.

4. As a manager you have a number of means of communicating to employees. What ways are at your disposal and why would you use one rather than another?
Answer - The chief means of conveying messages is oral communication. The advantages--speed and feedback. The major disadvantage--whenever the message has to be passed through a number of people there is a potential for distortion. Written communications include memos, letters, electronic mail, fax transmissions, organizational periodicals, notices placed on bulletin boards, or any other device that is transmitted via written words or symbols. Advantages--they're tangible and verifiable. Written communications are more likely to be well thought out, logical, and clear. Drawback--time consuming because it is more precise. The lack of feedback. Nonverbal communication--verbal messages also impart a nonverbal message. Nonverbal communication includes body movements, the intonations or emphasis we give to words, facial expressions, and the physical distance between the sender and receiver.

5. There are a number of common small-group networks. What are the strengths and weaknesses of each?
Answer - The three common types of small-group networks are shown in Exhibit 9-2. The chain rigidly follows the formal chain of command. The wheel relies on the leader to act as the central conduit for all the group's communication. The all-channel permits all group members to actively communicate with each other and is most often characterized in practice by the problem-solving task force. The effectiveness of each type of network depends on the goals of the group. If speed is important, the wheel and all-channel networks are most effective. For accuracy, the chain or wheel. The wheel is best for allowing leaders to emerge. If member satisfaction is important, the all-channel network is best and the wheel worst.

6. What is the grapevine and what important functions does it fulfill for managers and employees?
Answer - An informal system--information flows along the well-known grapevine and rumors can flourish. A classic study of the grapevine found that the grapevine was an important source of information, only 10 percent of those involved acted as liaison individuals. Information on events of general interest tended to flow between the major functional groups. The grapevine was about 75% accurate.

Rumors emerge as a response to situations that are important to us, where there is ambiguity, and under conditions that arouse anxiety. A rumor will persist either until the wants and expectations creating the uncertainty underlying the rumor are fulfilled or until the anxiety is reduced. The grapevine is an important part of any group or organization's communication network. It identifies for managers those confusing issues that employees consider important and that create anxiety. It acts as both a filter and a feedback mechanism, picking up the issues that employees consider relevant. For employees, the grapevine is particularly valuable for translating formal communications into their group's own jargon.

7. What are the common barriers to effective communication and how do they distort the communication process?
Answer - Filtering refers to a sender's purposely manipulating information so that the receiver will see it more favorably. The major determinant of filtering is the number of levels in an organization's structure. Selective perception-- the receiver, in the communication process, sees and hears things in a selective way based on his needs, motivations, experience/background, and other personal characteristics. The receiver also projects his interests and expectations into communications as he decodes them. Gender styles--Men and women use oral communication for different reasons. Men use talk to emphasize status women use it to create connection. Emotions--how the receiver feels at the time of receipt of a communication message will influence how he or she interprets it. Extreme emotions are most likely to hinder effective communication. Language--Age, education, and cultural background are variables that influence the language a person uses and the definitions he gives to words. The problem is that members in an organization usually don't know how those with whom they interact have modified the language. Nonverbal cues--nonverbal communication is almost always accompanied by oral communication. When nonverbal cues are inconsistent with the oral message the receiver becomes confused, and the clarity of the message suffers.

8. If you were given an overseas assignment with your company, what cross-cultural factors would you need to consider regarding your communication with others in that new culture?
Answer - The greater the differences in backgrounds between sender and receiver, the greater the differences in meanings attached to particular words or behaviors. Four rules to reduce misperceptions, misinterpretations, and misevaluation.
   - Assume differences until similarity is proved.
   - Emphasize description rather than interpretation or evaluation. Description is less based on the observer's culture and background than on the interpretation or evaluation.
   - Practice empathy. Before sending a message, put yourself in the receiver's shoes.
   - Treat your interpretation as a working hypothesis. Once you've developed an explanation for a new situation treat your interpretation as a hypothesis that needs further testing.

9. You are given the task of conducting communication training for new first line supervisors. What suggestions would you offer them for being more effective communicators?
Answer - Use feedback--many communication problems can be attributed directly to misunderstandings and inaccuracies. Simplify language--Structure messages in ways that will make them clear and understandable. Jargon can facilitate understanding when it is used with other group members who speak that language, but it can cause innumerable problems when used outside that

group. Listen actively--see Exhibit 9-4 for the steps. Constrain emotions--if we're emotionally upset over an issue, we're likely to misconstrue incoming messages. The best approach is to defer further communication until composure is regained. Watch your nonverbal cues--Assume that actions speak louder than words. Use the grapevine--You can't eliminate the grapevine, therefore use it and make it work for you. The grapevine is a valuable source of feedback.

10. Outline behaviors associated with providing effective feedback.
    Answer - See Exhibit 9-3.

11. Identify the behaviors related to effective active listening.
    Answer - See Exhibit 9-4.

EXERCISE

Are You Listening?

The purpose of this exercise is to give students the opportunity to both practice and experience active listening.

1. Conduct a mini-lecture on active listening emphasizing the key elements and then demonstrate it with a student in front of the class. Have the student talk about something he/she is comfortable with--his/her family, the roommate, food service at the school, etc. The listener should exhibit the following active listening behavior:
   - Make eye contact.
   - Exhibit affirmative facial expressions.
   - Ask questions.
   - Paraphrase.
   - Avoid interrupting.
2. Using birth month, pair the students.
   - Ask everyone who was born in January and July to hold up their hands. Pair them. Everyone born in February and August, etc. It's simply a different way to make pairs.
3. Have students sit facing each other with their backs to the left and right walls of the room.
4. Tell the students with their backs to the left wall that they are the speakers. The students with their backs to the right wall are the listeners.
5. Tell the speakers to think for a minute about their topic--they can choose anything appropriate [caution them to not discuss anything too personal, illegal, etc., even as a joke].
6. Tell the listeners they are to actively listen and facilitate the conversation through their active listening.
7. Tell them they have five minutes and have them begin.
8. Call time have them reverse roles. Have the new speakers talk for five minutes.
9. Call time.
10. Now ask them to prepare to answer two questions.
    - As the speaker--How did it feel to be listened to?
    - As a listener--What was the hardest thing about being an active listener?
11. Facilitate a discussion of their experiences. You will probably discover that:
    - Students are surprised at how good it felt to be listened to.
    - Students had a hard time not interjecting their own thoughts and ideas when listening.

CHAPTER 10 - LEADERSHIP AND CREATING TRUST

CHAPTER OBJECTIVES

After reading this chapter, you should be able to:

1. Summarize the conclusions of trait theories.
2. Identify the limitations of behavioral theories.
3. Describe the Fiedler Contingency model.
4. Summarize the path-goal theory.
5. List the contingency variables in the leader-participation model.
6. Explain gender differences in leadership styles.
7. Differentiate transformational from transactional leadership.
8. Identify the skills that visionary leaders exhibit.
9. Describe the four specific roles of effective team leaders
10. Summarize how leaders can build trust.

LECTURE OUTLINE

I. WHAT IS LEADERSHIP?

A. Defined

1. Leadership is the ability to influence a group toward the achievement of goals.
    a) This influence may be formal, such as that provided by the possession of managerial rank in an organization.
    b) Nonsanctioned leadership is the ability to influence that arises outside of the formal structure of the organization.
2. The leadership literature is voluminous, and much of it is confusing and contradictory.

II. TRAIT THEORIES

A. Introduction

1. On the basis of the general connotations in today's media, one might list qualities such as intelligence, charisma, decisiveness, enthusiasm, strength, bravery, integrity, self-confidence, etc.
2. The search for characteristics (such as those listed) that would differentiate leaders from nonleaders occupied the early psychologists who studied leadership.
3. Research efforts at isolating these traits resulted in a number of dead ends.
4. However, attempts to identify traits consistently associated with leadership have been more successful.
5. Six traits on which leaders differ from nonleaders:
    a) Drive and ambition.
    b) The desire to lead and influence others.
    c) Honesty and integrity.
    d) Self-confidence.
    e) Intelligence.
    f) In-depth technical knowledge related to their area of responsibility.
6. Traits alone are not sufficient for explaining leadership.
7. Their primary failing is that they ignore situational factors.
8. A major movement away from trait theories began as early as the 1940s. Leadership research from the late 1940s through the mid-1960s emphasized the preferred behavioral styles that leaders demonstrated.

III. BEHAVIORAL THEORIES

A. Introduction

1. The inability to find traits led researchers to look at the behaviors that specific leaders exhibited.
2. Researchers hoped the behavioral approach would provide more definitive answers and have some practical implications quite different from those of the trait approach.
   a) If behavioral studies were to turn up critical behavioral determinants of leadership, we could train people to be leaders.
   b) The difference between trait and behavioral theories, in terms of application, lies in their underlying assumptions.
      (1) If trait theories were valid, then leaders were basically born.
      (2) If there were specific behaviors that identified leaders, then we could teach leadership.
3. A number of studies looked at behavioral styles. The two most popular studies: the Ohio State group and the University of Michigan group.

B. Ohio State Studies

1. The most comprehensive and replicated of the behavioral theories resulted from research that began at Ohio State University in the late 1940s.
   a) Researchers sought to identify independent dimensions of leader behavior.
   b) They narrowed over a thousand dimensions into two categories that substantially accounted for most of the leadership behavior described by subordinates.
      (1) Initiating structure
      (2) Consideration
2. Initiating structure refers to the extent to which a leader is likely to define and structure his or her role and those of subordinates in the search for goal attainment.
   a) Organize work, work relationships, and goals
3. Consideration is described as the extent to which a person is likely to have job relationships characterized by mutual trust, respect for subordinates' ideas, and regard for their feelings.
   a) Showing concern for his followers' comfort, well being, status, and satisfaction
4. Research found that leaders high in initiating structure and consideration tended to achieve high subordinate performance and satisfaction more frequently than those who rated low on either initiating structure, consideration, or both.
5. But the high-high style did not always result in positive consequences--it leads to greater rates of grievances, absenteeism, and turnover and lower levels of job satisfaction for workers performing routine tasks.
6. The Ohio State studies suggested that the high-high style generally resulted in positive outcomes, but enough exceptions were found to indicate that situational factors needed to be integrated into the theory.

C. University of Michigan Studies

1. University of Michigan's Survey Research Center studies were done at about the same time as those being done at Ohio State with similar research objectives.
2. The Michigan group came up with two dimensions of leadership behavior:
   a) employee-oriented.
   b) production-oriented.
3. Leaders who were employee-oriented were described as emphasizing interpersonal relations; they took a personal interest in the needs of their subordinates and accepted individual differences among members.

4. The production-oriented leaders, in contrast, tended to emphasize the technical or task aspects of the job---their main concern was in accomplishing their group's tasks, and the group members were a means to that end.
5. Researchers strongly favored the leaders who were employee-oriented in their behavior.
   a) Employee-oriented leaders were associated with higher group productivity and higher job satisfaction.
   b) Production-oriented leaders tended to be associated with low group productivity and low worker satisfaction.

D. The Managerial Grid
1. Robert Blake and Jane Mouton developed a graphic portrayal of a two-dimensional view of leadership styles.
2. They proposed a managerial grid based on the styles of "concern for people" and "concern for production," which essentially represent the Ohio State dimensions of consideration and initiating structure or the Michigan dimensions of employee-oriented and production-oriented.
3. The grid.
   a) See Exhibit 10-1.
   b) Nine possible positions along each axis.
   c) Eighty-one different positions.
   d) Shows the factors that dominate a leader's thinking in regard to getting results.
4. Conclusions.
   a) Managers perform best under a 9,9 style.
   b) The grid offers a better framework for conceptualizing leadership style than for presenting any tangible new information.

E. Summary of Behavioral Theories
1. There was very little success in identifying consistent relationships between patterns of leadership behavior and group performance.
2. General statements could not be made.
3. What was missing was consideration of the situational factors that influence success or failure.

IV. CONTINGENCY THEORIES

A. Introduction
1. It became increasingly clear that predicting leadership success was more complex than isolating a few traits or preferable behaviors.
2. The failure to obtain consistent results led to a new focus on situational influences.
3. Many studies have attempted to isolate the critical situational factors that affect leadership effectiveness.
   a) Some of the more popular variables examined were: the type of task being performed, the style of the leader's immediate supervisor, group norms, time demands, and the organization's culture.
4. Three contingency theories have received the bulk of attention: Fiedler, path-goal, and leader-participation.
5. We also take a look at gender as a contingency variable.

B. The Fiedler Model
1. Fred Fiedler developed the first comprehensive contingency model for leadership.

2. His model proposes that effective group performance depends on the proper match between the leader's style of interacting with his or her subordinates and the degree to which the situation gives control and influence to the leader.
   a) Least-preferred co-worker (LPC) questionnaire purports to measure whether a person is task oriented or relationship oriented.
   b) He isolated three situational criteria---leader-member relations, task structure, and position power--that he believed can be manipulated so as to create the proper match with the behavioral orientation of the leader.
   c) Fiedler went significantly beyond trait and behavioral approaches by attempting to isolate situations, relating his personality measure to his situational classification, and then predicting leadership effectiveness as a function of the two.
3. Fiedler model
   a) An individual's basic leadership style is a key factor in leadership success.
   b) To find the basic style Fiedler created the LPC questionnaire.
      (1) 16 contrasting adjectives.
      (2) The questionnaire asks the respondent to think of all the co-workers he or she has ever had and to describe the one person he/she least enjoyed working with by rating that person on a scale of 1 to 8 for each of the 16 sets of contrasting adjectives.
   c) Fiedler's premise was that what you say about others tells more about you than it tells about the persons you're describing.
      (1) If the least-preferred co-worker was described in relatively positive terms (a high LPC score), then the respondent was primarily interested in good personal relations with co-workers.
      (2) In contrast, if the least-preferred co-worker is seen in relatively unfavorable terms (a low LPC score), the respondent is primarily interested in productivity and thus would be labeled task-oriented.
   d) Fiedler assumed that an individual's leadership style is fixed, either relationship-oriented or task-oriented.
   e) This assumption means that if a situation requires a task-oriented leader and the person in that leadership position is relationship-oriented, either the situation has to be modified or the leader replaced.
4. After an individual's basic leadership style has been assessed through the LPC, it is necessary to match the leader with the situation.
5. The three situational factors or contingency dimensions were identified by Fiedler:
   a) Leader-Member relations--The degree of confidence, trust, and respect subordinates have in their leader.
   b) Task structure--The degree to which the job assignments of subordinates are structured or unstructured.
   c) Position power--The degree of influence a leader has over power variables such as hiring, firing, discipline, promotions, and salary increases.
6. The next step--evaluate the situation in terms of the three contingency variables.
   a) Leader-member relations are either good or poor.
   b) Task structure either high or low.
   c) Position power either strong or weak.
7. Fiedler stated that the better the leader-member relations, the more highly structured the job, and the stronger the position power, the more control or influence the leader had.
8. By mixing the three contingency variables, there are potentially eight different situations or categories in which a leader could find himself or herself.

a) With knowledge of an individual's LPC and an assessment of the three contingency variables, the Fiedler model proposes matching them up to achieve maximum leadership effectiveness.

9. Fiedler studied more than 1,200 groups, comparing relationship versus task-oriented leadership styles in each of the eight situational categories.
   a) Task-oriented leaders tend to perform better than relationship-oriented leaders in situations that are very favorable to them and in situations that are very unfavorable.
   b) See Exhibit 10-2.
10. Application
   a) Seek to match leaders and situations.
   b) That situation would be defined by evaluating the three contingency factors of leader-member relations, task structure, and position power.
   c) An individual's leadership style is fixed.
   d) There are really only two ways in which to improve leader effectiveness.
      (1) First, you can choose the leader who best fits the situation.
      (2) The second alternative would be to change the situation to fit the leader.
11. Research finds conflicting results depending on the type of studies used.
   a) A generally positive conclusion-- there is considerable evidence to support the model.
   b) But additional variables are probably needed.
      (1) There are problems with the LPC and the practical use of the model that need to be addressed.
      (2) The contingency variables are complex and difficult for practitioners to assess.
12. Fiedler has clearly made an important contribution toward understanding leadership effectiveness.
   a) His model has been the object of much controversy and probably will continue to be.

C. Path-Goal Theory
1. One of the most respected approaches to leadership.
2. Developed by Robert House, a contingency model of leadership that extracts key elements from the Ohio State leadership research on initiating structure and consideration and the expectancy theory of motivation.
3. The essence of the theory is that it's the leader's job to assist his or her followers in attaining their goals and to provide the direction or support needed to ensure that their goals are compatible with the overall objectives of the group or organization.
   a) The term path-goal is derived from the belief that effective leaders clarify the path and reduce roadblocks and pitfalls for their followers.
   b) A leader's behavior is acceptable to subordinates to the degree that they view it as an immediate source of satisfaction or as a means of future satisfaction.
   c) A leader's behavior is motivational to the degree that it:
      (1) Makes subordinate need satisfaction contingent on effective performance.
      (2) Provides the coaching, guidance, support, and rewards that are necessary for effective performance.
4. House identified four leadership behaviors.
   a) The directive leader lets subordinates know what is expected of them, schedules work to be done, and gives specific guidance on how to accomplish tasks.
      (1) Parallels the Ohio State studies' initiating structure
   b) The supportive leader is friendly and shows concern for the needs of subordinates.
      (1) Essentially synonymous with the Ohio State studies' consideration
   c) The participative leader consults with subordinates and uses their suggestions before making a decision.

   d) The achievement-oriented leader sets challenging goals and expects subordinates to perform at their highest level.
   e) Path-goal theory implies that the same leader can display any or all of these behaviors depending on the situation.
5. See Exhibit 10-3.
   a) Path-goal theory proposes two classes of situational, or contingency variables.
   b) Those in the environment are outside the control of the leader (task structure, formal authority system, and work group).
   c) Factors in the second class are part of the personal characteristics of the subordinate (locus of control, experience, and perceived ability).
6. The theory proposes that leader behaviors should complement these contingency variables.
7. Hypotheses evolving out of path-goal theory.
   a) Directive leadership leads to greater satisfaction when tasks are ambiguous or stressful than when they are highly structured and well laid out.
   b) Supportive leadership results in high employee performance and satisfaction when subordinates are performing structured tasks (leadership complements environment).
   c) Directive leadership is likely to be redundant among subordinates with high ability or with considerable experience.
   d) The clearer and more bureaucratic the formal authority relationships, the more leaders should exhibit supportive behavior and de-emphasize directive behavior..
   e) Directive leadership will lead to higher employee satisfaction when there is substantive conflict within a work group.
   f) Subordinates with an internal locus of control (those who believe they control their own destiny) will be most satisfied with a participative style.
   g) Subordinates with an external locus of control will be most satisfied with a directive style.
   h) Achievement-oriented leadership will increase subordinates' expectations that effort will lead to high performance when tasks are ambiguously structured.
8. The evidence supports the logic underlying the theory.
   a) Employee performance and satisfaction are likely to be positively influenced when the leader compensates for things lacking in either the employee or the work setting.
   b) However, when the leader spends time explaining what is already clear or when the employee has the ability to handle them without help, the leader is seen as redundant or even insulting.
9. Path-goal theory's framework has been tested and appears to have moderate to high empirical support.

D. Leader-Participation Model
1. In 1973, Victor Vroom and Phillip Yetton developed a leader-participation model.
2. These researchers argued that leader behavior must adjust to reflect the task structure.
3. Vroom and Yetton's model was normative--it provided a sequential set of rules that should be followed in determining the form and amount of participation in decision making as determined by different types of situations.
4. The model was a decision tree incorporating seven contingencies (whose relevance could be identified by making "yes" or "no" choices) and five alternative leadership styles.
5. Vroom and Jago revised this model.
   a) The new model retains the same five alternative leadership styles but expands the contingency variables to twelve.
   b) See Exhibit 10-4.
6. Tests of both models have been encouraging.

7. Unfortunately, the model is far too complex for the typical manager.
    a) Vroom and Jago have developed a computer program to guide managers through all the decision branches in the revised model.

E. Gender as a Contingency Variable: Do Males and Females Lead Differently?
1. An extensive review of the literature suggests two conclusions regarding gender and leadership.
    a) The similarities tend to outweigh the differences.
    b) Women prefer a democratic leadership style, whereas men feel more comfortable with a directive style.
2. The similarities among men and women leaders are surprising.
    a) Because of career self-selection and organization selection.
    b) Just as people who choose careers in law enforcement or civil engineering have a lot in common, so do individuals who choose managerial roles/positions.
    c) Similarly, organizations tend to recruit and promote into leadership positions people who project leadership attributes.
3. Despite the previous conclusion, studies indicate some differences in the inherent leadership styles of women and men.
    a) Women encourage participation, share power and information, and attempt to enhance followers' self-worth.
    b) They prefer to lead through inclusion and rely on their charisma, expertise, contacts, and interpersonal skills to influence others.
    c) Men, on the other hand, are more likely to use a directive command-and-control style.
    d) They rely on the formal authority of their position for their influence base.
4. These findings need to be qualified.
    a) The tendency for female leaders to be more democratic than males declines when women are in male-dominated jobs.
    b) Apparently, group norms and masculine stereotypes of leaders override personal preferences.
5. It's tempting to assume that the noted differences between men and women would automatically work to favor men.
    a) It doesn't.
    b) In today's organizations, flexibility, teamwork, trust, and information sharing are replacing rigid structures, competitive individualism, control, and secrecy.
    c) The best managers listen, motivate, and provide support to their people.
    d) The leadership styles women typically use can make them better than men at negotiating.

V. TRAIT THEORIES UPDATED: CHARISMATIC LEADERSHIP

A. Transactional Leaders
1. These people guide or motivate their followers in the direction of established goals by clarifying role and task requirements.
2. There is another type of leader who inspires followers to transcend their own self-interests for the good of the organization and who is capable of having a profound and extraordinary effect on his or her followers.
    a) These are charismatic or transformational leaders.
    b) Ted Turner, Jesse Jackson, Mother Teresa, General Douglas MacArthur, and Franklin D. Roosevelt are of this latter type.
    c) By the force of their personal abilities, they transform their followers by raising the sense of the importance and value of their tasks.

B. Characteristics that Differentiate Charismatic Leaders from Noncharismatic Leaders
1. Self-confidence
   a) They have complete confidence in their judgment and ability.
2. A vision
   a) An idealized goal that proposes a better future than the status quo.
3. Strong convictions in that vision
   a) Perceived as willing to take on high personal risk, incur high costs, and engage in self-sacrifice to achieve their vision.
4. Extraordinary behavior
   a) Engage in behavior that is perceived as novel, unconventional, and counter to norms.
5. Image as a change agent
   a) Perceived as agents of radical change rather than as caretakers of the status quo.
6. Charismatic leaders impact his/her followers' attitudes and behavior.
   a) Followers of charismatic leaders were more self-assured, experienced more meaningfulness in their work, reported more support from their leaders, worked longer hours, saw their leaders as more dynamic, and had higher performance ratings than the followers of noncharismatic but effective leaders.
   b) People working under charismatic leaders were more productive and satisfied than those working under leaders who relied on the more traditional transactional behaviors of initiating structure and consideration.
7. These limited studies provide only a limited ability to generalize.

VI. VISIONARY LEADERSHIP

A. Definition
1. Visionary leadership goes beyond charisma.
2. Visionary leadership is the ability to create and articulate a realistic, credible, attractive vision of the future for an organization or organizational unit that grows out of and improves upon the present.
3. A review of various definitions finds that a vision differs from other forms of direction-setting in several ways:
   a) A vision has clear and compelling imagery that offers an innovative way to improve, which recognizes and draws on traditions, and connects to actions that people can take to realize change.
   b) Vision taps people's emotions and energy.
4. The key properties of a vision seem to be inspirational possibilities that are value centered, realizable, with superior imagery and articulation.
   a) A vision is likely to fail if it doesn't offer a view of the future that is clearly and demonstrably better for the organization and its members.
   b) Visions that have clear articulation and powerful imagery are more easily grasped and accepted.
5. Examples
   a) Rupert Murdoch vision of the future of the communication industry combining entertainment and media.
   b) Mary Kay Ash's vision of women as entrepreneurs selling products that improve their self-image gave impetus to her cosmetics company.
   c) Charles Schwab is currently attempting to redefine financial services by combining discount prices with comprehensive offerings.
6. Skills of visionary leaders.
   a) The ability to explain the vision to others.
   b) The ability to express the vision not just verbally but through the leader's behavior.
   c) The ability to extend the vision to different leadership contexts.

VII. TEAM LEADERSHIP

A. Leadership within a Team Context.

1. Many leaders are not equipped to handle the change to teams.
2. A consultant estimated that:
    a) probably 15 percent of managers are natural team leaders.
    b) another 15 percent could never lead a team because it runs counter to their personality.
    c) There's that huge group in the middle that can learn team leadership.
3. Most managers have to learn skills such as the patience to share information, to trust others, to give up authority, and to understand when to intervene.
4. Effective leaders have mastered the difficult balancing act of knowing when to leave their teams alone and when to intercede.
5. A recent study of 20 organizations that had reorganized themselves around teams found certain common responsibilities that all leaders had to assume.
    a) These included coaching, facilitating, handling disciplinary problems, and reviewing team/individual performance, training, and communicating.
6. A more meaningful way to describe the team leader's job is to focus on two priorities: managing the team's external boundary and facilitating the team process.
7. This is done through four specific roles.
    a) First, team leaders are liaisons with external constituencies--upper management, other internal teams, customers, and suppliers.
    b) Second, team leaders are trouble-shooters. When the team has problems and asks for assistance, team leaders sit in on meetings and help try to resolve the problems.
        (1) This rarely relates to technical or operation issues.
    c) Third, team leaders are conflict managers. When disagreements surface, they help process the conflict.
    d) Finally, team leaders are coaches.
        (1) They clarify expectations and roles, teach, offer support, cheerlead, and do whatever else is necessary to help team members.

VIII. IS LEADERSHIP ALWAYS RELEVANT?

A. Leadership May Not Always be Important

1. Numerous studies demonstrate that, in many situations, whatever behaviors leaders exhibit are irrelevant.
    a) Characteristics of subordinates such as their experience, training, professional orientation, or need for independence can neutralize the effect of leadership.
    b) People in jobs that are inherently unambiguous and routine or that are intrinsically satisfying may have little need for a leader.
    c) Organizational characteristics such as explicit formalized goals, rigid rules and procedures, or cohesive work groups can act in the place of formal leadership.
2. Supporters of the leadership concept have tended to place an undue burden on this variable for explaining and predicting behavior.
    a) It's too simplistic to consider subordinates as being guided to goal accomplishment solely on the basis of the behavior of their leader.
    b) It's important, therefore, to recognize explicitly that leadership is merely another independent variable in explaining organizational behavior.
3. Even charismatic leadership may not be a panacea.
    a) Charismatic leaders may be ideal for pulling a group or organization through a crisis, but they often perform poorly after the crisis subsides and ordinary conditions return.
    b) Charismatic managers are often self-possessed, autocratic, and given to thinking that their opinions have a greater degree of certainty than they merit.

(1) These behaviors then tend to drive good people away and can lead their organizations down dangerous paths.

IX. TRUST AND LEADERSHIP

A. What Is Trust?

1. Trust is a positive expectation that another will not--through words, actions, or decisions--act opportunistically.
2. The two most important elements of our definition are familiarity and risk.
    a) The phrase positive expectation in our definition assumes knowledge and familiarity about the other party.
        (1) Trust is a history-dependent process based on relevant but limited samples of experience.
        (2) It takes time to form, building incrementally and accumulating.
    b) The term opportunistic refers to the inherent risk and vulnerability in any trusting relationship.
        (1) Trust involves making oneself vulnerable.
        (2) But trust is not taking risk per se; rather it is a willingness to take risk.
3. Key dimensions that underlie the concept of trust. See Exhibit 10-5.
    a) Integrity refers to honesty and truthfulness. This one seems to be most critical.
    b) Competence encompasses an individual's technical and interpersonal knowledge and skills.
        (1) Does the person know what he or she is talking about?
    c) Consistency relates to an individual's reliability, predictability, and good judgment in handling situations.
    d) Loyalty is the willingness to protect and save face for another person.
        (1) Trust requires that you can depend on someone not to act opportunistically.
    e) The final dimension of trust is openness. Can you rely on the person to give you the full truth?
4. Trust appears to be a primary attribute associated with leadership. Trust and trust-worthiness modulate the leader's access to knowledge and cooperation.
    a) When followers trust a leader, they are willing to be vulnerable to the leader's actions.
5. Honesty, for instance, consistently ranks at the top of most people's list of characteristics they admire in their leaders.

B. Three Types of Trust

1. There are three types of trust in organizational relationships: deterrence-based, knowledge-based, and identification-based.
2. The following analysis assumes two parties are entering into a new relationship. They have no previous experiences to overcome; they're uncertain about each other; they believe they're vulnerable if they disclose too much too quickly; and they're uncertain about the future longevity of the relationship.
3. Deterrence-based trust.
    a) The most fragile relationships.
    b) One violation or inconsistency can destroy the relationship.
    c) This form of trust is based on fear of reprisal if the trust is violated.
    d) Deterrence-based trust will work only to the degree that punishment is possible, consequences are clear, and the punishment is actually imposed if the trust is violated.
    e) To be sustained, the potential loss of future interaction with the other party must outweigh the profit potential that comes from violating expectations.

f) Most new relationships begin on a base of deterrence.

4. Knowledge-Based Trust.
   a) Most organizational relationships are rooted in knowledge-based trust.
   b) Trust is based on the behavioral predictability that comes from a history of interaction.
   c) It exists when you have adequate information about someone to understand them well enough to be able to accurately predict their likely behavior.
   d) Relies on information rather than deterrence--of the other party and predictability of his or her behavior replaces the contracts, penalties, and legal arrangements more typical of deterrence-based trust.
   e) This knowledge develops over time.
   f) Trust is not necessarily broken by inconsistent behavior.
      (1) If you believe you can adequately explain or understand another's apparent violation, you can accept it, forgive the person, and move on in the relationship.
   g) Most manager-employee relationships are knowledge-based.
5. Identification-based trust.
   a) The highest level of trust is achieved when there is an emotional connection between the parties.
   b) It allows one party to act as an agent for the other and substitute for that person in interpersonal transactions.
   c) Controls are minimal at this level.
   d) The best example of identification-based trust is a long-term, happily married couple.
   e) You see identification-based trust occasionally in organizations among people who have worked together for long periods of time and have a depth of experience that allows them to know each other inside and out.
   f) This is also the type of trust that managers ideally seek in teams.

C. How Do You Build Trust?

1. Practice openness--Mistrust comes as much from what people don't know as from what they do know. Openness leads to confidence and trust.
2. Be fair--Before making decisions or taking actions, consider how others will perceive them in terms of objectivity and fairness.
3. Speak your feelings--Managers who convey only hard facts come across as cold and distant.
4. Tell the truth--If integrity is critical to trust, you must be perceived as someone who tells the truth.
5. Show consistency--People want predictability. Mistrust comes from not knowing what to expect.
6. Fulfill your promises---Trust requires that people believe that you are dependable.
7. Maintain confidences--You trust people who are discreet and upon whom you can rely. So if people make themselves vulnerable by telling you something in confidence, they need to feel assured that you will not discuss it with others or betray that confidence.
8. Demonstrate competence--Develop the admiration and respect of others by demonstrating technical and professional ability.

X. IMPLICATIONS FOR MANAGERS

1. Let's try to identify commonalties among the leadership theories and attempt to determine what, if any, practical value the theories hold for managers.
2. Careful examination discloses that the concepts of task and people often expressed in more elaborate terms that hold substantially the same meaning--permeate most of the theories. The task dimension is called just that by Fiedler, but it goes by the name of

"initiating structure" for the Ohio State group, "directive" by path-goal supporters, "production orientation" by the Michigan researchers, and "concern for production" by Blake and Mouton. The people dimension gets similar treatment, going under such aliases as "consideration," "supportive," and "employee-oriented" or 'relationship-oriented" leadership. Clearly, leadership behavior can be shrunk down to two dimensions--task and people--but researchers continue to differ as to whether the orientations are two ends of a single continuum or two independent dimensions.

3. Some traits have shown, over time, to be modest predictors of leadership effectiveness. But the fact that a manager possessed intelligence, drive, self-confidence, or the like would by no means assure us that his or her subordinates would be productive and satisfied employees. The ability of these traits to predict leadership success is just not that strong.
4. The early task--people approaches (the Ohio State, Michigan, and managerial grid theories) also offer us little substance. The strongest statement one can make on the basis of these theories is that leaders who rate high in people orientation should end up with satisfied employees. The research is too mixed to make predictions regarding employee productivity or the effect of a task orientation on productivity and satisfaction.
5. Controlled laboratory studies designed to test the Fiedler model, in aggregate, have generally supported the theory. But field studies provide more limited support. We suggest that only category II, V, VII, and VIII situations warrant the use of the LPC instrument to assess whether this is a leader--situation match and the use of that information to predict employee productivity and satisfaction.
6. The path-goal model provides a framework for explaining and predicting leadership effectiveness that has developed a solid, empirical foundation. It recognizes that a leader's success depends on adjusting his or her style to the environment and to the individual characteristics of followers.
7. In spite of the leader-participation model's complexity, efforts to validate it have been encouraging. One investigation, for example, found that leaders who were high in agreement with the model had subordinates with higher productivity and higher satisfaction than those leaders who were low in agreement with the model. For our purposes, its greatest contribution is in identifying a set of contingency variables that you should consider before choosing a leadership style.
8. Finally, we discussed the role that trust plays in leadership. Effective managers today must develop trusting relationships with those they seek to lead. Why? Because as organizations have become less stable and predictable, strong bonds of trust are replacing bureaucratic rules in defining expectations and relationships.

SUMMARY

1. Leadership is the ability to influence a group toward the achievement of goals. This influence may be formal, such as that provided by the possession of managerial rank in an organization.
2. The search for characteristics (such as those listed) that would differentiate leaders from nonleaders occupied the early psychologists who studied leadership.
3. The inability to find traits led researchers to look at the behaviors that specific leaders exhibited. The two most popular studies: the Ohio State group and the University of Michigan group. The Ohio State University studies narrowed over a thousand dimensions into two categories: initiating structure and consideration. The University of Michigan's Survey Research Center studies came up with two dimensions of leadership behavior: employee-oriented and production-oriented.
4. Robert Blake and Jane Mouton proposed a managerial grid based on the styles of "concern for people" and "concern for production," which essentially represent the Ohio State dimensions of consideration and initiating structure or the Michigan dimensions of employee-oriented and production-oriented.

5. There was very little success in identifying consistent relationships between patterns of leadership behavior and group performance. What was missing was consideration of the situational factors that influence success or failure.
6. The failure to obtain consistent results led to a new focus on situational influences. Three contingency theories have received the bulk of attention: Fiedler, path-goal, and leader-participation. Fred Fiedler's model proposes that effective group performance depends on the proper match between the leader's style of interacting with his or her subordinates and the degree to which the situation gives control and influence to the leader.
7. Path-goal theory is one of the most respected approaches to leadership. Developed by Robert House, the essence of the theory is that it's the leader's job to assist his or her followers in attaining their goals and to provide the direction or support needed to ensure that their goals are compatible with the overall objectives of the group or organization.
8. Another contingency model is the leader-participation model developed in 1973 by Victor Vroom and Phillip Yetton. These researchers argued that leader behavior must adjust to reflect the task structure. Unfortunately, the model is far too complex for the typical manager. Vroom and Jago have developed a computer program to guide managers through all the decision branches in the revised model.
9. An extensive review of the literature suggests two conclusions regarding gender and leadership. 1) The similarities tend to outweigh the differences. 2) Women prefer a democratic leadership style, whereas men feel more comfortable with a directive style. Studies also indicate some differences in the inherent leadership styles of women and men. 1) Women encourage participation, share power and information, and attempt to enhance followers' self-worth. 2) Men, on the other hand, are more likely to use a directive command-and-control style.
10. The transactional leaders guide or motivate their followers in the direction of established goals by clarifying role and task requirements. Transformational leaders inspire followers to transcend their own self-interests for the good of the organization and who is capable of having a profound and extraordinary effect on his or her followers.
11. Another type of leader is the visionary leader. Visionary leadership is the ability to create and articulate a realistic, credible, attractive vision of the future for an organization or organizational unit that grows out of and improves upon the present.
12. While a great deal is written about leadership, it may not always be important. Numerous studies demonstrate that, in many situations, whatever behaviors leaders exhibit are irrelevant.
13. Team leadership is becoming increasingly important to organizations and for managers to learn. Many leaders are not equipped to handle the change to teams. Most managers have to learn skills such as the patience to share information, to trust others, to give up authority, and to understand when to intervene.
14. Trust is critical to a manager's effectiveness. It is a positive expectation that another will not--through words, actions, or decisions--act opportunistically. The text outlines the key elements of trust in Exhibit 10-5. Trust appears to be a primary attribute associated with leadership. Trust and trust-worthiness modulate the leader's access to knowledge and cooperation. There are three types of trust in organizational relationships: deterrence-based, knowledge-based, and identification-based.

DISCUSSION QUESTIONS

1. What were the results of researchers' efforts to identify key leadership traits?
   Answer - On the basis of the general connotations in today's media, one might list qualities such as intelligence, charisma, decisiveness, enthusiasm, strength, bravery, integrity, self-confidence, etc. The search for characteristics (such as those listed) that would differentiate leaders from nonleaders occupied the early psychologists who studied leadership. Research identified traits consistently associated with leadership have been more successful. Six traits on which leaders differ from nonleaders: drive and ambition, the desire to lead and influence others, honesty and integrity, self-confidence, intelligence, and in-depth technical knowledge related to their area of responsibility.

Traits alone are not sufficient for explaining leadership. Their primary failing is that they ignore situational factors.

2. How did the studies at Ohio State and University of Michigan contribute to a behavioral understanding of leadership?
Answer - The inability to find traits led researchers to look at the behaviors that specific leaders exhibited. The difference between trait and behavioral theories, in terms of application, lies in their underlying assumptions. If trait theories were valid, then leaders were basically born. If there were specific behaviors that identified leaders, then we could teach leadership.

The most comprehensive and replicated of the behavioral theories resulted from research that began at Ohio State University in the late 1940s. Researchers sought to identify independent dimensions of leader behavior. 1) Initiating structure refers to the extent to which a leader is likely to define and structure his or her role and those of subordinates in the search for goal attainment. 2) Consideration is described as the extent to which a person is likely to have job relationships characterized by mutual trust, respect for subordinates' ideas, and regard for their feelings. Research found that leaders high in initiating structure and consideration tended to achieve high subordinate performance and satisfaction more frequently than those who rated low either on initiating structure, consideration, or both.

University of Michigan's Survey Research Center studies were done at about the same time as those being done at Ohio State with similar research objectives. The Michigan group came up with two dimensions of leadership behavior. 1) Leaders who were employee-oriented were described as emphasizing interpersonal relations; they took a personal interest in the needs of their subordinates and accepted individual differences among members. 2) The production-oriented leaders, in contrast, tended to emphasize the technical or task aspects of the job---their main concern was in accomplishing their group's tasks, and the group members were a means to that end. Researchers strongly favored the leaders who were employee-oriented in their behavior. Employee-oriented leaders were associated with higher group productivity and higher job satisfaction. Production-oriented leaders tended to be associated with low group productivity and low worker satisfaction.

3. Describe Fiedler's Contingency model.
Answer - The first comprehensive contingency model for leadership was developed by Fred Fiedler. His model proposes that effective group performance depends on the proper match between the leader's style of interacting with his or her subordinates and the degree to which the situation gives control and influence to the leader. Least-preferred co-worker (LPC) questionnaire purports to measure whether a person is task oriented or relationship oriented. He isolated three situational criteria---leader-member relations, task structure, and position power--that he believed can be manipulated so as to create the proper match with the behavioral orientation of the leader. Fiedler went significantly beyond trait and behavioral approaches by attempting to isolate situations, relating his personality measure to his situational classification, and then predicting leadership effectiveness as a function of the two. Fiedler assumed that an individual's leadership style is fixed, either relationship-oriented or task-oriented. This assumption means that if a situation requires a task-oriented leader and the person in that leadership position is relationship oriented, either the situation has to be modified or the leader replaced. Fiedler studied more than 1,200 groups, comparing relationship versus task-oriented leadership styles in each of the eight situational categories.

4. Why is the path-goal theory an improvement over other contingency-based theories of leadership?
Answer - One of the most respected approaches to leadership, developed by Robert House. The contingency model of leadership extracts key elements from the Ohio State leadership research on initiating structure and consideration and the expectancy theory of motivation. The essence of the theory is that it's the leader's job to assist his or her followers in attaining their goals and to provide

the direction or support needed to ensure that their goals are compatible with the overall objectives of the group or organization. The term path-goal is derived from the belief that effective leaders clarify the path and reduce roadblocks and pitfalls for their followers. A leader's behavior is acceptable to subordinates to the degree that they view it as an immediate source of satisfaction or as a means of future satisfaction. The evidence supports the logic underlying the theory. Employee performance and satisfaction are likely to be positively influenced when the leader compensates for things lacking in either the employee or the work setting. Path-goal theory's framework has been tested and appears to have moderate to high empirical support.

5. How does the leader-participation model contingency theory of leadership differ from other theories? Why don't managers use it more?
Answer - In 1973, Victor Vroom and Phillip Yetton developed a leader-participation model. These researchers argued that leader behavior must adjust to reflect the task structure. Vroom and Yetton's model was normative--it provided a sequential set of rules that should be followed in determining the form and amount of participation in decision making as determined by different types of situations. The model was a decision tree incorporating seven contingencies (whose relevance could be identified by making "yes" or "no" choices) and five alternative leadership styles. Vroom and Jago revised this model. The new model retains the same five alternative leadership styles but expands the contingency variables to twelve. The model is far too complex for the typical manager. Vroom and Jago have developed a computer program to guide managers through all the decision branches in the revised model.

6. Compare and contrast men and women as leaders. What are the implications for managers?
Answer - An extensive review of the literature suggests two conclusions regarding gender and leadership. The similarities tend to outweigh the differences. Women prefer a democratic leadership style, whereas men feel more comfortable with a directive style. Women encourage participation, share power and information, and attempt to enhance followers' self-worth. They prefer to lead through inclusion and rely on their charisma, expertise, contacts, and interpersonal skills to influence others. Men, on the other hand, are more likely to use a directive command-and-control style. They rely on the formal authority of their position for their influence base. Implications. The tendency for female leaders to be more democratic than males declines when women are in male-dominated jobs. It's tempting to assume that the noted differences between men and women would automatically work to favor men. In today's organizations, flexibility, teamwork, trust, and information sharing are replacing rigid structures, competitive individualism, control, and secrecy. The best managers listen, motivate, and provide support to their people. The leadership styles women typically use can make them better than men at negotiating. The similarities among men and women leaders are not surprising because of career self-selection and organization selection. Similarly, organizations tend to recruit and promote into leadership positions people who project leadership attributes.

7. Differentiate transformational from transactional leadership.
Answer - Transactional leaders guide or motivate their followers in the direction of established goals by clarifying role and task requirements. Transformational leaders, by the force of their personal abilities, transform their followers by raising the sense of the importance and value of their tasks. They inspire followers to transcend their own self-interests for the good of the organization and are capable of having a profound and extraordinary effect on their followers. There are six characteristics that distinguish transformation/charismatic leaders.
   - self-confidence--they have complete confidence in their judgment and ability.
   - a vision--an idealized goal that proposes a better future than the status quo.
   - extraordinary behavior--engage in behavior that is perceived as novel, unconventional, and counter to norms.

- strong convictions in that vision--Perceived as willing to take on high personal risk, incur high costs, and engage in self-sacrifice to achieve their vision
- image as a change agent--perceived as agents of radical change rather than as caretakers of the status quo.
- charismatic leader's impact his/her followers' attitudes and behavior.

8. What distinguishes a visionary leaders from a charismatic or other types of leaders?
Answer - In many ways they are similar but visionary leadership goes beyond charisma. Visionary leadership is the ability to create and articulate a realistic, credible, attractive vision of the future for an organization or organizational unit that grows out of and improves upon the present. There are three key skills of visionary leaders. 1) The ability to explain the vision to others. 2) The ability to express the vision not just verbally but through the leader's behavior. 3) The ability to extend the vision to different leadership contexts.

9. What roles do team leaders play in helping their teams work effectively?
Answer - Effective leaders have mastered the difficult balancing act of knowing when to leave their teams alone and when to intercede. This is done through four specific roles. First, team leaders are liaisons with external constituencies--upper management, other internal teams, customers, and suppliers. Second, team leaders are trouble-shooters. When the team has problems and asks for assistance, team leaders sit in on meetings and help try to resolve the problems. This rarely relates to technical or operation issues. Third, team leaders are conflict managers. When disagreements surface, they help process the conflict. Finally, team leaders are coaches. They clarify expectations and roles, teach, offer support, cheerlead, and do whatever else is necessary to help team members.

10. In what circumstances is leadership irrelevant?
Answer - Numerous studies demonstrate that, in many situations, whatever behaviors leaders exhibit are irrelevant. 1) Characteristics of subordinates such as their experience, training, professional orientation, or need for independence can neutralize the effect of leadership. 2) Characteristics of jobs, people in jobs that are inherently unambiguous and routine or that are intrinsically satisfying may have little need for a leader. 3) Organizational characteristics such as explicit formalized goals, rigid rules and procedures, or cohesive work groups can act in the place of formal leadership.

11. You are new on the job. You know the importance of trust for effective management. What can you do to build trust with your new employees?
Answer - Trust is a positive expectation that another will not--through words, actions, or decisions--act opportunistically. The two most important elements of our definition are familiarity and risk. Suggestions for building trust.
    - Practice openness--Mistrust comes as much from what people don't know as from what they do know. Openness leads to confidence and trust.
    - Be fair--Before making decisions or taking actions, consider how others will perceive them in terms of objectivity and fairness.
    - Speak your feelings--Managers who convey only hard facts come across as cold and distant.
    - Tell the truth--If integrity is critical to trust, you must be perceived as someone who tells the truth.
    - Show consistency--People want predictability. Mistrust comes from not knowing what to expect.
    - Fulfill your promises---Trust requires that people believe that you are dependable.
    - Maintain confidences--You trust people who are discreet and upon whom you can rely. So if people make themselves vulnerable by telling you something in confidence, they need to feel assured that you will not discuss it with others or betray that confidence.
    - Demonstrate competence--Develop the admiration and respect of others by demonstrating technical and professional ability.

EXERCISE

What Characterizes a Leader?

This exercise will show students different leadership styles in a fun way. It requires some significant preparation on your part.

1. Rent one or more of the following movies.
   - *Karate Kid* - Good for contingency leadership.
   - *Lawrence of Arabia* - Good for visionary leadership.
   - *Hoosiers* - Good for transactional leadership.
2. Preview the films on the VCR you will use in class and note where the following sections are. (By previewing you will reduce viewing time to 15-20 minutes out of each film.)
   - *Karate Kid* - When Miagi has Daniel washing, sanding, and painting and then shows tnat he's learned karate--high task low relationship. When they are on the inlet fishing and Daniel is standing on the boat practicing--moderate task, moderate relationship. And the tournament at the end of the film--high relationship, low task direction.
   - *Lawrence of Arabia* - The beginning of the film when Lawrence gets his assignment and declares its fun, when he is first riding in the desert and won't drink his water except when his guide does, and then when he is talking the tribal leader into riding across the desert to attack the port city and then later when he talks the second tribal leader into joining them. The pattern shows the development, execution, and creation commitment to a vision.
   - *Hoosiers* - Good for transactional leadership. When Gene Hackman is first coaching the players and tells them to leave if they don't want to work. Choose one or two scenes where he is dictating to them how to play, my way or the highway. Be sure to close with the tournament game where the players finally have enough confidence to tell him they want to do something different and he lets them. This last scene is important to show that transactional leadership does work, you just may not like the method.
3. You can use one or all three films, depending on time.
4. Lead a discussion after watching the clips from each film.
5. As an alternative, watch the entire movie (s), stopping the video periodically and discussing the elements of leadership displayed to that point.

CHAPTER 11 - POWER AND POLITICS

CHAPTER OBJECTIVES

After reading this chapter, you should be able to:

1. Define power.
2. Describe the five bases of power.
3. Explain what creates dependency in power relationships.
4. Describe how power is central to understanding sexual harassment.
5. Define political behavior.
6. Describe the importance of a political perspective.
7. Explain the factors contributing to political behavior in organizations.
8. Identify seven techniques for managing the impression you make on others.

LECTURE OUTLINE

I. A DEFINITION OF POWER

- A. Power
    1. Power refers to the capacity that A has to influence the behavior of B so that B does something he or she would not otherwise do.
    2. This definition implies:
        - a) A potential that need not be actualized to be effective.
        - b) A dependence relationship.
        - c) That B has some discretion over his or her own behavior.
    3. Power may exist but not be used. It is, therefore, a capacity or potential.
    4. Probably the most important aspect of power is that it is a function of dependence. The greater B's dependence on A, the greater is A's power in the relationship.
        - a) Dependence is based on alternatives that B perceives and the importance that B places on the alternatives that A controls.
    5. For A to get B to do something he or she otherwise would not do means B must have the discretion to make choices.

II. CONTRASTING LEADERSHIP AND POWER

- A. A Comparison
    1. The two concepts of power and leadership are closely intertwined. Leaders use power to attain group goals, and power is a means for facilitating their achievement.
    2. Differences
        - a) Power does not require goal compatibility, merely dependence.
        - b) Leadership requires some congruence between the goals of the leader and those being led.
        - c) Leadership research, for the most part, emphasizes style.
        - d) The research on power has tended to encompass a broader area and focus on tactics for gaining compliance.

III. BASES OF POWER

- A. Coercive Power
    1. The coercive power base is defined by French and Raven as being dependent on fear.
        - a) One reacts to this power out of fear of the negative results that might occur if one failed to comply.
        - b) It rests on the application, or the threat of application, of physical sanctions such as the infliction of pain, the generation of frustration through restriction of movement, or the control by force of basic physiological or safety needs.

    c) "Of all the bases of power available, the power to hurt others is possibly most often used, most often condemned, and most difficult to control ...."
2. At the organizational level, A has coercive power over B if A can dismiss, suspend, or demote B, assuming that B values his or her job.

B. Reward Power
1. The opposite of coercive power is reward power.
2. People comply with the wishes or directives of another because doing so produces positive benefits.
3. Rewards can be anything that another person values.
4. Coercive and reward power are actually counterparts.
    a) If you can remove something of positive value from another or inflict something of negative value upon him or her, you have coercive power over that person.
    b) If you can give someone something of positive value or remove something of negative value, you have reward power over that person.
    c) You don't need to be a manager to be able to exert influence through rewards.

C. Legitimate Power
1. In formal groups and organizations, probably the most frequent access to one or more of the power bases is one's structural position.
2. It represents the power a person receives as a result of his or her position in the formal hierarchy of an organization.
3. Positions of authority include coercive and reward powers.
4. Legitimate power is broader than the power to coerce and reward.
    a) It includes acceptance by members of an organization and of the authority of a position.

D. Expert Power
1. Expert power is influence wielded as a result of expertise, special skill, or knowledge.
2. Expertise has become one of the most powerful sources of influence as the world has become more technologically oriented.

E. Referent Power
1. Its base is identification with a person who has desirable resources or personal traits. If I admire and identify with you, you can exercise power over me because I want to please you.
2. Referent power develops out of admiration of another and a desire to be like that person.
3. Referent power explains why celebrities are paid millions of dollars to endorse products in commercials.

IV. DEPENDENCY: THE KEY TO POWER

A. The General Dependency Postulate
1. The greater B's dependency on A, the greater power A has over B.
    a) When you possess anything that others require but that you alone control, you make them dependent on you and, therefore, you gain power over them.
    b) Dependency, then, is inversely proportional to the alternative sources of supply.
2. If you can create a monopoly by controlling information, prestige, or anything that others crave, they become dependent on you.
3. Conversely, the more you can expand your options, the less power you place in the hands of others.

a) This principle explains, for example, why most organizations use many suppliers rather than give their business to only one.

B. What Creates Dependency?

1. Dependency is increased when the resource you control is important and scarce.
2. Importance
   a) To create dependency, therefore, you must control things that are perceived as important.
   b) The ability to reduce uncertainty increases a group's power and enhances its abilityt to create dependency.
3. Scarcity
   a) A resource needs to be perceived as scarce to create dependency.
   b) The need to obtain a scarce resource--such as, important knowledge--makes the high-ranking member dependent on the low-ranking member.
   c) Individuals in occupations in which the supply of personnel is low relative to demand can negotiate compensation and benefit packages far more attractive than can those in occupations for which there is an abundance of candidates.

V. POWER IN GROUPS: COALITIONS

A. Introduction

1. The natural way to gain influence is to become a powerholder.
   a) In many instances, doing so may be difficult, risky, costly, or impossible.
2. In such cases, efforts will be made to form a coalition of two or more "outs" who, by joining together, can each better themselves at the expense of those outside the coalition.
3. Predictions about the formation of coalitions.
   a) Coalitions in organizations often seek to maximize their size.
      (1) In organizations, the implementation of and commitment to the decision are at least as important as the decision itself.
      (2) It's necessary, therefore, for coalitions in organizations to seek a broad constituency to support the coalition's objectives, so the coalition must be expanded to encompass as many interests as possible.
   b) More coalitions will likely be created if there is a great deal of task and resource interdependence.
      (1) In contrast, there will be less interdependence among subunits and less coalition formation activity when subunits are largely self-contained or resources are abundant.
   c) Coalition formation will be influenced by the actual tasks that workers perform.
      (1) The more routine the task of a group or the work of individual jobs, the greater the likelihood that coalitions will form.

VI. POWER AND SEXUAL HARASSMENT

A. Sexual Harassment

1. Legally, sexual harassment is defined as unwelcome advances, requests for sexual favors, and other verbal or physical conduct, whether overt or subtle, of a sexual nature.
2. But there is a great deal of disagreement about what specifically constitutes sexual harassment.
3. Organizations have made considerable progress in the last few years toward limiting overt forms of sexual harassment.
4. The problems today are likely to surface around the more subtle forms of sexual harassment.
5. Most studies confirm that the concept of power is central to understanding sexual harassment.

   a) This seems to be true whether the harassment comes from a supervisor, a co-worker, or even a subordinate.
6. Because of power inequities sexual harassment by one's boss creates great difficulty for the person being harassed.
7. Co-workers don't have position power, but they can have influence and use it to sexually harass peers.
   a) In fact, although co-workers appear to engage in somewhat less severe forms of harassment than do supervisors, co-workers are the most frequent perpetrators of sexual harassment in organizations.
8. Harassment by subordinates doesn't get nearly the attention that harassment by a supervisor does, but it does occur.
   a) Usually the subordinate will devalue the superior through highlighting traditional gender stereotypes that reflect negatively on the person in power.
9. The topic of sexual harassment is about power.
   a) It's about one individual controlling or threatening another.
   b) It's wrong. It's illegal.

VII. POLITICS: POWER IN ACTION

A. A Definition of Political Behavior

1. Definitions for organizational politics have focused on the use of power to affect decision making in the organization or on behaviors by members that are self-serving and organizationally nonsanctioned.
2. We define political behavior in organizations as those activities that are not required as part of one's formal role in the organization but that influence or attempt to influence the distribution of advantages and disadvantages within the organization.
3. Key elements
   a) Political behavior is outside one's specified job requirements.
   b) The behavior requires some attempt to use one's power bases.
   c) Politics is concerned with the distribution of advantages and disadvantages within the organization.

B. The Importance of a Political Perspective

1. Those who fail to acknowledge political behavior ignore the reality that organizations are political systems.
2. A political view can explain much of what may seem to be irrational behavior in organizations.

C. Factors Contributing to Political Behavior

1. Individual Factors
   a) Researchers have identified certain personality characteristics, needs, and other individual factors that are likely to be related to political behavior.
   b) Employees who are authoritarian, have a high-risk propensity, or possess an external locus of control act politically with less regard for the consequences to the organization.
   c) A high need for power, autonomy, security, or status is also a major contributor to an employee's tendency to engage in political behavior.
2. Organizational Factors
   a) Political activity is probably more a function of the organization's culture than of individual differences.
   b) Evidence strongly indicates that certain cultures promote politics.

(1) Cultures characterized by low trust, role ambiguity, unclear performance evaluation systems, zero-sum reward allocation practices, democratic decision making, high pressures for performance, and self-serving senior managers will create opportunities for political activities to be nurtured.

c) The less trust there is within the organization, the higher the level of political behavior.

d) Role ambiguity means that the prescribed behaviors of the employee are not clear.

e) The greater the role ambiguity, the more one can engage in political activity with little chance of it being visible.

f) The more that organizations use subjective criteria in the appraisal, emphasize a single outcome measure, or allow significant time to pass between an action and its appraisal, the greater the likelihood an employee can get away with politicking.

g) The more an organization's culture emphasizes the zero-sum or win-lose approach to reward allocations, the more employees will be motivated to engage in politicking.

h) Many managers sought their positions in order to have legitimate power to make unilateral decisions. They fought hard and often paid high personal costs to achieve their influential positions. Sharing their power with others rubs directly against their desires. The result is that managers may use the required teams, committees, conferences, and group meetings in a superficial way--as arenas for maneuvering and manipulating.

i) The more pressure that employees feel to perform well, the more likely they are to engage in politicking.

j) When employees see the people on top engaging in political behavior, especially when they do so successfully and are rewarded for it, a climate is created that supports politicking.

D. Impression Management

1. People have an ongoing interest in how others perceive and evaluate them.
    a) North Americans spend billions of dollars on diets, health club memberships, cosmetics, and plastic surgery.
    b) Being perceived positively by others should have benefits for people in organizations.
        (1) In a political context, it might help sway the distribution of advantages in their favor.
2. The process by which individuals attempt to control the impression others form of them is called impression management.
3. Techniques
    a) Self-descriptions---Statements made by a person that describe such personal characteristics as traits, abilities, feelings, opinions, and personal lives.
    b) Conformity--Agreeing with someone else's opinion in order to gain his or her approval.
    c) Accounts---Excuses, justifications or other explanations of a predicament-creating event aimed at minimizing the apparent severity of the predicament.
    d) Apologies--Admitting responsibility for an undesirable event and simultaneously seeking to get a pardon for the action.
    e) Acclaiming--Explanation of favorable events by someone in order to maximize the desirable implications for that person.
    f) Flattery--Complimenting others about their virtues in an effort to make oneself appear perceptive and likable.
    g) Favors--Doing something nice for someone to gain that person's approval.

4. Keep in mind that nothing in IM implies that the impressions people convey are necessarily false.
    a) Misrepresentation can have a high cost. If the image claimed is false, you may be discredited.
    b) Individuals are more likely to misrepresent themselves in some situations than in others.
        (1) Highly uncertain or ambiguous situations provide relatively little information for challenging a fraudulent claim and reduce the risks associated with misrepresentation.
5. Effectiveness
    a) Only a few studies have been undertaken to test the effectiveness of IM techniques.
    b) The evidence demonstrates that using IM behaviors seems to work.
    c) Interviewing study.

E. The Ethics of Behaving Politically
1. Although there are no clear-cut ways to differentiate ethical from unethical politicking, there are some questions you should consider.
2. Exhibit 11-2 illustrates a decision tree to guide ethical actions.
    a) The first question you need to answer addresses self-interest versus organizational goals.
        (1) Ethical actions are consistent with the organization's goals.
3. The second question concerns the rights of other parties.
4. The final question that needs to be addressed is related to whether the political activity conforms to standards of equity and justice.
5. Unfortunately, the answers to the questions in Exhibit 11-2 are often argued in ways to make unethical practices seem ethical.
    a) Immoral people can justify almost any behavior.
    b) If you have a strong power base, recognize the ability of power to corrupt.

VIII. IMPLICATIONS FOR MANAGERS
1. If you want to get things done in a group or organization, it helps to have power. As a manager who wants to maximize your power, you will want to increase others' dependence on you. You can, for instance, increase your power in relation to your boss by developing knowledge or a skill that he or she needs and for which he or she perceives no ready substitute. But power is a two-way street. You will not be alone in attempting to build your power bases. Others, particularly subordinates, will be seeking to make you dependent on them. The result is a continual battle. While you seek to maximize others' dependence on you, you will be seeking to minimize your dependence on others. And, of course, others you work with will be trying to do the same.
2. The effective manager accepts the political nature of organizations. By assessing behavior in a political framework, you can better predict the actions of others and use this information to formulate political strategies that will gain advantages for you and your work unit.

SUMMARY

1. Power refers to the capacity that A has to influence the behavior of B so that B does something he or she would not otherwise do. Probably the most important aspect of power is that it is a function of dependence. The greater B's dependence on A, the greater is A's power in the relationship.
2. The two concepts of power and leadership are closely intertwined. Leaders use power to attain group goals, and power is a means for facilitating their achievement. There are several key differences.

3. There are five bases to power. The coercive power base is defined by French and Raven as being dependent on fear. The opposite of coercive power is reward power. People comply with the wishes or directives of another because doing so produces positive benefits. Legitimate power comes from one's structural position. Expert power is influence wielded as a result of expertise, special skill, or knowledge. Referent power's base is identification with a person who has desirable resources or personal traits.
4. A key element to power is dependency. When you possess anything that others require but that you alone control, you make them dependent on you and, therefore, you gain power over them. Dependency is increased when the resource you control is important and scarce. A resource needs to be perceived as scarce to create dependency.
5. The natural way to gain influence is to become a powerholder and forming a coalition is a way two or more "outs" can gain power. Coalitions in organizations often seek to maximize their size. Coalition formation will be influenced by the actual tasks that workers perform. The more routine the task of a group or the work of individual jobs, the greater the likelihood that coalitions will form.
6. Legally, sexual harassment is defined as unwelcome advances, requests for sexual favors, and other verbal or physical conduct, whether overt or subtle, of a sexual nature. But there is a great deal of disagreement about what specifically constitutes sexual harassment. Most studies confirm that the concept of power is central to understanding sexual harassment. Sexual harassment is about power. It's about one individual's controlling or threatening another. It's wrong. It's illegal.
7. Political behavior in organizations are those activities that are not required as part of one's formal role in the organization but that influence or attempt to influence the distribution of advantages and disadvantages within the organization.
8. The importance of a political perspective in an organization is that a political view can explain much of what may seem to be irrational behavior in organizations. Those who fail to acknowledge political behavior ignore the reality that organizations are political systems.
9. Political behavior occurs in organizations for a number of reasons. Researchers have identified certain personality characteristics, needs, and other individual factors that are likely to be related to political behavior. Political activity is probably more a function of the organization's culture than of individual differences. The greater the role ambiguity, the more one can engage in political activity with little chance of it being visible. The more that organizations use subjective criteria in the appraisal, the greater the likelihood an employee can get away with politicking. When employees see the people on top engaging in political behavior, especially when they do so successfully and are rewarded for it, a climate is created that supports politicking.
10. Impression management has become more important in organizations. It is the process by which individuals attempt to control the impression others form of them. Individuals manage the impressions they make through their self-descriptions, conformity, using justifications or other explanations of a predicament, apologies, etc.
11. Finally, it is important to think about the ethics of political behavior. Although there are no clear-cut ways to differentiate ethical from unethical politicking, there are some questions you should consider. Exhibit 11-2 illustrates a decision tree to guide ethical actions

DISCUSSION QUESTIONS

1. What is power?

   Answer - Power refers to the capacity that one person has to influence the behavior of another so that the second person does something he or she would not otherwise do. Power may exist but not be used. It is, therefore, a capacity or potential. Probably the most important aspect of power is that it is a function of dependence. The greater B's dependence on A, the greater is A's power in the relationship.

2. Contrast power and leadership.

Answer - Power refers to the capacity to influence the behavior of others. The concepts of power and leadership are closely intertwined. Leaders use power to attain group goals, and power is a means for facilitating their achievement. The differences are:

- Power does not require goal compatibility, merely dependence.
- Leadership requires some congruence between the goals of the leader and those led.
- Leadership research, for the most part, emphasizes style.
- The research on power has tended to encompass a broader area and focus on tactics for gaining compliance.

3. Manager's power can be based in several circumstances. What are the different bases of power and what are the advantages or disadvantages of using power in terms of its base or origin?
Answer - Coercive power--dependent on fear. It rests on the application, or the threat of application, of physical sanctions such as the infliction of pain, the generation of frustration through restriction of movement, or the control by force of basic physiological or safety needs. Reward power--the opposite of coercive power. People comply with the wishes or directives of another because doing so produces positive benefits. You don't need to be a manager to be able to exert influence through rewards. Legitimate power--the power base is one's structural position. It represents the power a person receives as a result of his or her position in the formal hierarchy of an organization. Positions of authority include coercive and reward powers. Legitimate power is broader than the power to coerce and reward. Expert power--Expert power is influence wielded as a result of expertise, special skill, or knowledge. Expertise has become one of the most powerful sources of influence as the world has become more technologically oriented. Referent power--Its base is identification with a person who has desirable resources or personal traits. If I admire and identify with you, you can exercise power over me because I want to please you. Referent power develops out of admiration of another and a desire to be like that person. Student's responses regarding advantages/disadvantages will be more of a value discussion than a factual discussion.

4. Power depends on dependency. As a manager how can you legitimately create dependency among your employees, peers, and your organization?
Answer - If you can create a monopoly by controlling information, prestige, or anything that others crave, they become dependent on you. Conversely, the more you can expand your options, the less power you place in the hands of others. Dependency is increased when the resource you control is important and scarce. To create dependency, therefore, you must control things that are perceived as important. The ability to reduce uncertainty increases a group's importance and, hence, its power but also what's important is situational. A resource needs to be perceived as scarce to create dependency. The need to obtain a scarce resource--such as important knowledge--makes the high-ranking member dependent on the low-ranking member.

5. What role do coalitions play in the developing of power bases, especially by individuals or groups that do not have a traditional base of power?
Answer - The natural way to gain influence is to become a powerholder. In such cases, efforts will be made to form a coalition of two or more "outs" who, by joining together, can each better themselves at the expense of those outside the coalition. Coalitions in organizations often seek to maximize their size. In organizations, the implementation of and commitment to the decision are at least as important as the decision itself. It's necessary, therefore, for coalitions in organizations to seek a broad constituency to support the coalition's objectives, so the coalition must be expanded to encompass as many interests as possible. More coalitions will likely be created if there is a great deal of task and resource interdependence. Coalition formation will be influenced by the actual tasks that workers perform. The more routine the task of a group or the work of individual jobs, the greater the likelihood that coalitions will form.

6. Why do researchers say that power not sex is central to understanding sexual harassment?
Answer - Legally, sexual harassment is defined as unwelcome advances, requests for sexual favors, and other verbal or physical conduct, whether overt or subtle, of a sexual nature. Most studies confirm that the concept of power is central to understanding sexual harassment. This seems to be true whether the harassment comes from a supervisor, a co-worker, or even a subordinate. Because of power inequities sexual harassment by one's boss creates great difficulty for the person being harassed. Co-workers don't have position power, but they can have influence and use it to sexually harass peers. In fact, although co-workers appear to engage in somewhat less severe forms of harassment than do supervisors, co-workers are the most frequent perpetrators of sexual harassment in organizations. Harassment by subordinates doesn't get nearly the attention that harassment by a supervisor does, but it does occur. Usually the subordinate will devalue the superior through highlighting traditional gender stereotypes that reflect negatively on the person in power.

7. How can you recognize political behavior in an organization?
Answer - The text defines political behavior in organizations as those activities that are not required as part of one's formal role in the organization but that influence or attempt to influence the distribution of advantages and disadvantages within the organization. There are three key elements. 1) Political behavior is outside one's specified job requirements. 2) The behavior requires some attempt to use one's power bases. 3) Politics is concerned with the distribution of advantages and disadvantages within the organization.

8. Why do managers and employees engage in political behavior in organizations?
Answer - There are individual and organizational factors that contribute to political behavior. <u>Individual factors</u>. Researchers have identified certain personality characteristics, needs, and other individual factors that are likely to be related to political behavior. Employees who are authoritarian, have a high-risk propensity, or possess an external locus of control act politically with less regard for the consequences to the organization. A high need for power, autonomy, security, or status is also a major contributor to an employee's tendency to engage in political behavior. <u>Organizational factors</u>. Political activity is probably more a function of the organization's culture than of individual differences. Evidence strongly indicates that certain cultures promote politics. Cultures characterized by low trust, role ambiguity, unclear performance evaluation systems, zero-sum reward allocation practices, democratic decision making, high pressures for performance, and self-serving senior managers will create opportunities for political activities to be nurtured. The greater the role ambiguity, the more one can engage in political activity with little chance of it being visible. The more that organizations use subjective criteria in the appraisal, emphasize a single outcome measure, or allow significant time to pass between an action and its appraisal, the greater the likelihood an employee can get away with politicking. The more an organization's culture emphasizes the zero-sum or win-lose approach to reward allocations, the more employees will be motivated to engage in politicking. Many managers sought their positions in order to have legitimate power to make unilateral decisions. They fought hard and often paid high personal costs to achieve their influential positions. Sharing their power with others rubs directly against their desires. The result is that managers may use the required teams, committees, conferences, and group meetings in a superficial way--as arenas for maneuvering and manipulating. The more pressure that employees feel to perform well, the more likely they are to engage in politicking. When employees see the people on top engaging in political behavior, especially when they do so successfully and are rewarded for it, a climate is created that supports politicking.

9. Regardless of the ethics of impression management, what things can a manager do to manage and enhance his/her image within an organization?
Answer - The process by which individuals attempt to control the impression others form of them is called impression management. There are seven techniques.

- Self-descriptions---Statements made by a person that describe such personal characteristics as traits, abilities, feelings, opinions, and personal lives.
- Conformity--Agreeing with someone else's opinion in order to gain his or her approval.
- Accounts---Excuses, justifications or other explanations of a predicament-creating event aimed at minimizing the apparent severity of the predicament.
- Apologies--Admitting responsibility for an undesirable event and simultaneously seeking to get a pardon for the action.
- Acclaiming--Explanation of favorable events by someone in order to maximize the desirable implications for that person.
- Flattery--Complimenting others about their virtues in an effort to make oneself appear perceptive and likable.
- Favors--Doing something nice for someone to gain that person's approval.

Keep in mind that nothing in IM implies that the impressions people convey are necessarily false. Misrepresentation can have a high cost. If the image claimed is false, you may be discredited.

10. Are there any ethical considerations to acting in a political manner within an organization that managers need to be aware of?
    Answer - Although there are no clear-cut ways to differentiate ethical from unethical politicking, there are some questions you should consider. Exhibit 11-2 illustrates a decision tree to guide ethical actions The first question you need to answer addresses self-interest versus organizational goals. Ethical actions are consistent with the organization's goals. The second question concerns the rights of other parties. The final question that needs to be addressed is related to whether the political activity conforms to standards of equity and justice.

EXERCISE

What is Your Power Base?

Our goal is for students to realize through practice what different forms of power look like and which ones they tend to gravitate toward using.

1. Have students read the following situation:
2. Choose students to role play the two positions, S.G.A. representative and Administration.
    - You can have two students fishbowl the exercise.
    - You can create two small teams; two S.G.A. representatives and three Administrators.
    - You can assign the role play to five small groups having each one play out one of the power positions.
3. Have the students role play for 10-12 minutes. Adjust the time as you see fit, sometimes the negotiation runs out more quickly and sometimes you can let it play out for 30 minutes.
4. The rest of the class should observe the role play and note:
    - What power-base was used by each person?
    - What else could they have done to make the position more powerful?
    - What did they do that didn't fit that power perspective?
    - Did they choose the most appropriate power base for this situation? Why?
5. Once the role play is completed, have the class discuss:
    - Important here is to show almost any power base can work.
    - Also, students will tend to have an orientation to one of the approaches.
    - Third, if both sides choose power approaches that lead to confrontation the negotiation will probably fail.

Power Play

You are a member of the Student Government Association's Executive Body at your college/university. You are an elected student representative, an Executive-level officer, but not the President of the S.G.A. You represent students in the business program/school. This program is a cash cow for the college/university in that it generates more tuition and grants than it consumes. Graduates tend to become wealthy alumni who make generous contributions. The business school/program and S.G.A. have built a close relationship with a number of these alumni. You also have been part of an undergraduate team that has enticed 20% more large corporations to interview at your campus through networking and personal contacts with the executives of these organizations.

The administration has implemented a campus-wide policy affecting all undergraduates that you want changed. [You may choose a current issue on campus, or leave the particulars ambiguous.] This policy is a special pain for business students. The policy came out of administration/alumni talks over the last year. Your chief administrator is a strong but reasonable person, who doesn't easily change direction but is willing to hear someone's perspective. The Chief Administrator is a bit feared by students, respected by faculty, and doesn't have the best relationship with alumni.

1. As the S.G.A. representative choose one of the four power bases and negotiate the elimination of or modification of this policy.
   - Choose the one you think has the most credibility given this situation.
   - Talk, negotiate, etc., as you think appropriate given this base of power.
   - Do not make overt statements that will give away your power base.
2. Do not reveal the power base you are using.
3. As the Chief Administrator choose a power base in response to the S.G.A. representative.
   - Choose the one you think has the most credibility given this situation.
   - Talk, negotiate, etc., as you think appropriate given this base of power.
   - Do not make overt statements that will give away your power base.

CHAPTER 12 - CONFLICT AND NEGOTIATION

CHAPTER OBJECTIVES

After reading this chapter, you should be able to:

1. Define conflict.
2. Differentiate between the traditional, human relations, and interactionist views of conflict.
3. Contrast functional and dysfunctional conflict.
4. Outline the conflict process.
5. Describe the five conflict-handling orientations.
6. Contrast distributive and integrative bargaining.
7. Identify decision biases that hinder effective negotiation.
8. Explain ways for individuals to improve their negotiating skills.

LECTURE OUTLINE

I. A DEFINITION OF CONFLICT

A. Definition

1. Multiple definitions of conflict.
2. Several common themes underlie most definitions.
   a) For there to be a conflict it must be perceived by the parties involved.
   b) Additional commonalties among most definitions of conflict are the concepts of opposition, scarcity, and blockage and the assumption there are two or more parties whose interests or goals appear to be incompatible.
   c) Resources--money, jobs, prestige, and power, for example--are not unlimited, and their scarcity encourages blocking behavior.
3. Differences between definitions tend to center around intent and whether conflict is limited only to overt acts.
   a) The intent issue is a debate over whether blockage behavior must be a determined action or whether it could occur as a result of fortuitous circumstances. As to whether conflict can refer only to overt acts, some definitions, for example, require signs of manifest fighting or open struggle as criteria for the existence of conflict.
4. Our definition of conflict acknowledges awareness (perception), opposition, scarcity, and blockage.
5. Further, we assume it to be a determined action, which can exist at either the latent or overt level.
6. We define conflict as a process in which an effort is purposely made by A to object to the efforts of B by some form of blocking that will result in frustrating B in attaining his or her goals or furthering his or her interests.

II. TRANSITIONS IN CONFLICT THOUGHT

A. The Traditional View

1. It was assumed that conflict was bad--something to be avoided.
2. The traditional view was consistent with the attitudes that prevailed about group behavior in the 1930s and 1940s.
3. According to studies such as those done at Hawthorne, conflict was a dysfunctional outcome resulting from poor communication, a lack of openness and trust between people, and the failure of managers to be responsive to the needs and aspirations of their employees.
4. The view that all conflict is bad is a simple approach and most of us still evaluate conflict situations on the basis of this outmoded standard.

B. The Human Relations View
   1. Conflict was a natural occurrence in all groups and organizations.
   2. Conflict should be accepted as it is inevitable.
   3. This view dominated conflict theory from the late 1940s through the mid-1970s.

C. The Interactionist View
   1. The current perspective on conflict.
   2. The interactionist approach encourages conflict on the grounds that a harmonious, peaceful, tranquil, and cooperative group is likely to become static, apathetic, and nonresponsive to needs for change and innovation.
   3. The major contribution of the interactionist approach, therefore, is encouraging group leaders to maintain an ongoing minimal level of conflict--enough to keep the group alive, self-critical, and creative.
   4. The text takes an interactionist view.
      a) Whether a conflict is good or bad depends on the type of conflict.
      b) It's necessary to differentiate between functional and dysfunctional conflicts.

III. DIFFERENTIATING FUNCTIONAL FROM DYSFUNCTIONAL CONFLICTS

A. Introduction
   1. The interactionist view does not propose that all conflicts are good.
      a) Some conflicts support the goals of the group and improve its performance; these are functional, constructive forms of conflict.
      b) There are also conflicts that hinder group performance; these are dysfunctional or destructive forms.
   2. The demarcation between functional and dysfunctional is neither clear nor precise.
      a) The type and level of conflict that creates healthy and positive involvement toward one group's goals may, in another situation, be highly dysfunctional.
   3. The important criterion is group performance.
      a) Since groups exist to attain a goal or goals, it is the impact of the conflict on the group, rather than on any single individual, that defines functionality.
   4. A group member may perceive an action as dysfunctional because the outcome is personally dissatisfying to him or her. For our analysis, however, it would be functional if it furthered the objectives of the group.

IV. THE CONFLICT PROCESS

A. See Exhibit 12-1, the conflict process

B. Stage I: Potential Opposition
   1. The first step in the conflict process is the presence of conditions that create opportunities for conflict to arise.
   2. Three general categories: communication, structure, and personal variables.
   3. Communication
      a) The communicative source represents those opposing forces that arise from semantic difficulties, misunderstandings, and 'noise" in the communication channels.
      b) One major misconception is that poor communication is the reason for conflicts.
      c) Poor communication is certainly not the source of all conflicts, though there is considerable evidence to suggest that problems in the communication process retard collaboration and stimulate misunderstanding.
      d) A review of the research suggests that semantic difficulties, insufficient exchange of information, and noise in the communication channel are all barriers to communication and potential antecedent conditions to conflict.

(1) Semantic difficulties arise as a result of differences in training, selective perception, and inadequate information about others.

e) The potential for conflict increases when either too little or too much communication takes place.

(1) It is possible to overcommunicate, resulting in an increase in the potential for conflict.

(2) The channel chosen for communicating can have an influence on stimulating opposition. The filtering process that occurs as information is passed between members and the divergence of communications from formal or previously established channels offer potential opportunities for conflict to arise.

4. Structure

a) The term structure is used, in this context, to include variables such as size; degree of routinization, specialization, and standardization in the tasks assigned to group members; heterogeneity of the group; leadership styles; reward systems; and the degree of dependence between groups.

b) Size and specialization act as forces to stimulate conflict.

c) There is some indication that a close style of leadership, that is, tight and continuous observation with restrictive control of the others' behaviors, increases conflict potential, but the evidence is not strong.

d) Too much reliance on participation may also stimulate conflict.

(1) Participation and conflict are highly correlated, apparently because participation encourages the promotion of differences.

(2) Reward systems, too, are found to create conflict when one member's gain is at another's expense.

(3) If a group is dependent on another group or if interdependence allows one group to win at another's expense, opposing forces are stimulated.

5. Personal Variables

a) The most important personal variables are individual value systems and individual idiosyncrasies and differences.

(1) The evidence indicates that certain personality types--for example, individuals who are highly authoritarian, dogmatic, and who demonstrate low self-esteem--lead to potential conflict.

b) Most important, and probably the most overlooked variable in the study of social conflict, is the notion of differing value systems.

(1) That is, people differ in the importance they give to values such as freedom, pleasure, hard work, self-respect, honesty, obedience, and equality.

(2) Differences in value systems are important sources of the potential for conflict.

C. Stage II: Cognition and Personalization

1. If the conditions cited in stage I generate frustration, then the potential for opposition becomes realized in the second stage.

2. One or more of the parties must be aware of the existence of the antecedent conditions.

3. Because a conflict is perceived does not mean it is personalized.

a) It is at the personal level where conflict is felt, when individuals become emotionally involved, that parties experience anxiety, tension, frustration, or hostility.

D. Stage III: Behavior

1. A member engages in action that frustrates the attainment of another's goals or prevents the furthering of the other's interests.

a) At this juncture, the conflict is out in the open.

2. Overt conflict covers a full range of behaviors---from subtle, indirect, and highly controlled forms of interference to direct, aggressive, violent, and uncontrolled struggle.
3. This is also when most conflict-handling behaviors are initiated.
4. Five conflict-handling approaches: competition, collaboration, avoidance, accommodation, and compromise.
   a) Competition. When one party seeks to achieve certain goals or to further personal interests, regardless of the impact on the parties to the conflict, he or she competes and dominates.
   b) Collaboration. When each of the parties in conflict desires to satisfy fully the concern of all parties, we have cooperation and the search for a mutually beneficial outcome.
      (1) In collaboration, the behavior of the parties is aimed at solving the problem and at clarifying the differences rather than accommodating various points of view.
   c) Avoidance. A party may recognize that a conflict exists but react by withdrawing from it or suppressing the conflict.
      (1) Indifference or the desire to evade overt demonstration of a disagreement can result in withdrawal.
   d) Accommodation. When the parties seek to appease their opponents, they may be willing to place their opponents' interests above their own.
      (1) In order to maintain the relationship, one party is willing to be self-sacrificing.
   e) Compromise. When each party to the conflict must give up something, sharing occurs, resulting in a compromised outcome. In compromising, there is no clear winner or loser.
      (1) The distinguishing characteristic of compromise, therefore, is the requirement that each party give up something.
5. The Impact of National Culture on Conflict Behavior.
   a) Your approach to handling conflict will, to some degree, be influenced by your cultural roots.
      (1) Americans, for example, have a reputation for being open, direct, and competitive. These characteristics are consistent with a society marked by relatively low uncertainty avoidance and high quantity-of-life rankings.
      (2) People in countries low in uncertainty avoidance feel secure and relatively free from threats of uncertainty. Their organizations, therefore, tend to be rather open and flexible.
      (3) Countries high in quality of life emphasize assertiveness. The cultural climate of low uncertainty avoidance and high quantity of life tends to shape a society that is open, direct, and competitive.
   b) This premise suggests that uncertainty avoidance and quantity/quality of life rankings would be fairly good predictors of which conflict styles are preferred in different countries.

E. Stage IV: Outcomes
1. Functional Outcomes
   a) Low or moderate levels of conflict could improve the effectiveness of a group.
   b) Conflict is constructive when it improves the quality of decisions, stimulates creativity and innovation, encourages interest and curiosity among group members, provides the medium through which problems can be aired and tensions released, and fosters an environment of self-evaluation and improvement.
      (1) Conflict can enhance the quality of decision making by allowing all points particularly the ones that are unusual or held by a minority, to be weighed in important decisions.

(2) Conflict is an antidote for groupthink.

c) Companies that have suffered because they had too little functional conflict.

(1) Sears, Roebuck.

(2) General Motors.

d) A comparison of six major decisions during the administrations of four U.S. presidents found that conflict reduced the chance that groupthink would overpower policy decisions.

e) There is further evidence that conflict leads to better and more innovative decisions, as well as increased group productivity.

2. Dysfunctional Conflict

a) Uncontrolled opposition breeds discontent, which acts to dissolve common ties and eventually leads to destruction of the group.

b) There is a substantial body of literature to document how the dysfunctional varieties of conflict can reduce group effectiveness.

c) Among the more undesirable consequences are a retarding of communication, reductions in group cohesiveness, and subordination of group goals to the primacy of infighting among members.

3. Research on conflict has yet to identify those situations in which conflict is more likely to be constructive than destructive.

4. Two hypotheses about the difference between functional and dysfunctional conflict.

a) The first is that extreme levels of conflict, exemplified by overt struggle or violence, are rarely, if ever, functional.

(1) Functional conflict is probably most often characterized by low to moderate levels of subtle and controlled opposition.

b) Second, the type of group activity should be another factor in determining functionality.

(1) We hypothesize that the more creative or unprogrammed the decision making of the group, the greater the probability that internal conflict will be constructive.

(2) Groups required to tackle problems demanding novel approaches--for example, in research or advertising--will benefit more from conflict than groups performing highly programmed activities such as work teams on an automobile assembly line.

V. NEGOTIATION

A. Definition

1. For our purposes, we define negotiation as a process in which two or more parties exchange goods or services and attempt to agree on the exchange rate for them.

2. In addition, we use the terms negotiation and bargaining interchangeably.

B. Bargaining Strategies

1. There are two general approaches to negotiation: distributive bargaining and integrative bargaining. See Exhibit 12-2.

2. Distributive Bargaining

a) Car purchase example.

b) The negotiating process in the example is called distributive bargaining.

c) Its most identifying feature is that it operates under zero-sum conditions.

(1) In the used car example, every dollar you can get the seller to cut from the car's price is a dollar you save.

d) The essence of distributive bargaining is negotiating over who gets what share of a fixed pie.

e) Probably the most widely cited example of distributive bargaining is in labor-management negotiations over wages.
f) Exhibit 12-3 - depicts the distributive bargaining strategy.
g) When engaged in distributive bargaining, one's tactics focus on trying to get one's opponent to agree to one's specific target point or to get as close to it as possible.

3. Integrative Bargaining
   a) Sales representative for a women's sportswear manufacturer example.
   b) This sales-credit negotiation is an example of integrative bargaining.
      (1) In contrast to distributive bargaining, integrative problem solving operates under the assumption that one or more settlements exist that can create a win-win solution.
   c) All things being equal, integrative bargaining is preferable to distributive bargaining. Because the former builds long-term relationships and facilitates working together in the future.
4. We don't see more integrative bargaining in organizations because of the conditions necessary for this type of negotiation.
   a) Parties who are open with information and candid about their concerns.
   b) A sensitivity by both parties to the other's needs.
   c) The ability to trust one another.
   d) A willingness by both parties to maintain flexibility.

C. Issues in Negotiation
1. Decision-Making Biases that Hinder Effective Negotiation.
   a) Irrational escalation of commitment. People tend to continue a previously selected course of action beyond what rational analysis would recommend.
   b) The mythical fixed pie. Bargainers assume that their gain must come at the expense of the other party.
   c) Anchoring and adjustments. People often have a tendency to anchor their judgments on irrelevant information, such as an initial offer. Many factors influence the initial positions people take when entering a negotiation.
   d) Framing negotiations. People tend to be overly affected by the way information is presented to them.
   e) Availability of information. Negotiators often rely too much on readily available information while ignoring more relevant data.
   f) The Winner's curse. The regret one feels after closing a negotiation. Because your opponent accepted your offer, you become concerned that you offered too much. This postnegotiation reaction is not unusual.
   g) Overconfidence. Many of the previous biases can combine to inflate a person's confidence in his or her judgment and choices. When people hold certain beliefs and expectations, they tend to ignore information that contradicts them.
2. The Role of Personality Traits in Negotiation.
   a) You try but can't predict an opponent's negotiating tactics even if you know something about his or her personality.
   b) Personality traits have no significant direct effect on either the bargaining process or negotiation outcomes.
      (1) You should concentrate on the issues and the situational factors in each bargaining episode and not on your opponent and his or her characteristics.
3. Cultural Differences in Negotiations.
   a) Negotiating styles clearly vary among national cultures.
   b) The French like conflict. They frequently gain recognition and develop their reputations by thinking and acting against others. As a result, the French tend to take

a long time in negotiating agreements, and they aren't overly concerned about whether their opponents like or dislike them.

c) The Chinese also draw out negotiations but for a different reason. They believe that negotiations never end. Like the Japanese, the Chinese negotiate to develop a relationship and a commitment to work together rather than to tie up every loose end.

d) Americans are known around the world for their impatience and their desire to be liked. Astute negotiators from other countries often turn these characteristics to their advantage by dragging out negotiations and making friendship conditional on the final settlement.

e) The cultural context of the negotiation significantly influences the amount and type of preparation for bargaining the relative emphasis on task versus interpersonal relationships; the tactics used, and even where the negotiation should be conducted.

f) The first study compared North Americans, Arabs, and Russians.

(1) North Americans tried to persuade by relying on facts and appealing to logic. They countered opponents' arguments with objective facts. They made small concessions early in the negotiation to establish a relationship and usually reciprocated opponents' concessions.

(2) North Americans treated deadlines as very important.

(3) The Arabs tried to persuade by appealing to emotion. They countered opponents' arguments with subjective feelings. They made concessions throughout the bargaining process and almost always reciprocated opponents' concessions. Arabs approached deadlines very casually.

(4) The Russians based their arguments on asserted ideals. They made few, if any, concessions. Any concession offered by an opponent was viewed as a weakness and was almost never reciprocated. Finally, the Russians tended to ignore deadlines.

g) The second study looked at verbal and nonverbal negotiation tactics exhibited by North Americans, Japanese, and Brazilians during half-hour bargaining sessions.

(1) Brazilians on average said No 83 times compared with 5 times for the Japanese and 9 times for the North Americans.

(2) The Japanese displayed more than 5 periods of silence lasting longer than 10 seconds during each 30-minute session.

(3) North Americans averaged 3.5 such periods; the Brazilians had none.

(4) The Japanese and North Americans interrupted their opponent about the same number of times, but the Brazilians interrupted two-and-a-half to three times more often than the North Americans and the Japanese.

(5) Finally, while the Japanese and the North Americans had no physical contact with their opponents during negotiations except for hand-shaking, the Brazilians touched each other almost five times every half hour.

VI. IMPLICATIONS FOR MANAGERS

A. Managing Conflict

1. Many people assume that conflict is related to lower group and organizational performance. That assumption is often false. Conflict can be either constructive or destructive to the functioning of a group or unit. When it's too high or too low, it hinders performance. An optimal level is one in which there is enough conflict to prevent stagnation, stimulate creativity, allow tensions to be released, and sow the seeds for change yet not so much as to be disruptive.
2. Advice to managers faced with excessive conflict. Don't assume that there's one conflict-handling approach that will always be best! You should select the resolution technique appropriate for each situation. Guidelines.

a) Use competition when quick, decisive action is vital (in emergencies); on important issues, where unpopular actions need implementing (in cost cutting, enforcing unpopular rules, discipline); on issues vital to the organization's welfare when you know you're right; and against people who take advantage of noncompetitive behavior.
b) Use collaboration to find an integrative solution when both sets of concerns are too important to be compromised; when your objective is to learn; to merge insights from people with different perspectives; to gain commitment by incorporating concerns into a consensus; and to work through feelings that have interfered with a relationship.
c) Use avoidance when an issue is trivial or when more important issues are pressing; when you perceive no chance of satisfying your concerns; when potential disruption outweighs the benefits of resolution; to let people cool down and regain perspective; when gathering information supercedes immediate decision; when others can resolve the conflict more effectively; and when issues seem tangential or symptomatic of other issues.
d) Use accommodation when you find you are wrong and to allow a better position to be heard, to learn, and to show your reasonableness; when issues are more important to others than to yourself and to satisfy others and maintain cooperation; to build social credits for later issues; to minimize loss when you are outmatched and losing; when harmony and stability are especially important; and to allow subordinates to develop by learning from mistakes.
e) Use compromise when goals are important but not worth the effort of potential disruption of more assertive approaches; when opponents with equal power are committed to mutually exclusive goals; to achieve temporary settlements to complex issues; to arrive at expedient solutions under time pressure; and as a backup when collaboration or competition is unsuccessful.

B. Improving Negotiation Skills

1. Recommendations for improving your effectiveness at negotiating.
   a) Research Your Opponent--Acquire as much information as you can about your opponent's interests and goals. What constituencies must he or she appease? What is his or her strategy?
   b) Begin with a Positive Overture--Research shows that concessions tend to be reciprocated and lead to agreements. As a result, begin bargaining with a positive overture--perhaps a small concession--and then reciprocate your opponent's concessions.
   c) Address the Problem, Not Personalities--Concentrate on the negotiation issues not on the personal characteristics of your opponent. It's your opponent's ideas or position that you disagree with, not him or her personally. Separate the people from the problem, and don't personalize differences.
   d) Pay Little Attention to Initial Offers--Treat initial offers as merely a point of departure. Everyone has to have an initial position. They tend to be extreme and idealistic. Treat them as such.
   e) Emphasize Win-Win Solutions--If conditions are supportive, look for an integrative solution. Frame options in terms of your opponent's interests and look for solutions that can allow both you and your opponent to declare a victory.
   f) Create an Open and Trusting Climate--Skilled negotiators are good listeners, ask questions, focus their arguments directly, are not defensive, and have learned to avoid words and phrases that can irritate an opponent.

SUMMARY

1 Conflict is a process in which an effort is purposely made by A to object the efforts of B by some form of blocking that will result in frustrating B in attaining his or her goals or furthering his or her interests. This definition of conflict acknowledges awareness (perception), opposition, scarcity, and blockage.

2 The thinking about conflict has gone through a number of changes. The traditional view assumed that conflict was bad--something to be avoided. The human relations view sees conflict as a natural occurrence in all groups and organizations. The current perspective on conflict is the interactionist view. It encourages conflict on the grounds that a harmonious, peaceful, tranquil, and cooperative group is likely to become static, apathetic, and nonresponsive to needs for change and innovation.

3 The interactionist view does not propose that all conflicts are good. Some conflicts support the goals of the group and improve its performance; these are functional, constructive forms of conflict. There are also conflicts that hinder group performance; these are dysfunctional or destructive forms. The demarcation between functional and dysfunctional is neither clear nor precise.

4 There is a conflict process model; the text outlines it in Exhibit 12-1. The first step in the conflict process is the presence of conditions that create opportunities for conflict to arise. Three general categories: communication, structure, and personal variables. If the conditions cited in stage I generate frustration, then the potential for opposition becomes realized in the second stage. A member engages in action that frustrates the attainment of another's goals or prevents the furthering of the other's interests, this is Stage III and at this juncture, the conflict is out in the open. The fourth and final step focuses on functional outcomes of the conflict.

5 There are two general approaches to negotiation: distributive bargaining and integrative bargaining. The essence of distributive bargaining is negotiating over who gets what share of a fixed pie. In contrast to distributive bargaining, integrative problem solving operates under the assumption that one or more settlements exist that can create a win-win solution.

6 We become ineffective in negotiation through irrational escalation of commitment, the mythical fixed pie, anchoring and adjustments, framing negotiations, availability of information, the Winner's curse, and overconfidence. Both personality traits and cultural differences also play a role in negotiation.

7 We can improve our negotiation skills through a number of tactical steps, such as: research your opponent, begin with a positive overture, addressing the problem, not personalities, paying little attention to initial offers, emphasizing win-win solutions, and creating an open and trusting climate.

DISCUSSION QUESTIONS

1 How does the definition of conflict used by the authors of your text differ from other traditional definitions of conflict?

Answer - There are multiple definitions of conflict. Several common themes underlie most definitions: conflict must be perceived by the parties to it, there must be opposition, scarcity, and blockage and the assumption that there are two or more parties whose interests or goals appear to be incompatible, and resources must be involved. Your author's definition of conflict acknowledges awareness (perception), opposition, scarcity, and blockage. Further, they assume it to be a determined action, which can exist at either the latent or overt level. They define conflict as a process in which an effort is purposely made by A to object the efforts of B by some form of blocking that will result in frustrating B in attaining his or her goals or furthering his or her interests. The text takes an interactionist view. Whether a conflict is good or bad depends on the type of conflict. It's necessary to differentiate between functional and dysfunctional conflicts.

2 How has management thinking about conflict changed over the years?

Answer - It was assumed that conflict was bad--something to be avoided. The traditional view was consistent with the attitudes that prevailed about group behavior in the 1930s and 1940s. According to studies such as those done at Hawthorne, conflict was a dysfunctional outcome resulting from poor communication, a lack of openness and trust between people, and the failure of managers to be responsive to the needs and aspirations of their employees. Then came the human relations view that conflict was a natural occurrence in all groups and organizations. This view dominated conflict theory from the late 1940s through the mid-1970s. The current perspective is the interactionist view, which encourages conflict on the grounds that a harmonious, peaceful, tranquil, and cooperative group is likely to become static, apathetic, and nonresponsive to needs for change and innovation. The major contribution of the interactionist approach, therefore, is encouraging group leaders to maintain an ongoing minimal level of conflict--enough to keep the group alive, self-critical, and creative.

3 How does functional conflict differ from dysfunctional conflict?
Answer - Some conflicts support the goals of the group and improve its performance; these are functional, constructive forms of conflict. There are also conflicts that hinder group performance; these are dysfunctional or destructive forms. The demarcation between functional and dysfunctional is neither clear nor precise. The important criterion is group performance. Since groups exist to attain a goal or goals, it is the impact of the conflict on the group, rather than on any single individual, that defines functionality. Conflict is constructive when it improves the quality of decisions, stimulates creativity and innovation, encourages interest and curiosity among group members, provides the medium through which problems can be aired and tensions released, and fosters an environment of self-evaluation and improvement. Conflict is an antidote for groupthink. Uncontrolled opposition breeds discontent, which acts to dissolve common ties and eventually leads to destruction of the group. There is a substantial body of literature to document how the dysfunctional varieties of conflict can reduce group effectiveness.

4 Describe the conflict process.
Answer - This process is outlined in Exhibit 12-1. The first step in the conflict process is the presence of conditions that create opportunities for conflict to arise. If the conditions cited in stage I generate frustration, then the potential for opposition becomes realized in the second stage. One or more of the parties must be aware of the existence of the antecedent conditions. A member engages in action that frustrates the attainment of another's goals or prevents the furthering of the other's interests. At this juncture, the conflict is out in the open. The fourth and final stage relates to functional outcomes. Low or moderate levels of conflict could improve the effectiveness of a group.

5 What conflict-handling behavior would be best in each of the following situations?
   a. A manager of marketing is in a conflict with another manager in his cross-functional project team. He'd like to resolve the conflict in a way so that he's on good working terms with his peer.
   b. Tom negotiates to win. He doesn't feel like he's really negotiated until he's left "some blood on the floor."
   c. Henry is in a disagreement with his boss' boss, the Executive VP. Henry doesn't really care about the matter and the Executive VP can make things difficult for Henry in his job in the future.
   d. Jane wants to go to Palm Beach for spring break, her parents are saying no. Her Dad's pretty worried that she would even ask because "of all the things college kids do down there." Jane wants to make peace because she really wants to go to Europe with a study group this summer.
   e. Althea and Maya both want a secretary for their departments but HR will only allocate one new personnel slot to their general area. Neither can really employ a full-time secretary but the company has spent its temporary help budget.

Answer -
   a. Collaboration. When each of the parties in conflict desires to fully satisfy the concern of all parties, we have cooperation and the search for a mutually beneficial outcome.
   b. Competition. When one party seeks to achieve certain goals or to further personal interests, regardless of the impact on the parties to the conflict, he or she competes and dominates.

c. Avoidance. A party may recognize that a conflict exists but react by withdrawing from it or suppressing the conflict. Indifference or the desire to evade overt demonstration of a disagreement can result in withdrawal.
d. Accommodation. When the parties seek to appease their opponents, they may be willing to place their opponents' interests above their own. In order to maintain the relationship, one party is willing to be self-sacrificing.
e. Compromise. When each party to the conflict must give up something, sharing occurs, resulting in a compromised outcome. In compromising, there is no clear winner or loser.

6 As a manager in another country what things do you need to consider when handling conflict?
Answer - Be aware that your approach to handling conflict will, to some degree, be influenced by your cultural roots. Americans, for example, have a reputation for being open, direct, and competitive. These characteristics are consistent with a society marked by relatively low uncertainty avoidance and high quantity-of-life rankings. People in countries low in uncertainty avoidance feel secure and relatively free from threats of uncertainty. Their organizations, therefore, tend to be rather open and flexible. Countries high in quality of life emphasize assertiveness. The cultural climate of low uncertainty avoidance and high quantity of life tends to shape a society that is open, direct, and competitive. This premise suggests that uncertainty avoidance and quantity/quality of life rankings would be fairly good predictors of which conflict styles are preferred in different countries.

7 Contrast distributive and integrative bargaining.
Answer - There are two general approaches to negotiation: distributive bargaining and integrative bargaining. The most identifying feature of distributive bargaining is that it operates under zero-sum conditions. The essence of distributive bargaining is negotiating over who gets what share of a fixed pie. When engaged in distributive bargaining, one's tactics focus on trying to get one's opponent to agree to one's specific target point or to get as close to it as possible. In contrast to distributive bargaining, integrative problem solving operates under the assumption that one or more settlements exist that can create a win-win solution. All things being equal, integrative bargaining is preferable to distributive bargaining, because the former builds long-term relationships and facilitates working together in the future. We don't see more integrative bargaining in organizations because of the conditions necessary for this type of negotiation: parties who are open with information and candid about their concerns, a sensitivity by both parties to the other's needs, the ability to trust one another, and a willingness by both parties to maintain flexibility.

8 What are the decision biases that can hinder effective negotiation?
Answer -

- Irrational escalation of commitment. People tend to continue a previously selected course of action beyond what rational analysis would recommend.
- The mythical fixed pie. Bargainers assume that their gain must come at the expense of the other party.
- Anchoring and adjustments. People often have a tendency to anchor their judgments on irrelevant information, such as an initial offer. Many factors influence the initial positions people take when entering a negotiation.
- Framing negotiations. People tend to be overly affected by the way information is presented to them.
- Availability of information. Negotiators often rely too much on readily available information while ignoring more relevant data.
- The Winner's curse. The regret one feels after closing a negotiation. Because your opponent accepted your offer, you become concerned that you offered too much. This postnegotiation reaction is not unusual.

- Overconfidence. Many of the previous biases can combine to inflate a person's confidence in his or her judgment and choices. When people hold certain beliefs and expectations, they tend to ignore information that contradicts them.

9 How do culture difference affect negotiation styles? Offer examples of those differences in specific countries.
Answer - Negotiating styles clearly vary among national cultures. The French like conflict. They frequently gain recognition and develop their reputations by thinking and acting against others. As a result, the French tend to take a long time in negotiating agreements, and they aren't overly concerned about whether their opponents like or dislike them. The Chinese also draw out negotiations but for a different reason. They believe that negotiations never end. Like the Japanese, the Chinese negotiate to develop a relationship and a commitment to work together rather than to tie up every loose end. Americans are known around the world for their impatience and their desire to be liked. Astute negotiators from other countries often turn these characteristics to their advantage by dragging out negotiations and making friendship conditional on the final settlement. North Americans tried to persuade by relying on facts and appealing to logic. They countered opponents' arguments with objective facts. They made small concessions early in the negotiation to establish a relationship and usually reciprocated opponents' concessions. North Americans treated deadlines as very important. The Arabs tried to persuade by appealing to emotion. They countered opponents' arguments with subjective feelings. They made concessions throughout the bargaining process and almost always reciprocated opponents' concessions. Arabs approached deadlines very casually. The Russians based their arguments on asserted ideals. They made few, if any, concessions. Any concession offered by an opponent was viewed as a weakness and was almost never reciprocated. Finally, the Russians tended to ignore deadlines.

10 You are preparing to negotiate for your first car purchase. What techniques could you use to improve the outcome of this negotiation?
Answer - Students' answers will vary. Some tactics, researching your opponent will clearly fit any situation. Other tactics such as address the problem not personality, may be somewhat irrelevant. Student justification is important.

- Research Your Opponent--Acquire as much information as you can about your opponent's interests and goals.
- Begin with a Positive Overture--Research shows that concessions tend to be reciprocated and lead to agreements.
- Address the Problem, Not Personalities--Concentrate on the negotiation issues not on the personal characteristics of your opponent.
- Pay Little Attention to Initial Offers--Treat initial offers as merely a point of departure. Everyone has to have an initial position. They tend to be extreme and idealistic.
- Emphasize Win-Win Solutions--If conditions are supportive, look for an integrative solution. Frame options in terms of your opponent's interests and look for solutions that can allow both you and your opponent to declare a victory.
- Create an Open and Trusting Climate--Skilled negotiators are good listeners, ask questions, focus their arguments directly, are not defensive, and have learned to avoid words and phrases that can irritate an opponent.

EXERCISE

Conflict-Management Style Survey*

Instructions: Answer the following questions from a single frame of reference--work-related conflicts, family conflicts, or social conflicts. Allocate 10 points among the four alternative answers given for each of the fifteen items below.

Example: When the people I supervise become involved in a personal conflict, I usually:

Intervene to settle the dispute.	Call a meeting to talk over the problem.	Offer to help if I can.	Ignore the problem.	
3	6	1	0	= 10

Be certain that your answers add up to 10.

1. When someone I care about is actively hostile toward me--yelling, threatening, abusive--I tend to:

Respond in a hostile manner.	Try to persuade the person to give up the hostile behavior.	Stay and listen as long as possible.	Walk away.
_____	_____	_____	_____

2. When someone who is unimportant to me is actively hostile toward me, i.e., yelling, threatening, abusive, etc., I tend to:

Respond in a hostile manner.	Try to persuade the person to give up the hostile behavior.	Stay and listen as long as possible.	Walk away.
_____	_____	_____	_____

3. When I observe people in conflicts in which anger, threats, hostility, and strong opinions are present, I tend to:

Become involved and take a position.	Attempt to mediate.	Observe to see what happens.	Leave as quickly as possible.
_____	_____	_____	_____

4. When I perceive another person as meeting his/her needs at my expense, I am apt to:

Work to do anything I can to change that person.	Rely on persuasion and "facts" when attempting to have that person change.	Work hard at changing how I relate to that person.	Accept the situation as it is.
_____	_____	_____	_____

5. When involved in an interpersonal dispute, I generally:

Draw the other into issues between seeing the problem as I do.	Examine the a workable us as logically as possible.	Look hard for course and let the compromise.	Let time take itsperson problem work itself out.
_____	_____	_____	_____

6. The quality that I value the most in dealing with conflict would be:

Emotional strength and security.	Intelligence.	Love and openness.	Patience
_____	_____	_____	_____

7. Following a serious altercation with someone I care for deeply, I:

Strongly desire to go back and settle things my way.	Want to go back and work it out--whatever it takes.	Worry about it a lot but not initiate/plan for further contact.	Let it lie and not plan
_____	_____	_____	_____

8. When I see a serious conflict developing between two people I care about, I tend to:

Express my disappointment that this had to happen,	Attempt to persuade them to resolve their differences.	Watch to see what develops.	Leave the scene.
_____	_____	_____	_____

9. When I see a serious conflict developing between two people who are unimportant to me, I tend to:

Express my disappointment that this happened.	Attempt to persuade them to resolve their differences.	Watch to see what develops.	Leave the scene.
_____	_____	_____	_____

10. The feedback that I receive from most people about how I behave when faced with conflict and opposition indicates that I:

Try hard to get my way.	Try to work out differences cooperatively.	Am easygoing and take a soft or conciliatory position.	Usually avoid the conflict.
_____	_____	_____	_____

11. When communicating with someone with whom I am having a serious conflict, I:

Try to overpower the other person with my speech.	Talk a little bit more than I listen.	Am an active listener (feeding back words and feelings).	Am a passive listener (agreeing and apologizing).
_____	_____	_____	_____

12. When involved in an unpleasant conflict, I:

Use humor with the other party.	Make an occasional quip or joke about the situation.	Relate humor only to myself.	Suppress all attempts at humor.
_____	_____	_____	_____

13. When someone does something that irritates me (e.g., smokes in a nonsmoking area or crowds in line in front of me), my tendency in communicating with the offending person is to:

Insist that the person look me in the eye.	Look the person directly in the eye and maintain eye contact.	Maintain intermittent eye contact.	Avoid looking directly at the person.
_____	_____	_____	_____

14.

Stand close and make physical contact.	Use my hands and body to illustrate my points.	Stand close to the person without touching him or her.	Stand back and keep my hands to myself.
_____	_____	_____	_____

15.

Use strong, direct language and tell the person to stop.	Try to persuade the person to stop.	Talk gently and tell the person what my feelings are.	Say and do nothing.
_____	_____	_____	_____

CONFLICT-MANAGEMENT STYLE SURVEY SCORING AND INTERPRETATION SHEET

Instructions: When you have completed all fifteen items, add your scores vertically, resulting in four column totals. Put these on the blanks below.

Totals: ______ ______ ______ ______
Column 1 Column 2 Column 3 Column 4

Your highest score is your dominant conflict management strategy. All of us use all four strategies at one time or another. Your dominant style is the one you prefer and will certainly come out in more intense conflict situations. Knowing your style will help you be more effective in dealing with conflict.

Four conflict-handling approaches: competition, collaboration, avoidance, and accommodation.

Column 1. Competition. When one party seeks to achieve certain goals or to further personal interests, regardless of the impact on the parties to the conflict, he or she competes and dominates.

Column 2. Collaboration. When each of the parties in conflict desires to satisfy fully the concern of all parties, we have cooperation and the search for a mutually beneficial outcome. In collaboration, the behavior of the parties is aimed at solving the problem and at clarifying the differences rather than accommodating various points of view.

Column 3. Accommodation. When the parties seek to appease their opponents, they may be willing to place their opponents' interests above their own. In order to maintain the relationship, one party is willing to be self-sacrificing.

Column 4. Avoidance. A party may recognize that a conflict exists but react by withdrawing from it or suppressing the conflict. Indifference or the desire to evade overt demonstration of a disagreement can result in withdrawal.

Now total your scores for Columns 1 and 2 and Columns 3 and 4.

Column 1 + Column 2 ________ = Score A Column 3 + Column 4 ________ = Score B

If Score A is significantly higher than Score B (25 points or more), it may indicate a tendency toward assertive conflict management. A significantly higher B score signals a more conciliatory approach.

* Adapted from the work of Marc Robert, in the 1987 University Associates, Inc.

CHAPTER 13 - FOUNDATIONS OF ORGANIZATION STRUCTURE

CHAPTER OBJECTIVES

After reading this chapter, students should be able to:

1. Identify the six key elements that define an organization's structure.
2. Describe a simple structure.
3. Explain the characteristics of a bureaucracy.
4. Describe a matrix organization.
5. Explain the characteristics of a "virtual" organization.
6. Summarize why managers want to create boundaryless organizations.
7. List the factors that favor different organization structures.
8. Explain the behavioral implications of different organization structures.

LECTURE OUTLINE

I. WHAT IS ORGANIZATION STRUCTURE?

A. Defined

1. An organization structure defines how job tasks are formally divided, grouped, and coordinated.
2. Six key elements--work specialization, departmentalization, chain of command, span of control, centralization and decentralization, and formalization.
    a) See Exhibit 13-1.

B. Work Specialization

1. Early in this century, Henry Ford became rich and famous by building automobiles on an assembly line.
    a) By breaking jobs up into small standardized tasks, which could be performed over and over again, Ford was able to produce cars at the rate of one every ten seconds, while using employees who had relatively limited skills.
2. The term work specialization or division of labor describes the degree to which tasks in the organization are subdivided into separate jobs.
3. By the late 1940s, most manufacturing jobs in industrialized countries were being done with high work specialization.
    a) Management saw this as a means to make the most efficient use of employees' skills.
    b) Employee skills at performing a task successfully increase through repetition.
    c) Training for specialization is more efficient from the organization's perspective. It is easier and less costly to find and train workers to do specific and repetitive tasks than to do a broad range of diverse tasks.
4. For much of the first half of this century, managers viewed work specialization as an unending source of increased productivity but, by the 1960s, there was increasing evidence that a good thing can be carried too far.
    a) The point was reached of human diseconomies--boredom, fatigue, stress, low productivity, poor quality, increased absenteeism, and high turnover--which more than offset the economic advantages.
    b) See Exhibit 13-2.
5. Managers then began to increase productivity by enlarging the scope of job activities and by giving employees a variety of activities to do, allowing them to do a whole job, etc.
6. Today managers recognize the economies work specialization provides as well as the problems it creates when it's carried too far.

C. Departmentalization
1. Grouping jobs together so that common tasks can be coordinated.
2. One of the most popular ways is by functions performed.
   a) The major advantage--is economies of scale by placing people with common skills and orientations into common units.
3. Tasks can also be departmentalized by the type of product the organization produces.
   a) The major advantage to this type of grouping is increased accountability for product performance, since all activities related to a specific product are under the direction of a single manager.
4. Another departmentalization is on the basis of geography or territory.
   a) If an organization's customers are scattered over a large geographical area, then this form of departmentalization can be valuable.
5. Process departmentalization groups people by the specific phase they perform in the production process.
   a) Because each process requires different skills, this method offers a basis for the homogeneous categorizing of activities.
6. A final category, is the particular type of customer.
   a) The assumption underlying customer departmentalization is that customers in each department have a common set of problems and needs that can best be met by having specialists for each.
7. Large organizations may use all of the forms of departmentalization.
8. Two general trends, however, seem to be gaining momentum in the past decade.
   a) Customer departmentalization has grown in popularity. In order to better monitor the needs of customers and serve them.
   b) The second trend is that rigid functional departmentalization is being complemented by teams that cross over traditional departmental lines.

D. Chain of Command
1. In the 1970s, the chain-of-command was a basic cornerstone in organizational design.
2. The chain of command is an unbroken line of authority that extends from the top of the organization to the lowest echelon and clarifies who reports to whom.
3. It answers questions for employees such as, "Who do I go to if I have a problem?" and "Who am I responsible to?"
4. Two complementary concepts: authority and unity of command.
   a) Authority refers to the rights inherent in a managerial position to give orders and expect the orders to be obeyed.
   b) The unity-of-command principle helps preserve the concept of an unbroken line of authority. It states that a person should have one and only one superior to whom he or she is directly responsible.
5. The concepts of chain of command, authority, and unity of command have substantially less relevance today because of advancements in computer technology and the trend toward empowering employees.

E. Span of Control
1. All things being equal, the wider or larger the span, the more efficient the organization.
   a) See Exhibit 13-3 as an example.
2. Wider spans are more efficient in terms of cost. But at some point wider spans reduce effectiveness.
3. Narrow spans of control of five or six employees permits a manager to maintain close control.
4. Narrow spans have three major drawbacks.

a) They're expensive because they add levels of management.
b) They make vertical communication in the organization more complex.
c) Third, narrow spans of control encourage overly tight supervision and discourage employee autonomy.

5. The trend in recent years has been toward wider spans of control.
   a) To ensure that performance doesn't suffer organizations have been investing heavily in employee training.

F. Centralization and Decentralization

1. The term centralization refers to the degree to which decision making is concentrated at a single point in the organization.
   a) The concept includes only formal authority--the rights inherent in one's position.
   b) If top management makes the organization's key decisions with little or no input from lower-level personnel, then the organization is centralized.
   c) The more that lower-level personnel provide input or are actually given the discretion to make decisions, the more decentralization there is.
2. In a decentralized organization, action can be taken more quickly to solve problems, more people provide input into decisions, and employees are less likely to feel alienated from those who make the decisions that affect their work lives.
3. There has been a marked trend toward decentralizing decision making.

G. Formalization

1. Formalization refers to the degree to which jobs within the organization are standardized.
   a) If a job is highly formalized, then the job incumbent has a minimum amount of discretion over what is to be done, when it is to be done, and how he or she should do it.
      (1) Employees can be expected always to handle the same input in exactly the same way, resulting in a consistent and uniform output.
      (2) There are explicit job descriptions, lots of organizational rules, and clearly defined procedures covering work processes in organizations that have a high degree of formalization.
   b) Where formalization is low, job behaviors are relatively nonprogrammed and employees have a great deal of freedom to exercise discretion in their work.
   c) Standardization not only eliminates the possibility of employees' engaging in alternative behaviors, but it removes the need for employees even to consider alternatives.
2. The degree of formalization can vary widely among organizations and within organizations.

II. COMMON ORGANIZATIONAL DESIGNS

A. Three Common Organizational Designs

B. The Simple Structure

1. The simple structure is characterized most by what it is not rather than what it is.
   a) Not elaborate.
   b) Low degree of departmentalization.
   c) Wide spans of control.
   d) Little formalization.
2. The simple structure is a "flat" organization; it usually has only two or three vertical levels, a loose body of employees, and one individual in whom the decision-making authority is centralized.

a) It's most widely practiced in small businesses in which the manager and the owner are one and the same.
b) Preferred in time of temporary crisis because it centralizes control.

3. Strengths
   a) Its simplicity.
   b) It's fast, flexible, inexpensive to maintain, and accountability is clear.
4. Weakness
   a) Difficult to maintain in anything other than small organizations.
   b) As size increases, decision making typically becomes slower.
   c) It's risky--everything depends on one person.

C. The Bureaucracy
1. Standardization--the key that underlies all bureaucracies.
2. The bureaucracy is characterized by:
   a) highly routine operating tasks achieved through specialization.
   b) very formalized rules and regulations.
   c) tasks that are grouped into functional departments.
   d) centralized authority.
   e) narrow spans of control.
   f) decision making that follows the chain of command.
3. Strengths
   a) Primary strength--the ability to perform standardized activities efficiently.
   b) Bureaucracies can get by nicely with less talented and, hence, less costly---middle- and lower-level managers.
   c) The pervasiveness of rules and regulations substitutes for managerial discretion.
4. Weaknesses
   a) Specialization creates sub-unit conflicts. Functional unit goals can override the overall goals of the organization.
   b) Having to deal with people who work in these organizations: obsessive concern with following the rules.
5. The peak of bureaucracy's popularity was probably in the 1950s and 1960s.
   a) The majority of large organizations still take on basic bureaucratic characteristics, particularly specialization and high formalization.
   b) However, spans of control have generally been widened, authority has become more decentralized, and functional departments have been supplemented with an increased use of teams.
   c) Another trend is toward breaking bureaucracies up into smaller, though fully functioning, minibureaucracies.

D. The Matrix Structure
1. Used in advertising agencies, aerospace firms, research and development laboratories, construction companies, hospitals, etc.
2. The matrix combines two forms of departmentalization---functional and product.
3. The strength of functional departmentalization
   a) Putting like specialists together.
4. Weaknesses
   a) It is difficult to coordinate the specialists' tasks so that their diverse projects are completed on time and within budget.
5. Product departmentalization, on the other hand, has exactly the opposite strengths and weaknesses.

a) It facilitates coordination of specialists so that they can meet deadlines and budget targets, and further, it provides clear responsibility for all activities related to a product.
b) But activities and costs are duplicated.

6. The most obvious structural characteristic of the matrix is that it breaks the unity-of-command concept.
   a) Exhibit 13-4 shows the matrix form as used in a college of business administration.
7. Strengths
   a) The ability to facilitate coordination among multiple complex and interdependent activities.
      (1) As an organization gets larger, its information-processing capacity can become overloaded.
      (2) The direct and frequent contact between different specialties in the matrix can make for better communication and more flexibility.
   b) The matrix reduces bureaupathologies. The dual lines of authority reduce tendencies of departmental members to become so busy protecting their little worlds that the organization's overall goals become secondary.
   c) It facilitates the efficient allocation of specialists.
   d) The matrix achieves the advantages of economies of scale by providing the organization with both the best resources and an effective way of ensuring their efficient deployment.
8. Disadvantages
   a) The confusion it creates.
   b) Its propensity to foster power struggles.
   c) The stress it places on individuals.
      (1) When you dispense with the unity-of-command concept, ambiguity is significantly increased, and ambiguity often leads to conflict.

III. NEW OPTIONS

A. Three Structural Designs

B. The Team Structure

1. An organization that uses teams as its central coordination device has a team structure.
2. The primary characteristics of the team structure are that it breaks down departmental barriers and decentralizes decision making to the level of the work team.
3. In smaller companies, the team structure can define the entire organization.
4. More often the team structure complements what is typically a bureaucracy.

C. The Virtual Organization

1. Why own when you can rent? That's the essence of the virtual organization--a small, core organization that outsources major business functions. In structural terms, the virtual organization is highly centralized, with little or no departmentalization.
2. This is a quest for maximum flexibility. These "virtual" organizations have created networks of relationships that allow them to contract out manufacturing, distribution, marketing, or any other business function that management feels can be done better or cheaper by others.
3. The virtual organization stands in sharp contrast to the typical bureaucracy.
4. Exhibit 13-5 shows a virtual organization.
   a) The core of the organization is a small group of executives, overseeing in-house activities and coordinating relationships with the other external organizations.
5. The major advantage to the virtual organization is its flexibility.

6. The primary drawback to this structure is that it reduces management's control over key parts of its business.

D. The Boundaryless Organization

1. General Electric chairman, Jack Welch, coined the term boundaryless organization to describe what he wanted GE to become.
   a) The boundaryless organization seeks to eliminate the chain of command, have limitless spans of control, and replace departments with empowered teams.
2. By removing vertical boundaries, management flattens the hierarchy.
   a) Status and rank are minimized.
   b) And the organization looks more like a silo than a pyramid.
   c) Cross-hierarchical teams, participative decision-making practices, and the use of 360-degree performance appraisals are examples of what GE is doing to break down vertical boundaries.
3. Functional departments create horizontal boundaries.
   a) Reduce these barriers with cross-functional teams and organizing activities around processes.
   b) Cut through horizontal barriers using lateral transfers and rotating people into and out of different functional areas. This approach turns specialists into generalists.
4. When fully operational, the boundaryless organization also breaks down barriers to external constituencies and barriers created by geography.
5. Globalization, strategic alliances, customer-organization linkages, and telecommuting are all examples of practices that reduce external boundaries.
6. The one common technological thread that makes the boundaryless organization possible is a networked computer.
   a) They allow people to communicate across intraorganizational and interorganizational boundaries.

IV. WHY DO STRUCTURES DIFFER?

A. Exhibit 13-6

1. There are two extreme models of organization structure.
   a) Mechanistic--generally synonymous with the bureaucracy in that it has extensive departmentalization, high formalization, a limited information network (mostly downward communication), and little participation by low-level members in decision making.
   b) Organic--looks like a boundaryless organization. Flat, uses cross-hierarchical and cross-functional teams, has low formalization, possesses a comprehensive information network, involves high participation in decision making.

B. Strategy

1. An organization's structure is a means to help management achieve its objectives.
2. Strategy and structure should be closely linked--structure should follow strategy.
3. Strategy frameworks focus on three strategy dimensions--innovation, cost minimization, and imitation.
   a) An innovation strategy does not mean a strategy merely for simple or cosmetic changes from previous offerings but rather one for meaningful and unique innovations.
   b) An organization that is pursuing a cost-minimization strategy tightly controls costs, refrains from incurring unnecessary innovation or marketing expenses, and cuts prices in selling a basic product.

c) Organizations following an imitation strategy try to capitalize on the best of both of the previous strategies.
   (1) They seek to minimize risk and maximize opportunity for profit. Their strategy is to move into new products or new markets only after viability has been proved by innovators.
   (2) They take the successful ideas of innovators and copy them.

4. Linking strategy and structure.
   a) Innovators need the flexibility of the organic structure.
   b) Cost minimizers seek the efficiency and stability of the mechanistic structure.
   c) Imitators combine the two structures. They use a mechanistic structure in order to maintain tight controls and low costs in their current activities, and at the same time they create organic sub-units in which to pursue new undertakings.

C. Organization Size
1. An organization's size significantly affects its structure.
   a) Large organizations--those typically employing 2,000 or more tend to have more specialization, more departmentalization, more vertical levels, and more rules and regulations than do small organizations.
   b) But the relationship isn't linear.
   c) Size affects structure at a decreasing rate.

D. Technology
1. The term technology refers to how an organization transfers its inputs into outputs.
2. Every organization has at least one technology for converting financial, human, and physical resources into products or services.
3. The bottom line on numerous studies on the technology-structure relationship.
   a) The common theme that differentiates technologies is their degree of routineness.
   b) Technologies tend toward either routine or nonroutine activities.
      (1) The former is characterized by automated and standardized operations.
      (2) Nonroutine activities are customized. They include such varied operations as furniture restoring, custom shoe making, and genetic research.
4. The relationship between technology and structure.
   a) Routine tasks are associated with taller and more departmentalized structures.
5. The relationship between technology and formalization, however, is stronger.
   a) Studies consistently show routineness to be associated with the presence of rule manuals, job descriptions, and other formalized documentation.

E. Environmental Uncertainty
1. An organization's environment is composed of those institutions or forces that are outside the organization and potentially affect the organization's performance.
2. The environment is considered a key determinant of structure.
3. An organization's structure is affected by its environment because of environmental uncertainty.
4. Relationship of environmental uncertainty to different structural arrangements.
   a) The more dynamic and uncertain the environment, the greater the need for flexibility.
   b) Organic structure will lead to higher organizational effectiveness.
   c) Conversely, in stable and predictable environments, the mechanistic form will be the structure of choice.

V. ORGANIZATION STRUCTURE AND EMPLOYEE BEHAVIOR

A. Affects of Structure on Behavior

1. The conclusion of a review of the evidence linking organization structures to employee performance and satisfaction shows that you can't generalize.
   a) Not everyone prefers the freedom and flexibility of organic structures.
   b) Some people are most productive and satisfied with mechanistic structures.
2. The evidence generally indicates that work specialization contributes to higher employee productivity but at the price of reduced job satisfaction.
3. Work specialization is not an unending source of higher productivity.
   a) Problems start to surface, and productivity begins to suffer, when the human diseconomies of doing repetitive and narrow tasks overtake the economies of specialization.
4. Some individuals want work that makes minimal intellectual demands and provides the security of routine. For these people, high work specialization is a source of job satisfaction.

B. Span of Control

1. There is no evidence to support a relationship between span of control and employee performance.
2. It is intuitively attractive to argue that wide spans lead to higher employee performance because they provide more distant supervision and more opportunity for personal initiative, but the research fails to support this notion.
3. It is impossible to state that any particular span of control is best for producing high performance or high satisfaction among subordinates due to individual differences.
4. However, there is some evidence indicating that a managers' job satisfaction increases as the number of subordinates he or she supervises increases.

C. Centralization

1. There is strong evidence linking centralization and job satisfaction.
   a) The less centralization the greater amount of participative decision making.
   b) Evidence suggests that participative decision making is positively related to job satisfaction.
   c) But, again, individual differences surface.
2. The decentralization-satisfaction relationship is strongest with employees who have low self-esteem.
3. To maximize employee performance and satisfaction, take individual differences into account.

VI. IMPLICATIONS FOR MANAGERS

1. An organization's internal structure contributes to explaining and predicting employee behavior. The structural relationships in which people work have an important bearing on their attitudes and behavior.
2. To the degree that an organization's structure reduces ambiguity for employees and clarifies such concerns as "What am I supposed to do?" "How am I supposed to do it?" "Who do I report to?" and "Who do I go to if I have a problem?," it shapes their attitudes and facilitates and motivates them to higher levels of performance.
3. Of course, structure also constrains employees to the extent that it limits and controls what they do. Organizations structured around high levels of formalization and specialization, the chain of command, etc., give employees little autonomy. In contrast, organizations that are structured around limited specialization, low formalization, wide

spans of control, and the like provide employees greater freedom and, thus, will be characterized by greater behavioral diversity.

SUMMARY

1 An organization structure defines how job tasks are formally divided, grouped, and coordinated and is defined itself by six key elements--work specialization, departmentalization, chain of command, span of control, centralization and decentralization, and formalization.

2 The simple structure is characterized most by what it is not rather than what it is: not elaborate, low degree of departmentalization, wide spans of control, and little formalization. The simple structure is a "flat" organization; it usually has only two or three vertical levels, a loose body of employees, and one individual in whom the decision-making authority is centralized.

3 The bureaucracy is marked by standardization. They are also characterized by: highly routine operating tasks achieved through specialization, very formalized rules and regulations, tasks that are grouped into functional departments, centralized authority, narrow spans of control, etc.

4 The matrix combines two forms of departmentalization---functional and product. Used in advertising agencies, aerospace firms, research and development laboratories, construction companies, hospitals, etc.

5 Why own when you can rent? That's the essence of the virtual organization--a small, core organization that outsources major business functions. In structural terms, the virtual organization is highly centralized, with little or no departmentalization.

6 The boundaryless organization seeks to eliminate the chain of command, have limitless spans of control, and replace departments with empowered teams. By removing vertical boundaries, management flattens the hierarchy. When fully operational, the boundaryless organization also breaks down barriers to external constituencies and barriers created by geography. Globalization, strategic alliances, customer-organization linkages, and telecommuting are all examples of practices that reduce external boundaries.

7 There are two very different models of organization structure. Mechanistic--generally synonymous with the bureaucracy in that it has extensive departmentalization, high formalization, a limited information network (mostly downward communication), and little participation by low-level members in decision making. Organic--looks like a boundaryless organization. Flat, uses cross-hierarchical and cross-functional teams, has low formalization, possesses a comprehensive information network, involves high participation in decision making.

8 An organization's structure is a means to help management achieve its objectives. Strategy and structure should be closely linked--structure should follow strategy. Strategy frameworks focus on three strategy dimensions--innovation, cost minimization, and imitation and the structural design that works best with each?

9 The conclusion of a review of the evidence linking organization structures to employee performance and satisfaction shows that you can't generalize. The evidence generally indicates that work specialization contributes to higher employee productivity but at the price of reduced job satisfaction. Work specialization is not an unending source of higher productivity. Some individuals want work that makes minimal intellectual demands and provides the security of routine. For these people, high work specialization is a source of job satisfaction.

DISCUSSION QUESTIONS

1 Identify the six key elements that define an organization's structure.

Answer - An organization structure defines how job tasks are formally divided, grouped, and coordinated. Six key elements--work specialization, departmentalization, chain of command, span of control, centralization and decentralization, and formalization. The term work specialization or division of labor describes the degree to which tasks in the organization are subdivided into separate jobs. Departmentalization is the grouping of jobs together so those common tasks can be coordinated. The chain of command is an unbroken line of authority that extends from the top of the organization to the lowest echelon and clarifies who reports to whom. Span of control. All things being equal, the wider or larger the span, the more efficient the organization. Wider spans are more efficient in terms of cost. But at some point wider spans reduce effectiveness. Narrow spans of control of five or six employees permits a manager to maintain close control. The term centralization refers to the degree to which decision making is concentrated at a single point in the organization. In a decentralized organization, action can be taken more quickly to solve problems, more people provide input into decisions, and employees are less likely to feel alienated from those who make the decisions that affect their work lives. Formalization refers to the degree to which jobs within the organization are standardized.

2 What characterizes a simple organizational structure? What are its strengths and weaknesses?
Answer - The simple structure is characterized most by what it is not rather than what it is. The simple structure is a "flat" organization; it usually has only two or three vertical levels, a loose body of employees, and one individual in whom the decision-making authority is centralized. It's most widely practiced in small businesses in which the manager and the owner are one and the same. Preferred in time of temporary crisis because it centralizes control. Its strengths--simplicity, it's fast, flexible, inexpensive to maintain, and accountability is clear. Its weakness--difficult to maintain in anything other than small organizations. As size increases, decision making typically becomes slower. It's risky--everything depends on one person.

3 Explain the characteristics of a bureaucracy.
Answer - The bureaucracy is characterized by: highly routine operating tasks achieved through specialization, very formalized rules and regulations, tasks that are grouped into functional departments, centralized authority, narrow spans of control, and decision making that follows the chain of command. Its primary strength--the ability to perform standardized activities efficiently. Bureaucracies can get by nicely with less talented and, hence, less costly---middle- and lower-level managers. The pervasiveness of rules and regulations substitutes for managerial discretion. Its weaknesses--it creates sub-unit conflicts, functional unit goals can override the overall goals of the organization, and having to deal with people who work in these organizations with an obsessive concern with following the rules.

4 Describe a matrix organization.
Answer - The matrix structure is used in advertising agencies, aerospace firms, research and development laboratories, construction companies, hospitals, etc. It combines two forms of departmentalization---functional and product. The strength of functional departmentalization--putting like specialists together. Weaknesses--it is difficult to coordinate the specialists' tasks so that their diverse projects are completed on time and within budget. Product departmentalization, on the other hand, has exactly the opposite strengths and weaknesses.

5 Why would a company decide to use a "virtual" organizational structure?
Answer - The essence of the virtual organization--a small, core organization that outsources major business functions. In structural terms, the virtual organization is highly centralized, with little or no departmentalization. This is a quest for maximum flexibility. These "virtual" organizations have created networks of relationships that allow them to contract out manufacturing, distribution, marketing, or any other business function that management feels can be done better or cheaper by others. The major advantage to the virtual organization is its flexibility. The primary drawback to this structure is that it reduces management's control over key parts of its business.

6 Why would managers want to create boundaryless organizations?
Answer - The boundaryless organization seeks to eliminate the chain of command, have limitless spans of control, and replace departments with empowered teams. By removing vertical boundaries,

management flattens the hierarchy. Status and rank are minimized. And the organization looks more like a silo than a pyramid. Cross-hierarchical teams, participative decision-making practices, and the use of 360-degree performance appraisals are examples of what GE is doing to break down vertical boundaries. When fully operational, the boundaryless organization also breaks down barriers to external constituencies and barriers created by geography. The one common technological thread that makes the boundaryless organization possible is a networked computer. They allow people to communicate across intraorganizational and interorganizational boundaries.

7 Why do organizational structures differ?
Answer - There are several key elements that shape organizational structure. Strategy--an organization's structure is a means to help management achieve its objectives. Strategy and structure should be closely linked--structure should follow strategy. Strategy frameworks focus on three strategy dimensions--innovation, cost minimization, and imitation and the structural design that works best with each. Size--Organization's size significantly affects its structure. Large organizations--those typically employing 2,000 or more tend to have more specialization, more departmentalization, more vertical levels, and more rules and regulations than do small organizations. Size affects structure at a decreasing rate. Technology--The term technology refers to how an organization transfers its inputs into outputs. Every organization has at least one technology for converting financial, human, and physical resources into products or services. Environmental uncertainty--An organization's environment is composed of those institutions or forces that are outside the organization and potentially affect the organization's performance. The environment is considered a key determinant of structure.

8 What behavioral implications of different organization structures should managers be aware of?
Answer - The conclusion of a review of the evidence linking organization structures to employee performance and satisfaction shows that you can't generalize. Not everyone prefers the freedom and flexibility of organic structures. Some people are most productive and satisfied with mechanistic structures. The evidence generally indicates that work specialization contributes to higher employee productivity but at the price of reduced job satisfaction. Work specialization is not an unending source of higher productivity. Problems start to surface, and productivity begins to suffer, when the human diseconomies of doing repetitive and narrow tasks overtake the economies of specialization. Some individuals want work that makes minimal intellectual demands and provides the security of routine. For these people, high work specialization is a source of job satisfaction. There is no evidence to support a relationship between span of control and employee performance. It is impossible to state that any particular span of control is best for producing high performance or high satisfaction among subordinates due to individual differences. There is strong evidence linking centralization and job satisfaction. The less centralization the greater amount of participative decision making. Evidence suggests that participative decision making is positively related to job satisfaction.

EXERCISE

University Structure

Students will learn how to analyze organizational structure by examining the structure of their current college/university. [If you can find a local business through the Chamber of Commerce or Kiwanis Club, etc., consider substituting them for the university.]

1. Divide the class into groups of 3-5 students, six groups in total.
2. As a class, create a form for analysis of your selected organization(s).
    - Use the elements and their corresponding questions as listed on page 184, Figure 13-1, to create the form.
    - Use a scale of 1 (low) to 5 (high) for each category, i.e., 1- low work specialization, 5 - high departmentalization, etc.
    - Leave space for written comments explaining the rating and giving details of the structural element.
3. If you are analyzing a large organization, give each team one structural element to study.
4. If you are analyzing a small organization have each team look at the entire organization.
5. Each team should prepare to report orally or in writing of their findings.
    - If written reports are used students should give a summary to the class upon submission of their report.
6. The reports should address:
    - How is the organization currently structured?
    - What type of organizational structure is it--organic/mechanistic, simple, bureaucratic, matrix?
    - Could this organization benefit from a new organizational structure--virtual, team, or boundaryless? How would it benefit?
7. As a class, discuss the groups' findings and come to a consensus on the restructuring action, if any, needed to be taken by the organization(s).

CHAPTER 14 - TECHNOLOGY AND WORK DESIGN

CHAPTER OBJECTIVES

After reading this chapter, students should be able to:

1. Contrast reengineering and total quality management
2. Describe the implications of flexible manufacturing systems for people who work within them
3. Identify who is affected by worker obsolescence
4. Explain the job characteristics model
5. Contrast the social information-processing model with the job characteristics model
6. Describe how a job can be enriched
7. Explain the argument that jobs may be becoming obsolete

LECTURE OUTLINE

I. TECHNOLOGY
   A. Technology in the Workplace
      1. Technology was how an organization transfers its inputs into outputs.
         a) The term has become widely used to describe machinery and equipment that use sophisticated electronics and computers to produce those outputs.
      2. The common theme--they substitute machinery for human labor in transforming inputs into outputs has been going on since the Industrial Revolution in the mid-1800s.
      3. No coverage of the behavior of people at work is complete without discussing how recent advances in technology are changing the workplace and affecting the work lives of employees.
      4. Four specific issues
         a) Total quality management and continuous improvement processes.
         b) Reengineering.
         c) Flexible manufacturing systems.
         d) Worker obsolescence.

   B. Quality and Continuous Improvement Processes
      1. TQM is a philosophy of management that's driven by the constant attainment of customer satisfaction through the continuous improvement of all organizational processes.
      2. 99.9 percent error-free performance examples
         a) The U.S. Post Office would lose 2,000 pieces of mail an hour.
         b) U.S. doctors would perform 500 incorrect surgical procedures each week.
         c) There would be two plane crashes a day at O'Hare Airport in Chicago
      3. TQM programs seek to achieve continuous process improvements so that variability is constantly reduced increasing the uniformity of the product or service.
         a) This results in lower costs and higher quality.
      4. Continuous improvement runs counter to the typical American management.
         a) Work projects are linear--with a beginning and an end.
         b) The search for continuous improvement creates a race without a finish line.
      5. How will employees be affected?
         a) Increased stress from a work climate that no longer accepts complacency with the status quo.
         b) A race with no finish line can never be won--a situation that creates constant tension.
         c) The pressures from an unrelenting search for process improvements can create anxiety and stress in some employees.
         d) The most significant implication for employees is that management will look to them as the prime source for improvement ideas.

e) Employee involvement programs are part of TQM.

C. Reengineering Work Processes
1. How you would do things if you could start all over from scratch?
a) It comes from the process of taking apart an electronics product and designing a better version.
b) Michael Hammer applied the term to organizations.
c) As applied to organizations, reengineering means that management should start with a clean sheet of paper in rethinking and redesigning those processes by which the organization creates value and does work, ridding itself of operations that have become antiquated.
2. Three key elements
a) An organization's distinctive competencies define what it is that the organization does better than its competition.
(1) The importance of identifying distinctive competencies is that they guide decisions regarding what activities are crucial to the organization's success.
b) Assess the core processes that clearly add value to the organization's distinctive competencies.
(1) These are the processes that transform materials, capital, information, and labor into products and services that the customer values.
(2) Process value analysis typically uncovers a whole lot of activities that add little or nothing of value and whose only justification is "we've always done it this way."
c) Reorganize around horizontal processes.
(1) Using cross-functional and self-managed teams.
(2) Focusing on processes rather than functions.
3. One of the goals of reengineering is to minimize the necessary amount of management.
4. Reengineering Versus TQM
a) Both emphasize processes and customer satisfaction.
b) Otherwise they diverge radically.
c) The means the two approaches use are totally different.
5. TQM
a) Incremental improvements.
b) TQM relies on bottom-up, participative decision making.
6. Reengineering
a) Quantum leaps in performance.
b) Reengineering is initially driven by top management.
c) When completed, the workplace is largely self-managed. But getting there is a very autocratic, nondemocratic process.
d) Reengineering's supporters argue that it has to be this way because the level of change that the process demands is highly threatening to people, and they aren't likely to accept it voluntarily.
7. Implications for Employees.
a) Reengineering is rapidly gaining momentum in business and industry.
(1) A recent survey found that, among manufacturing firms, 44 percent of respondents indicated they are now reengineering or considering doing so.
(2) Among utilities and insurance companies, the responses were 48 and 52 percent, respectively.
b) Companies are being forced to reengineer their work processes in order to survive.
c) Reengineering will eliminate between 1 million and 2.5 million jobs each year.
(1) Staff support jobs, especially middle managers, will be most vulnerable.

(2) So, too, will clerical jobs in service industries.

d) These new jobs will typically require a wider range of skills, include more interaction with customers and suppliers, offer greater challenge, contain increased responsibilities, and provide higher pay.

e) The three- to five-year period it takes to implement reengineering is usually tough on employees.

D. Flexible Manufacturing Systems

1. In a global economy, manufacturing organizations that can respond rapidly to change have a competitive advantage.
2. The unique characteristic of flexible manufacturing systems is that by integrating computer-aided design, engineering, and manufacturing, they can produce low-volume products for customers at a cost comparable to what had been previously possible only through mass production.
   a) Flexible manufacturing systems are, in effect, repealing the laws of economies of scale.
3. Some automated plants can build a wide variety of flawless products and switch from one product to another on cue from a central computer.
   a) John Deere has a $1.5 billion automated factory that can turn out 10 basic tractor models with as many as 3,000 options without plant shutdowns for retooling.
   b) National Bicycle Industrial Co., which sells its bikes under the Panasonic brand, uses flexible manufacturing to produce any of 11,231,862 variations on 18 models of racing, road, and mountain bikes in 199 color patterns and an almost unlimited number of sizes.
4. The affect of flexible manufacturing systems on the workers.
   a) Workers in flexible manufacturing plants need more training and higher skills than assembly-line workers.
   b) There are fewer employees, so each has to be able to do a greater variety of tasks.
   c) Employees in flexible plants are typically organized into teams and given considerable decision-making discretion.
   d) These plants tend to have organic structures. They decentralize authority into the hands of the operating teams.

E. Worker Obsolescence

1. Changes in technology have cut the shelf life of most employees' skills.
   a) Repetitive tasks--like those traditionally performed on assembly lines and by low-skilled office clerks--will continue to be automated.
   b) Some jobs will be upgraded--the traditional secretary to administrative assistant.
2. Reengineering is producing significant increases in employee productivity.
   a) Employees, who are computer illiterate, have poor interpersonal skills, or can't work autonomously, will increasingly find themselves ill prepared for the demands of new technologies.
3. Obsolescence doesn't exclude the managerial ranks.
   a) Middle managers who merely acted as conduits are being eliminated.
   b) The new model will emphasize good listening, coaching, motivation, and team-support skills.

F. Work Design

1. The way that tasks are combined to create individual jobs has a direct influence on employee performance and satisfaction.
2. In this section, we'll look at task characteristics theories and work redesign.

G. Task Characteristics Theories

1. OB researchers have developed task characteristics theories that seek to identify task characteristics of jobs, how these characteristics are combined to form different jobs, and the relationship of these task characteristics to employee motivation, satisfaction, and performance.
2. The three most important-requisite task attributes theory, the job characteristics model, and the social information-processing model.
3. Requisite Task Attributes Theory
    a) The task characteristics approach began with the pioneering work of Arthur Turner and Paul Lawrence in the mid-1960s.
    b) They predicted that employees would prefer jobs that were complex and challenging.
    c) They defined job complexity in terms of six task characteristics: (1) variety, (2) autonomy, (3) responsibility, (4) knowledge and skill, (5) required social interaction, and (6) optional social interaction.
4. Their findings confirmed their absenteeism prediction.
    a) Turner and Lawrence concluded that workers in larger communities had a variety of nonwork interests and thus were less involved in and motivated by their work.
    b) In contrast, workers from smaller towns had fewer nonwork interests and were more receptive to the complex tasks of their jobs.
5. The importance of Turner and Lawrence's requisite task attributes theory.
    a) They demonstrated that employees did respond differently to different types of jobs.
    b) They provided a preliminary set of task attributes by which jobs could be assessed.
    c) They focused attention on the need to consider the influence of individual differences on employees' reaction to jobs.
6. The Job Characteristics Model
    a) Turner and Lawrence's requisite task attributes theory laid the foundation for the dominant framework for defining task characteristics and understanding their relationship to employee motivation, performance, and satisfaction.
    b) In the JCM, any job can be described in terms of five core job dimensions.
        (1) Skill variety--The degree to which the job requires a variety of different activities so the worker can use a number of different skills and talents.
        (2) Task identity--The degree to which the job requires completion of a whole and identifiable piece of work.
        (3) Task significance--The degree to which the job has a substantial impact on the lives or work of other people.
        (4) Autonomy--The degree to which the job provides substantial freedom, independence, and discretion to the individual in scheduling the work and in determining the procedures to be used in carrying it out.
        (5) Feedback--The degree to which carrying out the work activities required by the job results in the individual's obtaining direct and clear information about the effectiveness of his or her performance.
    c) Exhibit 14-1 shows examples of job activities that rate high and low for each characteristic.
    d) Exhibit_14-2 presents the model.
        (1) The first three dimensions--skill variety, task identity, and task significance--combine to create meaningful work.
        (2) Jobs that possess autonomy give the job incumbent a feeling of personal responsibility for the results and that, if a job provides feedback, the employee will know how effectively he or she is performing.
        (3) From a motivational standpoint, the model says that internal rewards are obtained by an individual when she learns (knowledge of results) that she personally

(experienced responsibility) has performed well on a task that she cares about (experienced meaningfulness).

e) The more that these three psychological states are present, the greater will be the employee's motivation, performance, and satisfaction and the lower his or her absenteeism and likelihood of leaving the organization.

f) Individuals with a high growth need are more likely to experience the psychological states when their jobs are enriched than are their counterparts with a low growth need.

7. The job characteristics model has been well researched and the evidence supports the general framework of the theory.
   a) There is still considerable debate around the five specific core dimensions in the JCM and the validity of growth need strength as a moderating variable.
8. Probable conclusions
   a) People who work on jobs with high-core job dimensions are generally more motivated, satisfied, and productive than are those who do not.
   b) Job dimensions operate through the psychological states in influencing personal and work outcome variables rather than influencing the outcomes directly.
9. Social Information-Processing Model
   a) People respond to their jobs as they perceive them rather than to the objective jobs themselves.
   b) The SIP model argues that employees adopt attitudes and behaviors in response to the social cues provided by others with whom they have contact.
      (1) These others can be co-workers, supervisors, friends, family members, or customers.
   c) A number of studies generally confirm the validity of the SIP model.
      (1) It has been shown that employee motivation and satisfaction can be manipulated by such subtle actions as a co-worker or boss commenting on the existence or absence of job features like difficulty, challenge, and autonomy.

H. Work Redesign
1. Job Rotation
   a) If employees suffer from overroutinization of their work, one alternative is to use job rotation (or what many now call cross-training).
2. The strengths of job rotation are that it reduces boredom and increases motivation through diversifying the employee's activities.
3. It can also have indirect benefits for the organization since employees with a wider range of skills give management more flexibility in scheduling work, adapting to changes, and filling vacancies.
4. Drawbacks
   a) Increased training costs
   b) Productivity is reduced
   c) It creates disruptions--members of the work group have to adjust to the new employee.
   d) It can demotivate intelligent and ambitious trainees who seek specific responsibilities in their chosen specialty.
5. Job Enlargement
   a) Increasing the number and variety of tasks that an individual performed resulted in jobs with more diversity.
   b) Efforts at job enlargement met with less than enthusiastic results.
      (1) "Before I had one lousy job. Now, through enlargement, I have three."
   c) There have been some successful applications of job enlargement.

(1) U.S. Shoe Co. created modular work areas to replace production lines in over half of its factories. The result has been footwear produced more efficiently and with greater attention to quality.

6. Job Enrichmen
   a) Job enrichment refers to the vertical expansion of jobs.
   b) It increases the degree to which the worker controls the planning, execution, and evaluation of his or her work.
   c) An enriched job organizes tasks so as to allow the worker to do a complete activity, increases the employee's freedom and independence, increases responsibility, and provides feedback, so an individual will be able to assess and correct his or her own performance.
   d) How to enrich an employee's job.
      (1) See Exhibit 14-3.
      (2) Combine tasks. This measure increases skill variety and task identity.
      (3) Create natural work units. This increases employee "ownership" of the work.
      (4) Establish client relationships. Managers should try to establish direct relationships between workers and their clients to increase skill variety, autonomy, and feedback for the employee.
      (5) Expand jobs vertically. Vertical expansion gives employees responsibilities and control that were formerly reserved for management.
      (6) Open feedback channels. Ideally, feedback about performance should be received directly as the employee does the job, rather than from management on an occasional basis.
   e) Example of effect--Lawrence Buettner, job enrichment program for his international-trade banking department at First Chicago Corporation.
      (1) Productivity has more than tripled, employee satisfaction has soared, and transaction volume has risen more than 10 percent a year.
      (2) Increased skills have translated into higher pay for the employees who are performing the enriched jobs.
   f) The overall evidence generally shows that job enrichment reduces absenteeism and turnover costs and increases satisfaction, but on the critical issue of productivity the evidence is inconclusive.

II. CHANGING THE WAY WE LOOK AT JOBS

A. Introduction
   1. Before 1800, very few people had a job. People worked hard raising food or making things at home. They had no regular hours, no job descriptions, no bosses, and no employee benefits.
   2. The Industrial Revolution and the creation of large manufacturing companies that brought about the concept of what we have come to think of as jobs.
   3. But the conditions that created the job are disappearing.
   4. Customized production is pushing out mass production; most workers now handle information, not physical products; and competitive conditions are demanding rapid response to changing markets.

B. What's Actually Disappearing
   1. In a fast-moving economy, jobs are rigid solutions to an elastic problem.
   2. When the work that needs doing changes constantly, organizations can't afford the inflexibility that traditional jobs bring with them.
   3. In 25 years or so, it's possible that very few people will have jobs as we have come to know them.

a) There will be part-time and temporary work situations.
b) Organizations will be essentially made up of hired guns--contingent employees (temporaries, part-timers, consultants, and contract workers) who join project teams created to complete a specific task.
c) Computers, pagers, cellular phones, modems, and the like will allow people to work for multiple employers at the same time in locations throughout the world.
(1) In place of security and predictability, they'll have flexibility and autonomy.

4. There are certainly pressures moving employers in this direction.
a) However, labor unions and others with a vested interest in the status quo will seek to hinder the move.
b) There are already companies--for instance, Intel and Microsoft--who are moving toward creating these jobless work environments.
c) Employees in these firms are typically assigned to a project when they're hired.
d) At any given time, most employees are working on multiple projects, under several team leaders, keeping different schedules, being in various places, and performing several different tasks.
e) These employees don't look to job descriptions or a supervisor for direction.

III. IMPLICATIONS FOR MANAGERS

1. Technology is changing people's jobs and their work behavior. TQM and its emphasis on continuous process improvement can increase employee stress as individuals find that performance expectations are constantly being increased. Reengineering is eliminating millions of employees and completely reshaping the jobs of those who remain. Flexible manufacturing systems require employees to learn new skills and accept increased responsibilities.
2. An understanding of work design can help managers design jobs that positively affect employee motivation. Jobs that offer autonomy, feedback, and similar complex task characteristics help to satisfy the individual goals of those employees who desire greater control over their work. Of course, consistent with the social information-processing model, the perception that task characteristics are complex is probably more important in influencing an employee's motivation than are the objective task characteristics themselves. The key, then, is to provide employees with cues that suggest that their jobs score high on factors such as skill variety, task identity, autonomy, and feedback.

SUMMARY

1 TQM is a philosophy of management that's driven by the constant attainment of customer satisfaction through the continuous improvement of all organizational processes. TQM programs seek to achieve continuous process improvements so that variability is constantly reduced increasing the uniformity of the product or service.

2 Reengineering work processes applied to organizations means that management should start with a clean sheet of paper in rethinking and redesigning those processes by which the organization creates value and does work, ridding itself of operations that have become antiquated.

3 The unique characteristic of flexible manufacturing systems is that by integrating computer-aided design, engineering, and manufacturing, they can produce low-volume products for customers at a cost comparable to what had been previously possible only through mass production. Flexible manufacturing systems are, in effect, repealing the laws of economies of scale.

4 Changes in technology have cut the shelf life of most employees' skills. Obsolescence doesn't exclude the managerial ranks. Work design is the way that tasks are combined to create individual jobs has a direct influence on employee performance and satisfaction.

5 OB researchers have developed task characteristics theories that seek to identify task characteristics of jobs, how these characteristics are combined to form different jobs, and the relationship of these

task characteristics to employee motivation, satisfaction, and performance. The three most important are the requisite task attributes theory, the job characteristics model, and the social information-processing model.

6 Turner and Lawrence's requisite task attributes theory laid the foundation for the dominant framework for defining task characteristics and understanding their relationship to employee motivation, performance, and satisfaction. In the JCM, any job can be described in terms of five core job dimensions: skill variety, task identity, task significance, autonomy, and feedback. The job characteristics model has been well researched and the evidence supports the general framework of the theory.

7 The social information-processing model (SIP) argues that people respond to their jobs, as they perceive them rather than to the objective jobs themselves. The SIP model argues that employees adopt attitudes and behaviors in response to the social cues provided by others with whom they have contact. A number of studies generally confirm the validity of the SIP model.

8 Work redesign has several techniques within it that managers can use to increase worker motivation. If employees suffer from overroutinization of their work, one alternative is to use job rotation (or what many now call cross-training). Job enlargement, increasing the number and variety of tasks that an individual performed resulted in jobs with more diversity. Job enrichment refers to the vertical expansion of jobs. It increases the degree to which the worker controls the planning, execution, and evaluation of his or her work.

9 In today's fast-moving economy, jobs are rigid solutions to an elastic problem. When the work that needs doing changes constantly, organizations can't afford the inflexibility that traditional jobs bring with them. In 25 years or so, it's possible that very few people will have jobs as we have come to know them.

DISCUSSION QUESTIONS

1 Your company wants to engage in an improvement process. You make high quality products and control your costs fairly well. The company is well-established in its industry and has managed to keep its workforce fairly "lean." Would you recommend a TQM or a reengineering approach and why?

Answer - In this case the best solution is TQM, the company needs to improve what it's doing not radically change things. TQM is a philosophy of management that's driven by the constant attainment of customer satisfaction through the continuous improvement of all organizational processes. TQM programs seek to achieve continuous process improvements so that variability is constantly reduced increasing the uniformity of the product or service. Reengineering starts from scratch. There are three key elements. 1) An organization's distinctive competencies define what it is that the organization does better than its competition. 2) Assess the core processes that clearly add value to the organization's distinctive competencies. 3) Reorganize around horizontal processes.

2 Explain the implications of flexible manufacturing systems for your employees if you choose to implement such a process.

Answer - The unique characteristic of flexible manufacturing systems is that by integrating computer-aided design, engineering, and manufacturing, they can produce low-volume products for customers at a cost comparable to what had been previously possible only through mass production. Flexible manufacturing systems are, in effect, repealing the laws of economies of scale. Workers in flexible manufacturing plants need more training and higher skills than assembly-line workers. There are fewer employees, so each has to be able to do a greater variety of tasks. Employees in flexible plants are typically organized into teams and given considerable decision-making discretion. These plants tend to have organic structures. They decentralize authority into the hands of the operating teams.

3 What is worker obsolescence and who is/will be impacted by it?
Answer - Changes in technology have cut the shelf life of most employees' skills. Repetitive tasks will continue to be automated. Some jobs will be upgraded--the traditional secretary to administrative assistant. Employees who are computer illiterate, have poor interpersonal skills, or can't work autonomously will increasingly find themselves ill-prepared for the demands of new technologies. Obsolescence will also affect the managerial ranks. Middle managers who merely acted as conduits are being eliminated. The new model will emphasize good listening, coaching, motivation, and team-support skills.

4 You are responsible for a customer service telemarketing unit with 50 employees. They tend to do the same tasks each day, answer the phones, answering questions, finding answers from other sources if they don't know the answer, etc. You are the sole supervisor of this large group. Using the job characteristics model describe how you might improve their jobs in order to improve motivation, performance, and job satisfaction.
Answer - Students' answer will show significant variety depending on how much they assume. The "mini-case" is deliberately written to leave room for making assumptions. Students should cover most elements of the model. In the JCM, any job can be described in terms of five core job dimensions.

- Skill variety--The degree to which the job requires a variety of different activities so the worker can use a number of different skills and talents.
- Task identity--The degree to which the job requires completion of a whole and identifiable piece of work.
- Task significance--The degree to which the job has a substantial impact on the lives or work of other people.
- Autonomy--The degree to which the job provides substantial freedom, independence, and discretion to the individual in scheduling the work and in determining the procedures to be used in carrying it out.
- Feedback--The degree to which carrying out the work activities required by the job results in the individual's obtaining direct and clear information about the effectiveness of his or her performance.

5 What is the value of the social information-processing model for managers?
Answer - According to the social information-processing model people respond to their jobs as they perceive them rather than to the objective jobs themselves. The SIP model argues that employees adopt attitudes and behaviors in response to the social cues provided by others with whom they have contact. These others can be co-workers, supervisors, friends, family members, or customers. It has been shown that employee motivation and satisfaction can be manipulated by such subtle actions as a co-worker or boss commenting on the existence or absence of job features like difficulty, challenge, and autonomy.

6 Why would a company use job rotation as a work redesign strategy?
Answer - If employees suffer from overroutinization of their work, one alternative is to use job rotation (or what many now call cross-training). The strengths of job rotation are that it reduces boredom and increases motivation through diversifying the employee's activities. It can also have indirect benefits for the organization since employees with a wider range of skills give management more flexibility in scheduling work, adapting to changes, and filling vacancies.

7 In what ways can a job be enriched?
Answer - Job enrichment refers to the vertical expansion of jobs. It increases the degree to which the worker controls the planning, execution, and evaluation of his or her work. An enriched job organizes tasks so as to allow the worker to do a complete activity, increases the employee's freedom and

independence, increases responsibility, and provides feedback, so an individual will be able to assess and correct his or her own performance.

- See Exhibit 14-3.
- Combine tasks. This measure increases skill variety and task identity.
- Create natural work units. This increases employee "ownership" of the work.
- Establish client relationships. Managers should try to establish direct relationships between workers and their clients to increase skill variety, autonomy, and feedback for the employee.
- Expand jobs vertically. Vertical expansion gives employees responsibilities and control that were formerly reserved to management.
- Open feedback channels. Ideally, feedback about performance should be received directly as the employee does the job, rather than from management on an occasional basis?

8 How is the work world changing?
Answer - Customized production is pushing out mass production; most workers now handle information, not physical products; and competitive conditions are demanding rapid response to changing markets. When the work that needs doing changes constantly, organizations can't afford the inflexibility that traditional jobs bring with them. In 25 years or so, it's possible that very few people will have jobs as we have come to know them. There will be part-time and temporary work situations. Organizations will be essentially made up of hired guns"--contingent employees (temporaries, part-timers, consultants, and contract workers) who join project teams created to complete a specific task. Computers, pagers, cellular phones, modems, and the like will allow people to work for multiple employers at the same time in locations throughout the world.

EXERCISE

The Impact of Technology

Students should be stretched to think about how technology has and will change teaching and the learning process. As a class, discuss the following questions. If any of these situations already exist, ask students, to discuss how their implementation has changed their learning processes. Students should answer five questions in their discussion.

1. How has [or would] the implementation of this technology improved the specific process?
2. How has [or would] the implementation of this caused problems in the specific process?
3. How has [or would] this technology change the institution?
4. How has [or would] interpersonal relationships be affected?
5. What would it take to implement this technology? [In terms of training, equipment, money, attitude change, etc.]

Situations

1. Online registration using the Internet. Students must access the class registration process from any computer that has Internet capability. Students receive immediate confirmation of their schedule, any changes that need to be made, and they can pay their bill by typing in their credit card information.
2. Providing all students on campus with their own laptop or desktop computer that is theirs to take when they leave the campus. Students may choose laptop or desktop.
3. All faculty are required to use computer technology in their classes in some form--presentation of lecture, use of simulation, posting of assignments on the class Web site, providing e-mail or chatroom access to them, etc.
4. All assignments are submitted electronically by students, graded electronically by faculty, and returned to students electronically. The campus is made virtually paperless.

CHAPTER 15 - PERFORMANCE APPRAISAL AND REWARD SYSTEMS

CHAPTER OBJECTIVES

After reading this chapter, students should be able to:

1. Explain the purposes of performance appraisal.
2. Identify the advantages of using behaviors rather than traits in appraising performance.
3. Explain the most popular performance evaluation criteria.
4. Identify who, in addition to the boss, can do performance evaluations.
5. Describe the potential problems in performance appraisal and actions that can correct those problems.
6. Explain why managers often dislike giving performance reviews.
7. Outline the various types of rewards.
8. Explain the links between performance appraisals, rewards, and employee behavior.

LECTURE OUTLINE

I. PERFORMANCE APPRAISAL

A. Purposes of Performance Appraisal

1. Management uses appraisals for general personnel decisions.
   a) Promotions, transfers, and terminations
   b) Second, appraisals identify training and development needs.
2. Used as a criterion against which selection and development programs are validated.
   a) The effectiveness of training and development programs can be determined by using performance appraisals to assess subsequent employee job performance.
3. Appraisals also provide feedback to employees on how the organization views their performance.
4. Used as the basis for reward allocations.
   a) Decisions about who gets merit pay increases and other rewards are typically determined by performance appraisals.

B. Performance Appraisal and Motivation

1. The expectancy model of motivation offers the best explanation of what conditions the amount of effort an individual will exert on his or her job.
2. A vital component of this model is performance, specifically the effort-performance and performance-reward linkages.
3. If employees know what is expected of them, how their performance will be measured, and they feel confident that their efforts will result in a satisfactory performance as defined by the criteria by which they are being measured then they will be motivated.
4. They also must feel confident that if they perform as they are being asked, they will receive rewards.

C. What Do We Evaluate?

1. The performance criteria or criterion used to evaluate employee performance will have a major influence on what employees do.
2. Public employment agency example.
3. Management consultant specializing in police research example.
4. The three most popular sets of performance appraisal criteria--individual task outcomes, behaviors, and traits.
5. Individual Task Outcomes
   a) If ends count, rather than means, then management should evaluate an employee's task outcomes.

b) Behaviors. In many cases, it's difficult to identify specific outcomes that can be directly attributable to an employee's actions.
(1) In such instances, it is not unusual for management to evaluate the employee's behavior.
c) Traits. The weakest set of criteria, yet still widely used by organizations.
(1) Traits such as having a good attitude, showing confidence, being dependable etc.

D. Who Should Do the Evaluating?
1. By tradition, a manager's authority typically has included appraising subordinates' performance.
2. Others may actually be able to do the job better.
3. Immediate Superior
a) The employee's immediate boss conducts about 95 percent of all performance evaluations at the lower and middle levels of the organization.
(1) Many bosses feel unqualified to evaluate the unique contributions of each of their subordinates.
(2) Others resent being asked to "play God" with their employees' careers.
(3) Organizations using self-managed teams, telecommuting, and other organizing devices, distance bosses from their employees.
4. Peers
a) Peer evaluations are one of the most reliable sources of appraisal data.
(1) Peers are close to the action.
(2) Using peers as raters results in several independent judgments, whereas a boss can offer only a single evaluation.
(3) And the average of several ratings is often more reliable than a single evaluation.
b) On the down side, peer evaluations can suffer from co-workers' unwillingness to evaluate one another and from biases of friendship or animosity.
5. Self-Evaluation
a) Employees evaluating their own performance is consistent with values such as self-management and empowerment.
b) Self-evaluations get high marks from employees themselves.
c) They suffer from overinflated assessment and self-serving bias.
d) Self-evaluations are often low in agreement with superiors' ratings.
6. Immediate Subordinates
a) Immediate subordinates' evaluations can provide accurate and detailed information about a manager's behavior because the evaluators typically have frequent contact with the manager.
b) The problem--fear of reprisal from bosses given unfavorable evaluations. Respondent anonymity is crucial if these evaluations are to be accurate.
7. The Comprehensive Approach: The 360-Degree Appraisal.
a) The latest approach to performance evaluation.
b) Performance feedback comes from the full circle of an employee's daily contacts.
c) The number of appraisals can be as few as three or as many as twenty-five, with most organizations collecting five to ten per employee.
8. A recent survey found that 26 percent of U.S. companies use some form of 360-degree feedback as part of the review process.
9. Its appeal--it fits well with organizations using teams, employee involvement, and TQM programs.

E. Performance Appraisal Method
1. Written Essays

a) The simplest method of appraisal is to write a narrative describing an employee's strengths, weaknesses, past performance, potential, and suggestions for improvement.
b) No complex forms or extensive training needed but the results often reflect the ability of the writer.

2. Critical Incidents
   a) Critical incidents focus the evaluator's attention on those behaviors that are key in making the difference between executing a job effectively or ineffectively.
   b) The appraiser writes down anecdotes that describe what the employee did that was especially effective or ineffective.
   c) The key here is that only specific behaviors are cited.
3. Graphic Rating Scales
   a) One of the oldest and most popular methods.
   b) A set of performance factors--quantity and quality of work, depth of knowledge, cooperation, loyalty, etc., are listed.
   c) The evaluator rates each on an incremental scale, typically five points.
   d) They don't provide the depth of information that essays or critical incidents do.
   e) They are less time-consuming to develop and administer.
   f) They also allow for quantitative analysis and comparison.
4. Behaviorally Anchored Rating Scales
   a) These scales combine major elements from the critical incident and graphic rating scale approaches.
      (1) The employee is rated on the basis of items along a continuum, but the points are examples of actual behavior on the given job rather than general descriptions or traits.
   b) Behaviorally anchored rating scales specify definite, observable, and measurable job behavior.
   c) These behavioral examples are then translated into a set of performance dimensions, each dimension having varying levels of performance.
5. Multiperson Comparisons
   a) These rankings evaluate one individual's performance against another's.
   b) It is a relative rather than an absolute measuring device.
   c) Three most popular--group order ranking, individual ranking, and paired comparisons
      (1) The group order ranking requires the evaluator to place employees into a particular classification, such as top one-fifth or second one-fifth.
      (2) The individual ranking approach ranks in order employees from best to worst. This approach allows for no ties.
      (3) The paired comparison approach compares each employee with every other employee and rates each as either the superior or the weaker member of the pair. After all paired comparisons are made, each employee is assigned a summary ranking based on the number of superior scores he or she achieved. This ensures that each employee is compared against every other, but it can become unwieldy when many employees are being compared.
   d) Multiperson comparisons can be combined with one of the other methods to blend the best from both absolute and relative standards.

F. Potential Problems
   1. To the degree that the following factors are prevalent, an employee's evaluation is likely to be distorted.
   2. Single Criterion
      a) The typical employee's job is made up of a number of tasks.

b) If performance is assessed by a single criterion measure, the result would be a limited evaluation of that job.
c) When employees are appraised on a single job criterion employees will concentrate on the single criterion to the exclusion of other relevant factors.

3. Leniency Error
   a) Every appraiser has his or her own value system that acts as a standard against which appraisals are made.
   b) Some evaluators mark high--a positive leniency error and others low-- a negative leniency error.
      (1) When positively lenient an individual's performance is rated higher than it actually should be.
      (2) A negative leniency error understates performance.
   c) If the same person appraised all individuals in an organization, there would be no problem.
   d) Any error factor would be applied equally to everyone.
   e) The difficulty arises when we have different raters with different leniency errors making judgments.
4. Halo Error
   a) This is the tendency for an evaluator to let the assessment of an individual on one trait influence his or her appraisal of that person on other traits.
      (1) Students tend to rate a faculty member as outstanding on all criteria when they are particularly appreciative of a few things he or she does in the classroom.
      (2) Similarly, a few bad habits such as showing up late for lectures or being slow in returning papers might result in students' appraising the instructor as lousy across the board.
5. Similarity Error
   a) This is when evaluators rate other people by giving special consideration to those qualities that they perceive in themselves.
      (1) Those who demonstrate this characteristic tend to benefit, while others are penalized.
6. Low Differentiation
   a) Regardless of whom the appraiser evaluates and what traits are used, all of his or her evaluations seem similar.
      (1) Low differentiators tend to ignore or suppress differences, perceiving the universe as more uniform than it really is.
      (2) High differentiators, on the other hand, tend to utilize all available information to the utmost extent and thus are better able to perceive anomalies and contradictions.
7. Forcing Information to Match Nonperformance Criteria.
   a) Rarely advocated, sometimes the formal appraisal takes place after the decision about the individual's performance has been made.
   b) Decisions are often arrived at before objective information to support that decision has been gathered.

G. Overcoming the Problems

1. Use Multiple Criteria.
   a) Since successful performance on most jobs requires doing a number of things well, all those things should be identified and evaluated.
   b) The more complex the job, the more criteria that will need to be identified and evaluated.
2. De-emphasize Traits.

a) Traits have little or no performance relationship.
b) Traits such as loyalty, initiative, courage, reliability, and self-expression are intuitively appealing characteristics in employees.
c) Another weakness is the judgment of what the trait is.

3. Emphasize Behavior.
   a) Whenever possible, it is better to use measures based on behavior rather than traits for appraisals.
   b) Measures based on behavior focus on specific examples--both good and bad--of performance, we avoid the problem of using inappropriate substitutes for actual performance.
   c) When appraising specific examples of behavior, we increase the likelihood that two or more evaluators will see the same thing.
4. Document Performance Behaviors in a Journal
   a) By keeping a journal of specific critical incidents for each employee, evaluators tend to make more accurate judgments.
   b) They reduce leniency and halo errors.
5. Use Multiple Evaluators
   a) As the number of evaluators increases, the probability of attaining accurate information increases.
6. Appraise Selectively
   a) If raters make appraisals on only those dimensions on which they are in a good position to rate, we increase interrater agreement and make the evaluation a more valid process.
   b) We recommend that appraisers should be as close as possible, in terms of organizational level, to the individual being evaluated.
   c) The specific application of these concepts would result in having immediate supervisors or co-workers as the major contributors to the appraisal and asking them to evaluate those factors that they are best qualified to judge.
7. Train Appraisers
   a) By training appraisers, we can make them more accurate raters.
   b) Common errors such as halo and leniency have been minimized or eliminated.
   c) But the effects of training do appear to diminish over time, so regular training refresher sessions may be needed.

H. Don't Forget Performance Feedback.

1. Employees like to know how they are doing. They expect feedback.
2. Typically, they get it in the annual review. But this review frequently creates problems.
   a) It's a problem merely because managers put off such reviews.
   b) The annual review is troublesome if the manager saves up information related to performance and unloads it during the appraisal review.
3. Much of this problem can be avoided by giving feedback to employees on an ongoing basis.
4. Regardless of how often management needs to offer performance feedback to employees.
5. Appraising another person's performance is one of the most emotionally charged of all management activities.
   a) Statistically speaking, half of all employees are below the median.
   b) The average employee's estimate of his or her own performance level generally falls around the 75th percentile.
6. Employees tend to be unrealistic and inflate the assessment of their own performance placing the manager in the uncomfortable position, even with good news.

I. What about Team Performance Evaluations
   1. Performance evaluation concepts have been almost exclusively developed with individual employees in mind.
   2. Four suggestions for a performance appraisal system for teams.
      a) Tie the team results to the organizational goals.
      b) Begin with the team's customers and the work process the team follows to satisfy their needs.
      c) Measure both team and individual performance.
      d) Train the team to create its own measures. This ensures that everyone understands his or her role on the team and helps the team develop into a more cohesive unit

J. Performance Appraisal in a Global Context
   1. Caution must be used in generalizing across cultures.
   2. To illustrate, consider three elements of culture--a person's relationship to the environment, time orientation, and focus of responsibility.
      a) American and Canadian organizations hold people responsible for their actions because people in these countries believe they can dominate their environment.
      b) In Middle Eastern countries, on the other hand, performance appraisals aren't likely to be widely used, because managers in these countries tend to see people as subjugated to their environment.
      c) Some countries, such as the United States, have a short-term time orientation and conduct annual performance appraisals.
      d) In Japan, however, where people hold a long-term time frame, performance appraisals may occur only at five- or ten-year intervals.
      e) Israel's culture values group activities much more than does the culture of the United States or Canada.
      f) North American managers focus on the individual in performance appraisals, and their counterparts in Israel are likely to emphasize group contributions and performance.

II. REWARD SYSTEMS

A. Rewards are Important in Influencing Employee Behavior

B. Determinants of Rewards
   1. Most organizations believe that their reward systems are designed to reward merit.
   2. The problem lies in defining merit.
   3. Performance
      a) Performance is the measurement of results. Did you get the job done?
      b) Whether this criterion is valid in representing performance is not relevant to our definition as long as rewards are allocated on the basis of factors that are directly linked to doing the job successfully.
      c) For many jobs, productivity is used as a single criterion.
   4. Effort
      a) Organizations rarely make their rewarding of effort that explicit, yet it is certainly a major determinant in the reward distribution.
      b) This represents the classical example of rewarding means rather than ends.
   5. Seniority
      a) Seniority, job rights, and tenure dominate most civil service systems in the United States.
      b) These factors don't play as important a role in business corporations, but the length of time on the job is still a major factor in determining the allocation of rewards.

c) Its greatest virtue is that it is easy to determine.

6. Skills Held
   a) Allocating rewards on the basis of the skills of the employee.
   b) When individuals enter an organization, their skill level is usually a major determinant of the compensation they will receive.
   c) The relationship of demand and supply for particular skills in the community can significantly influence the rewards the organization must expend to acquire those skills.
7. Job Difficulty
   a) The complexity of the job can be a criterion by which rewards are distributed.
   b) Jobs that are difficult to perform or are undesirable because of stress or unpleasant working conditions may have to carry with them higher rewards in order to attract workers to them.
8. Discretionary Time
   a) The greater the discretion called for on a job, the greater the impact of mistakes and the greater the need for good judgment.
   b) In a job that has been completely programmed there is less judgment, and lower rewards can be offered to attract people to take these positions.
   c) As discretionary time increases, greater judgmental abilities are needed, and rewards must commensurately be expanded.

C. Types of Rewards

1. The types of rewards that an organization can allocate are more complex than is generally thought.
   a) There is direct compensation. But there are also indirect compensation and nonfinancial rewards.
2. Intrinsic rewards are those that individuals receive for themselves. They are largely a result of the worker's satisfaction with his or her job.
3. Extrinsic rewards include direct compensation, indirect compensation, and nonfinancial rewards. Of course, an employee expects some form of direct compensation: a basic wage or salary, overtime and holiday premium pay, etc.
4. Nonfinancial rewards. The organization will provide employees with indirect compensation: insurance, paid holidays and vacations, services, and perquisites. As these are generally made uniformly available to all employees at a given job level, regardless of performance, they are really not motivating rewards.
5. Where indirect compensation is controllable by management and is used to reward performance, then it clearly needs to be considered as a motivating reward.
   a) Company-paid membership in a country club.
   b) Access to company-owned automobiles and aircraft.
6. These forms of indirect compensations can be motivating rewards.
7. As with direct compensation, indirect compensation may be viewed in an individual, group, or organizational context.
   a) If rewards are to be linked closely with performance, however, we should expect individual rewards to be emphasized.
   b) If a certain group of managers within the organization has made a significant contribution, a blanket reward might be appropriate.
8. The classification of nonfinancial rewards tends to be a smorgasbord of desirable 'things" that are potentially at the disposal of the organization.
   a) The creation of nonfinancial rewards is limited only by managers' ingenuity and ability to assess 'payoffs" to the individuals.
   b) What one employee views as highly desirable, another finds superfluous.

(1) Some workers are very status conscious.
(2) Some employees value having their lunch at particular time.
(3) Some value working with congenial colleagues or getting a desired work assignment.

III. IMPLICATIONS FOR MANAGERS

1. Managers choose how employees are appraised and rewarded. Because these decisions affect the behavior of employees, care should be taken to ensure that the organization's appraisal and reward systems encourage the kinds of behaviors that management desires.
2. People do not work gratis. They expect payoffs: salary, benefits, promotion opportunities, recognition, social contact, and so forth. If employees perceive that their efforts are accurately appraised and if they further perceive that the rewards they value are closely linked to their appraisals, management will have optimized the motivational properties from the organization's appraisal and reward procedures and policies.
3. We can conclude that rewards are likely to lead to effective performance and satisfaction when they are (1) perceived as equitable by the employee, (2) tied to performance, and (3) tailored to the needs of the individual. These conditions should foster a minimum of dissatisfaction among employees, reduced absenteeism and turnover, and increased organizational commitment.
4. If these conditions don't exist, the probability of withdrawal behavior increases, and the prevalence of marginal or barely adequate performance increases. If workers perceive that their efforts are not recognized or rewarded, and if they view their alternatives as limited, they may continue working but perform at a level considerably below their capabilities.

SUMMARY

1 Performance appraisals are used for several purposes; general personnel decisions, to pinpoint employee skills and competencies that are currently inadequate, as a criterion against which selection and development programs are validated, to provide feedback to employees, and as the basis for reward allocations.

2 The expectancy model of motivation offers the best explanation of what conditions the amount of effort an individual will exert on his or her job. A vital component of this model is performance, specifically the effort-performance and performance-reward linkages.

3 The performance criteria or criterion used to evaluate employee performance, will have a major influence on what employees do. The three most popular sets of performance appraisal criteria are-individual task outcomes, behaviors, and traits.

4 Traditionally, a manager's authority typically includes appraising subordinates' performance. The employee's immediate boss conducts about 95 percent of all performance evaluations at the lower and middle levels of the organization. Peer evaluations are one of the most reliable sources of appraisal data. Having employees evaluate their own performance is consistent with values such as self-management and empowerment. Immediate subordinates' evaluations can provide accurate and detailed information about a manager's behavior because the evaluators typically have frequent contact with the manager.

5 Managers have a variety of performance appraisal systems to choose from. The simplest method of appraisal is written narrative. Critical incidents focus key behaviors. Graphic rating scales is one of the oldest and most popular methods. Behaviorally anchored rating scales combine major elements from the critical incident and graphic rating scale approaches. And finally, multiperson comparisons, a ranking process. The three most popular--group order ranking, individual ranking, and paired comparisons.

6 An employee's evaluation can be distorted for a number of reasons: by a single criterion, through a leniency error, by the tendency to let one trait influence the appraisal, when there is low differentiation, and finally, the forcing of information to match nonperformance criteria.
7 Distortion, problems, and rating errors can be corrected in a number of ways including: using multiple criteria, de-emphasizing traits, using measures based on behavior rather than traits, keeping a journal of specific critical incidents for each employee, using multiple evaluators, make appraisals on only those dimensions on which can be evaluated factually, and by training appraisers.
8 Employees like to know how they are doing. Typically, they get it in the annual review. But this review frequently creates problems because managers put off such reviews. Much of this problem can be avoided by giving feedback to employees on an ongoing basis.
9 When conducting performance appraisals in a global context caution must be used. Managers need to consider three elements of culture--a person's relationship to the environment, time orientation, and focus of responsibility.
10 Rewards are important in influencing employee behavior. Most organizations believe that their reward systems are designed to reward merit. The problem lies in defining merit. Organizations rarely make their rewarding of effort that explicit, yet it is certainly a major determinant in the reward distribution. The types of rewards that an organization can allocate are more complex than is generally thought. Intrinsic rewards are those that individuals receive for themselves. Extrinsic rewards include direct compensation, indirect compensation, and nonfinancial rewards.

DISCUSSION QUESTIONS

1 As a manager in a small start up company you are tasked with creating a performance appraisal system for hourly employees. As you design this program how could you use the data it would gather?
Answer - You can use the appraisals for general personnel decisions--promotions, transfers, and terminations. Second, appraisals identify training and development needs. They also can be used to pinpoint employee skills and competencies that are currently inadequate but can be remedied if appropriate programs are developed. It can be used as a criterion against which selection and development programs are validated. Appraisals also provide feedback to employees on how the organization views their performance. And, they can be used as the basis for reward allocations.

2 How can appraising performance be motivational for employees?
Answer - The expectancy model of motivation offers the best explanation of what conditions the amount of effort an individual will exert on his or her job. A vital component of this model is performance, specifically the effort-performance and performance-reward linkages. If employees know what is expected of them, how their performance will be measured, and they feel confident that their efforts will result in a satisfactory performance as defined by the criteria by which they are being measured then they will be motivated.

3 In designing your performance appraisal system what performance criteria could you use? Why would you use one rather than another?
Answer - Students' can make an argument for several criteria. They need to cover the following points regardless of the criteria they argue for. The performance criteria or criterion used to evaluate employee performance, will have a major influence on what employees do. The three most popular sets of performance appraisal criteria--individual task outcomes, behaviors, and traits.

- Individual task outcomes--if ends count, rather than means, then management should evaluate an employee's task outcomes.
- Behaviors--in many cases, it's difficult to identify specific outcomes that can be directly attributable to an employee's actions.
- Traits--the weakest set of criteria, yet still widely used by organizations.

4 In this small company we've been discussing, who should do the evaluation? How would you choose who should do the evaluating? Be realistic, this company has four managers and 25 employees.
Answer - Students probably should choose a traditional approach initially and perhaps argue for movement to peer or 360 feedback as the company grows. The big issue is what can realistic be done by very busy people in a small company. By tradition, a manager's authority typically has included appraising subordinates' performance. The employee's immediate boss conducts about 95 percent of all performance evaluations at the lower and middle levels of the organization. Peer evaluations are one of the most reliable sources of appraisal data. Using peers as raters results in several independent judgments, whereas a boss can offer only a single evaluation. On the down side, peer evaluations can suffer from co-workers' unwillingness to evaluate one another and from biases of friendship or animosity. Having employees evaluate their own performance is consistent with values such as self-management and empowerment. Self-evaluations get high marks from employees themselves. They suffer from overinflated assessment and self-serving bias. Immediate subordinates' evaluations can provide accurate and detailed information about a manager's behavior because the evaluators typically have frequent contact with the manager. The problem--fear of reprisal from bosses given unfavorable evaluations. Respondent anonymity is crucial if these evaluations are to be accurate.

5 In this small company, what would be the most effective performance appraisal method?
Answer - Again, the primary issue is practicality. So, written essays, graphic rating scales, and multiperson comparisons would probably work best. The simplest method of appraisal is to write a narrative describing an employee's strengths, weaknesses, past performance, potential, and suggestions for improvement. No complex forms or extensive training needed but the results often reflect the ability of the writer. Critical incidents focus the evaluator's attention on those behaviors that are key in making the difference between executing a job effectively or ineffectively. Graphic rating scales are one of the oldest and most popular methods. A set of performance factors--quantity and quality of work, depth of knowledge, cooperation, loyalty, etc., are listed. Behaviorally anchored rating scales combine major elements from the critical incident and graphic rating scale approaches. The employee is rated on the basis of items along a continuum, but the points are examples of actual behavior on the given job rather than general descriptions or traits. Multiperson comparisons evaluate one individual's performance against another's. It is a relative rather than an absolute measuring device. The three most popular are group order ranking, individual ranking, and paired comparisons.

6 What are the potential problems in performance appraisal and what actions can correct those problems?
Answer - To the degree that the following factors are prevalent, an employee's evaluation is likely to be distorted. If performance is assessed by a single criterion measure, the result would be a limited evaluation of that job. Some evaluators mark high--a positive leniency error and others low--a negative leniency error. The halo error is the tendency for an evaluator to let the assessment of an individual on one trait influence his or her appraisal of that person on other traits. Similarity error happens when evaluators rate other people by giving special consideration to those qualities that they perceive in themselves. Regardless of whom the appraiser evaluates and what traits are used, all of his or her evaluations seem similar. The final problem error is forcing information to match nonperformance criteria.

These problems can be overcome by doing several things. 1) The more complex the job, the more criteria that will need to be identified and evaluated. 2) De-emphasize traits, 3) Whenever possible, it is better to use measures based on behavior rather than traits for appraisals. 4) By keeping a journal of specific critical incidents for each employee, evaluators tend to make more accurate judgments. 5) As the number of evaluators increases, the probability of attaining accurate information increases. 6) If raters make appraisals on only those dimensions which they are in a good position to rate, we increase interrater agreement and make the evaluation a more valid process. 7) By training appraisers, we can make them more accurate raters.

7 Why do managers often dislike giving performance reviews?
Answer - Employees like to know how they are doing. Typically, they get it in the annual review. But this review frequently creates problems. Much of this problem can be avoided by giving feedback to employees on an ongoing basis. Appraising another person's performance is one of the most emotionally charged of all management activities. Statistically speaking, half of all employees are below the median. The average employee's estimate of his or her own performance level generally falls around the 75th percentile. Employees tend to be unrealistic and inflate the assessment of their own performance placing the manager in the uncomfortable position, even with good news.

8 If you wanted to use team performance appraisals in your performance appraisal system what changes would you need to make?
Answer - Performance evaluation concepts have been almost exclusively developed with individual employees in mind. Four suggestions for a performance appraisal system for teams. 1) Tie the team results to the organizational goals. 2) Begin with the team's customers and the work process the team follows to satisfy their needs. 3) Measure both team and individual performance. 4) Train the team to create its own measures. This ensures that everyone understands his or her role on the team and helps the team develop into a more cohesive unit

9 In developing rewards as part of your performance evaluation system what determinants would you use and why?
Answer - Students' answers should reflect both an orientation toward rewarding merit and a realization of the problem in defining merit. Performance is the measurement of results. Whether this criterion is valid in representing performance is not relevant to our definition; as long as rewards are allocated on the basis of factors that are directly linked to doing the job successfully. Organizations rarely make their rewarding of effort that explicit, yet it is certainly a major determinant in the reward distribution. Seniority, etc. doesn't play an important a role in business corporations, but the length of time on the job is still a major factor in determining the allocation of rewards. Allocating rewards on the basis of the skills of the employee is usually a major determinant of the compensation they will receive. The complexity of the job can be a criterion by which rewards are distributed. The greater the discretion called for on a job, the greater the impact of mistakes and the greater the need for good judgment.

10 As a final step in your performance appraisal system what types of rewards might you might offer and why?
Answer - The types of rewards that an organization can allocate are more complex than is generally thought. There are direct, indirect, and nonfinancial rewards. Intrinsic rewards are those that individuals receive for themselves. They are largely a result of the worker's satisfaction with his or her job. Extrinsic rewards include direct compensation, indirect compensation, and nonfinancial rewards. Nonfinancial rewards: the organization will provide employees with indirect compensation such as: insurance, paid holidays and vacations, services, and perquisites. As these are generally made uniformly available to all employees at a given job level, regardless of performance, they are really not motivating rewards. Where indirect compensation is controllable by management and is used to reward performance, then it clearly needs to be considered as a motivating reward. The classification of nonfinancial rewards tends to be a smorgasbord of desirable 'things" that are potentially at the disposal of the organization. The creation of nonfinancial rewards is limited only by managers' ingenuity and ability to assess payoffs to the individuals.

EXERCISE

Promoting Excellence in Teaching

Students should learn the complexities of creating an administration performance appraisal system. Without referring the current system used by your college/university, students should design a performance appraisal system for faculty and administrators. This can be done as an individual, team, or class exercise. It is written as a team exercise.

1. Break the class into groups of five.
2. Using this chapter as their outline they should create a performance evaluation system for either [or both] faculty and administrators.
3. Students should provide a written and oral report outlining their system and justifying it.
4. Their plan should realistically address the following:
   - How will their system motivate faculty [administrators] to be more effective?
   - What will be evaluated? Why?
   - Who will do the evaluating? How often? Why?
   - How will the appraisal be conducted, i.e., what method or methods? [They should create a sample instrument--BARS, essay, etc.]
   - What would it take to implement such a system?
     - In terms of people.
     - In terms of training.
     - In terms of financial cost.
     - Changes in reward/compensation structure of your institution.
   - What specific problems would their recommendation create?
   - How would they address the problems?
5. After each student team presents, they should lead the rest of the class in a discussion of how their proposal can be improved and implemented. Especially important is how realistic is their proposal.
6. The discussion should focus on the difficulties of designing a fair and realistic system, not any blunders the students make.

CHAPTER 16 - ORGANIZATIONAL CULTURE

CHAPTER OBJECTIVES

After reading this chapter, students should be able to:

1. Define the common characteristics making up organizational culture.
2. Contrast strong and weak cultures.
3. Identify the functional and dysfunctional effects of organizational culture on people.
4. List the factors that maintain an organization culture.
5. Clarify how culture is transmitted to employees.
6. Contrast organizational culture with national culture.
7. Explain the paradox of diversity.

LECTURE OUTLINE

I. DEFINING ORGANIZATIONAL CULTURE

A. Organizational culture

1. Organizational culture refers to a system of shared meaning held by members that distinguishes the organization from other organizations.
2. This system of shared meaning is, on closer examination, a set of key characteristics that the organization values.
3. Seven primary characteristics are:
    - a) Innovation and risk taking. The degree to which employees are encouraged to be innovative and take risks.
    - b) Attention to detail. The degree to which employees are expected to exhibit precision, analysis, and attention to detail.
    - c) Outcome orientation. The degree to which management focuses on results or outcomes rather than on the techniques and processes used to achieve those outcomes.
    - d) People orientation. The degree to which management decisions take into consideration the effect of outcomes on people within the organization.
    - e) Team orientation. The degree to which work activities are organized around teams rather than individuals.
    - f) Aggressiveness. The degree to which people are aggressive and competitive rather than easy going.
    - g) Stability. The degree to which organizational activities emphasize maintaining the status quo in contrast to growth.
4. Each of these characteristics exists on a continuum from low to high.
5. Appraising the organization on these seven characteristics, gives a composite picture of the organization's culture.
    - a) Exhibit 16-1 demonstrates how these characteristics can be mixed to create highly diverse organizations.

B. Culture Is a Descriptive Term

1. Organizational culture is concerned with how employees perceive the seven characteristics, not whether they like them.
2. This point differentiates the concept of organizational culture from that of job satisfaction.
3. Research on job satisfaction seeks to measure affective responses to the work environment. It is concerned with how employees feel about the organization's expectations, reward practices, methods for handling conflict, and the like.

C. Do Organizations Have Uniform Cultures?
1. Organizational culture represents a common perception held by the organization's members.
2. There can be subcultures within any given culture.
3. Most large organizations have a dominant culture and numerous sets of subcultures.
    a) A dominant culture expresses the core values that are shared by a majority of the organization's members.
        (1) It is this macro view of culture that gives an organization its distinct personality.
    b) Subcultures tend to develop in large organizations to reflect common problems, situations, or experiences that members face.
        (1) These subcultures are likely to be defined by department designations and geographical separation.
4. If organizations had no dominant culture and were composed only of numerous subcultures, the value of organizational culture as an independent variable would be significantly lessened.

D. Strong Versus Weak Cultures
1. It has become increasingly popular to differentiate between strong and weak cultures.
2. The argument is that strong cultures have a greater impact on employee behavior and are more directly related to reduced turnover.
3. A strong culture is characterized by the organization's core values being both intensely held and widely shared.
    a) The more members who accept the core values and the greater their commitment to those values, the stronger the culture is.
    b) A strong culture will have a greater influence on the behavior.
4. One specific result of a strong culture should be low employee turnover.
    a) A strong culture demonstrates high agreement among members about what the organization stands for.

II. WHAT DOES CULTURE DO?

A. Culture's Functions
1. It has a boundary-defining role; that is, it creates distinctions between one organization and others.
2. It conveys a sense of identity for organization members.
3. Culture facilitates the generation of commitment to something larger than one's individual self-interest.
4. It enhances social system stability.
5. Culture is the social glue that helps hold the organization together by providing appropriate standards for what employees should say and do.
6. Finally, culture serves as a sense-making and control mechanism that guides and shapes the attitudes and behavior of employees.
    a) Culture defines the rules of the game.
7. Who is offered a job, who is appraised as a high performer, and who gets a promotion are strongly influenced by the individual-organization fit, that is, whether the applicant or employee's attitudes and behavior are compatible with the culture.

B. Culture as a Liability
1. Culture enhances organizational commitment and increases the consistency of employee behavior.
2. From an employee's standpoint, culture is valuable because it reduces ambiguity.

3. Culture is a liability when the shared values do not agree with those that will further the organization's effectiveness.
   a) This is most likely to occur when the organization's environment is dynamic.
   b) When the environment is undergoing rapid change, the organization's entrenched culture may no longer be appropriate.
   c) Consistency of behavior is an asset to an organization in a stable environment.

III. CREATING AND SUSTAINING CULTURE

A. How a Culture Begins

1. An organization's current customs, traditions, and general way of doing things are largely due to what it has done before and the degree of success it had with those endeavors.
   a) The ultimate source of an organization's culture is its founders.
2. The founders of an organization.
   a) They have a vision of what the organization should be.
   b) They are unconstrained by organizational history or ideologies.
   c) The small size of any new organization further facilitates the founders' imposition of their vision on all organizational members.
   d) The organization's culture results from the interaction between the founders' biases and assumptions and what the original members learn subsequently from their own experiences.
3. Microsoft's culture is largely a reflection of co-founder and current CEO, Bill Gates.
   a) Gates himself is aggressive, competitive, and highly disciplined.
   b) Those are the same adjectives often used to describe the software giant he heads.
4. Other contemporary examples--Akio Morita at Sony, Fred Smith at Federal Express, Mary Kay at Mary Kay Cosmetics, and Richard Branson at the Virgin Group.

B. Keeping a Culture Alive

1. Once a culture is in place, practices within the organization act to maintain it by exposing employees to a set of similar experiences.
   a) An organization's human resource practices reinforce its culture.
2. Three forces play a particularly important part in sustaining a culture--selection practices, the actions of top management, and socialization methods.
3. Selection
   a) The explicit goal of the selection process is to identify and hire individuals who have the knowledge, skills, and abilities to perform the jobs within the organization successfully.
   b) With multiple candidates, the final decision about who is hired will be significantly influenced by the decision maker's judgment of how well the candidates will fit into the organization.
   c) This results in the hiring of people who have common values.
   d) The selection process also gives applicants information about the organization.
   e) Candidates who perceive a conflict between their values and those of the organization can self-select themselves out of the applicant pool.
   f) Example--Applicants for entry-level positions in brand management at Procter & Gamble
   g) Example--Applicants for positions at Compaq Computer
4. Top Management
   a) The actions of top management have a major impact on an organization's culture.
   b) What they say and how they behave establish norms that filter down through the organization.
   c) Example--Xerox Corp. chief executive from 1961 to 1968 Joseph C. Wilson.

(1) An aggressive, entrepreneurial type, he oversaw Xerox's staggering growth on the basis of its 914 copier, one of the most successful products in American history.
(2) Wilson's replacement as CEO was C. Peter McColough, a Harvard MBA with a formal management style.
   (a) He instituted bureaucratic controls and a major change in Xerox's culture.
(3) By the time McColough stepped down in 1982, Xerox had become stodgy and formal, with lots of politics and turf battles and layers of watchdog managers.
(4) His replacement was David T. Kearns, who believed that the culture he had inherited hindered Xerox's ability to compete.
   (a) He trimmed Xerox down by cutting 15,000 jobs, delegated decision making downward, and refocused the organization's culture etc.
(5) The current CEO, Paul Aliaire, has again sought to reshape Xerox's culture.
   (a) He has reorganized the corporation around a worldwide marketing department, has unified product development and manufacturing divisions, and has replaced half of the company's top management team with outsiders.

5. Socialization
   a) No matter how good a job the organization does in recruiting and selection, new employees are not fully indoctrinated in the organization's culture.
   b) New employees are potentially the most likely to disturb the beliefs and customs that are in place.
   c) The organization will, therefore, want to help new employees adapt to its culture. This adaptation process is called socialization.
   d) Example--Marine boot camp.
   e) The most critical socialization stage is at the time of entry into the organization.
      (1) Employees who fail to learn the essential or pivotal role behaviors risk being labeled nonconformists or rebels and, ultimately, being expelled.
6. Socialization's three stages--pre-arrival, encounter, and metamorphosis.
   a) The first stage encompasses all the learning that occurs before a new member joins the organization.
   b) In the second stage, the new employee sees what the organization is really like and confronts the likelihood that expectations and reality may diverge.
   c) In the third stage, the relatively long-lasting changes take place. The new employee masters the skills required for his or her job, successfully performs his or her new roles, and makes the adjustments to his or her work group's values and norms.
7. Exhibit 16-2 depicts this process.
   a) The prearrival stage occurs before the employee joins the organization; he or she arrives with an established set of values, attitudes, and expectations.
      (1) These cover both the work to be done and the organization from prior socialization in training and in school.
      (2) The selection process is part of prearrival, organizations use it to inform prospective employees about the organization as a whole and to ensure the inclusion of the right type.
   b) Entry into the organization begins the encounter stage.
      (1) Now the individuals confront the possible dichotomy between their expectations--about their job, co-workers, boss, and the organization in general and reality.
      (2) If expectations were accurate, the encounter stage is a reaffirmation.
      (3) Often this is not the case. Where expectations and reality differ, new employees must undergo socialization that will detach them from previous assumptions and replace them with an "acceptable" set.

(4) At the extreme, new members may become totally disillusioned with the actualities of their job and resign.

c) New members must work out any problems discovered during the encounter stage. They may have to go through changes or the metamorphosis stage.

(1) Exhibit 16-3 presents an organization's socialization options for fostering metamorphosis.

(2) Metamorphosis and the entry socialization process are complete when new members have become comfortable with the organization and their job.

(3) They have internalized the norms of the organization and their work group, and they understand and accept those norms.

(4) New members feel accepted by their peers as trusted and valued individuals.

(5) Exhibit 16--2 shows, successful metamorphosis should have a positive impact on the new employees' productivity and their commitment to the organization and reduce their propensity to leave the organization.

C. Summary: How Cultures Form

1. Exhibit 16-4 summarizes how an organization's culture is established and sustained.

a) The original culture is derived from the founder's philosophy.

b) This strongly influences the criteria used in hiring.

c) The actions of the current top management set the general climate of what is acceptable behavior and what is not.

d) Employee socialization depends on the degree of success achieved in matching new employees' values to those of the organization in the selection process and top management's preference for socialization methods.

IV. HOW EMPLOYEES LEARN CULTURE

A. Stories

1. Example--Henry Ford II was chairman of the Ford Motor Co.--remember "It's my name that's on the building." The message was clear: Henry Ford II ran the company.

2. Example--Nordstrom refunding a customer's money for tires, a product the story didn't sell because, "but we do whatever we need to do to make the customer happy. I mean it when I say we have a no-questions-asked return policy." Nordstrom then picked up the telephone and called a friend in the auto parts business to see how much he could get for the tires.

3. Stories such as these contain a narrative of events about the organization's founders, rule breaking, rags-to-riches successes, reductions in the workforce, relocation of employees, reactions to past mistakes, and organizational coping. These stories anchor the present in the past and provide explanations and legitimacy for current practices.

B. Rituals

1. Rituals are repetitive sequences of activities that express and reinforce the key values of the organization, what goals are most important, which people are important and which are expendable.

2. Example--College faculty

3. Example--Mary Kay Cosmetics' annual award meeting.

a) A cross between a circus and a Miss America pageant, the meeting takes place over a couple of days in a large auditorium, on a stage in front of a large, cheering audience, with all the participants dressed in glamorous evening clothes.

b) Saleswomen are rewarded with an array of flashy gifts---gold and diamond pins, fur stoles, and pink Cadillacs---based on their success in achieving sales quotas.

c) This "show" acts as a motivator by publicly recognizing outstanding sales performance.
d) The ritual aspect reinforces Mary Kay's personal determination and optimism.
e) It conveys to her salespeople that reaching their sales quota is important and that through hard work and encouragement they, too, can achieve success.

C. Material Symbols

1. Example--Fullers and Lampreia are two of Seattle's most highly rated and expensive restaurants. But, although they're less than ten blocks apart, the two restaurants convey a very different feel.
   a) Fullers is formal to the point of being "stuffy." It has a museum-quality decor. The staff is formally attired, serious, focused, and stiff.
   b) In contrast, Lampreia is casual and low-key. It has a stylish but minimalist decor. The staff's casual dress and style are consistent with the decor.
   c) Both Fullers and Lampreia consistently receive honors for their food and service, require reservations days, and sometimes weeks, ahead of time; and cost at least $80 for dinner for two.
   d) The material symbols convey messages to new employees.
      (1) At Fullers, the message is that we're serious, formal, and conservative.
      (2) The message at Lampreia, on the other hand, is that we're relaxed and open.
2. Messages can also be conveyed by material symbols bestowed on executives.
   a) Chauffeur-driven limousines and unlimited use of the corporate jet.
   b) Executives at other firms may get a Chevrolet (with no driver) and the plane seat is in the economy section of a commercial airliner.
3. Other examples of material symbols include the size of offices, their furnishings, executive perks, the use of employee lounges or on-site dining facilities, etc.
4. These material symbols convey to employees who is important, the degree of egalitarianism desired by top management, and the kinds of behavior (for example, risk taking, conservative, authoritarian, participative, individualistic, social) that are appropriate.

D. Language

1. Many organizations and units within organizations use language as a way to identify members of a culture or subculture.
2. Example--Knight-Ridder Information, a California-based data redistributor: accession number (a number assigned each individual record in a data base); KWIC (a set of key-words-in-context); and relational operator (searching a data base for names or key terms in some order).
3. Librarians are a rich source of terminology foreign to people outside their profession. They sprinkle their conversations liberally with acronyms such as ARL (Association for Research Libraries), OCLC (a center in Ohio that does cooperative cataloging), and OPAC (for on-line patron accessing catalog).
4. Organizations often develop unique terms to describe common business matters.
5. New employees are frequently overwhelmed with acronyms and jargon that, after six months on the job, have become fully part of their language.

V. MANAGING CULTURAL CHANGE

1. Because an organization's culture is made up of relatively stable characteristics, it's difficult to change.
   a) It develops over many years and is rooted in deeply held values.
2. A number of forces maintain a given culture.

a) Written statements about the organization's mission and philosophy.
b) The design of physical spaces and buildings.
c) The dominant leadership style.
d) Historical selection criteria, past promotion practices, entrenched rituals.
e) Popular stories about key people and events, etc.

3. Changing an organization's culture is difficult, it isn't impossible.
4. Conditions for effective cultural change.
   a) A dramatic crisis exists or is created. This is the shock that undermines the status quo and calls into question the relevance of the current culture.
      (1) A surprising financial setback, the loss of a major customer, or a dramatic technological breakthrough by a competitor.
      (2) Some executives purposely create a crisis in order to stimulate cultural change.
   b) Turnover in leadership. New top leadership, which can provide an alternative set of key values, is usually needed to make cultural change work.
      (1) A new CEO from outside the organization is more likely to introduce new cultural values.
      (2) An outside CEO, in contrast to promoting someone from within the organization, also conveys a message to employees that change is in the wind.
   c) Young and small organizations. Cultural change is more likely to take if the organization is both young and small.
      (1) Cultures in younger organizations are less entrenched.
      (2) It's easier to communicate new values.
   d) Weak culture. The more widely held a culture is and the higher the agreement among members on its values, the more difficult it will be to change.
5. Even when the above conditions are favorable, managers shouldn't look for immediate or dramatic shifts in their organization's culture. Cultural change is a lengthy process which should be measured in years rather than months.

VI. CREATING AN ETHICAL ORGANIZATIONAL CULTURE

A. The Nature of Cultural Influences an Organization's Ethical Climate

1. An organizational culture most likely to shape high ethical standards is high in risk tolerance, low to moderate in aggressiveness, and focuses on means as well as outcomes.
2. If the culture is strong and supports high ethical standards, it should have a very powerful and positive influence on employee behavior.
3. Example--Johnson & Johnson, has a strong culture that has long stressed corporate obligations to customers, employees, the community, and shareholders, in that order.
   a) Poisoned Tylenol case.
4. Practices for creating a more ethical culture.
   a) Be a visible role model--Employees will look to top-management behavior as a benchmark for appropriate behavior.
   b) Communicate ethical expectations---An organizational code of ethics should state the organization's primary values and the ethical rules that employees are expected to follow.
   c) Provide ethical training--Use training sessions to reinforce the organization's standards of conduct, to clarify what practices are and are not permissible, and to address possible ethical dilemmas.
   d) Visibly reward ethical acts and punish unethical ones--Performance appraisals of managers should include a point-by-point evaluation of how their decisions measured against the organization's code of ethics.

e) Provide protective mechanisms--The organization needs to provide formal mechanisms so that employees can discuss ethical dilemmas and report unethical behavior without fear of reprimand.

VII. ORGANIZATIONAL CULTURE VERSUS NATIONAL CULTURE

1. National culture must be taken into account if accurate predictions are to be made about organizational behavior in different countries.
   a) But does national culture override an organization's culture?
2. The research indicates that national culture has a greater impact on employees than does their organization's culture.
3. This conclusion has to be qualified to reflect the self-selection that goes on in hiring.
   a) A British multinational corporation, for example, is likely to be less concerned with hiring the "typical Italian" for its Italian operations than in hiring an Italian who fits with the corporation's way of doing things.
   b) The employee selection process will be used by multinationals to find and hire job applicants who are a good fit with their organization's dominant culture even if such applicants are somewhat atypical citizens of their country.

VIII. ORGANIZATIONAL CULTURE AND THE PARADOX OF DIVERSITY

A. A Contemporary Challenge for Managers.

1. Socializing new employees who, because of race, gender, ethnic, or other differences, are not like the majority of the organization's members creates what we call the paradox of diversity.
   a) Management wants new employees to accept the organization's core cultural values. But at the same time, management wants to openly acknowledge and demonstrate support for the differences that these employees bring to the workplace.
2. Strong cultures put considerable pressure on employees to conform. They limit the range of values and styles that are acceptable.
3. The dilemma--organizations hire diverse individuals because of the alternative strengths these people bring to the workplace, yet these diverse behaviors and strengths are likely to diminish in strong cultures as people attempt to fit in.
4. Management's challenge in this paradox of diversity is to balance these two conflicting goals.

IX. IMPLICATIONS FOR MANAGERS

1. Culture has a strong influence on employee behavior. What can management do to design a culture that molds employees in the way management wants?
2. When an organization is just being established, management has a great deal of influence.
   a) There are no established traditions. The organization is small.
   b) There are few, if any, subcultures.
   c) Everyone knows the founder and is directly touched by his or her vision.
   d) Management has the opportunity to create a culture that will best facilitate the achievement of the organization's goals.
3. When the organization is well established, so, too, is its dominant culture.
   a) It becomes very resistant to change.
   b) Strong cultures are particularly resistant to change because employees become so committed to them.
   c) If a given culture needs to be changed there may be little management can do.
   d) Under the most favorable conditions, cultural changes have to be measured in years, not weeks or months.

e) The "favorable conditions" are the existence of a dramatic crisis, turnover in the organization's top leadership, an organization that is both young and small, and a dominant culture that is weak.

SUMMARY

1 Organizational culture refers to a system of shared meaning held by members that distinguishes the organization from other organizations. Organizational cultures have seven primary characteristics; innovation and risk taking, attention to detail, outcome orientation, people orientation, team orientation, aggressiveness, and stability. Organizational culture represents a common perception held by the organization's members.

2 It has become increasingly popular to differentiate between strong and weak cultures. A strong culture is characterized by the organization's core values being both intensely held and widely shared.

3 Organizational culture has a boundary-defining role; that is, it creates distinctions between one organization and others. It conveys a sense of identity for organization members.

4 Culture enhances organizational commitment and increases the consistency of employee behavior. Culture is a liability when the shared values do not agree with those that will further the organization's effectiveness.

5 An organization's current customs, traditions, and general way of doing things are largely due to what it has done before and the degree of success it had with those endeavors. The ultimate source of an organization's culture is its founders.

6 Once a culture is in place, practices within the organization act to maintain it by exposing employees to a set of similar experiences. Three forces play a particularly important part in sustaining a culture--selection practices, the actions of top management, and socialization methods.

7 Organizations transmit their cultures to their employees in several ways. Stories contain a narrative of events about the organization's founders, etc., and they anchor the present in the past and provide explanations and legitimacy for current practices. Rituals are repetitive sequences of activities that express and reinforce the key values of the organization, what goals are most important, which people are important and which are expendable. The material symbols convey messages to new employees. Messages can also be conveyed by material symbols bestowed on executives. Many organizations and units within organizations use language as a way to identify members of a culture or subculture. Because an organization's culture is made up of relatively stable characteristics, it's difficult to change. It develops over many years and is rooted in deeply held values. Therefore certain conditions need to exist for there to be effective cultural change. A dramatic crisis exists or is create. A turnover in leadership.

8 An organizational culture most likely to shape high ethical standards is high in risk tolerance, low to moderate in aggressiveness, and focuses on means as well as outcomes. If the culture is strong and supports high ethical standards, it should have a very powerful and positive influence on employee behavior.

9 National culture--must be taken into account if accurate predictions are to be made about organizational behavior in different countries. The research indicates that national culture has a greater impact on employees than does their organization's culture.

10 Socializing of new employees who are not like the majority of the organization's members creates the paradox of diversity. Management wants new employees to accept the organization's core cultural values. But at the same time, management wants to openly acknowledge and demonstrate support for the differences that these employees bring to the workplace.

DISCUSSION QUESTIONS

1 What elements define an organization's culture?
Answer - Organizational culture refers to a system of shared meaning held by members that distinguishes the organization from other organizations. Seven primary characteristics. 1) Innovation and risk taking. The degree to which employees are encouraged to be innovative and take risks. 2)

Attention to detail. The degree to which employees are expected to exhibit precision, analysis, and attention to detail. 3) Outcome orientation. The degree to which management focuses on results or outcomes rather than on the techniques and processes used to achieve those outcomes. 4) People orientation. The degree to which management decisions take into consideration the effect of outcomes on people within the organization. 5) Team orientation. The degree to which work activities are organized around teams rather than individuals. 6) Aggressiveness. The degree to which people are aggressive and competitive rather than easy going. 7) Stability. The degree to which organizational activities emphasize maintaining the status quo in contrast to growth.

2 How many cultures and what type of cultures can an organization have?
Answer - Organizational culture represents a common perception held by the organization's members. There can be subcultures within any given culture. Most large organizations have a dominant culture and numerous sets of subcultures. A dominant culture expresses the core values that are shared by a majority of the organization's members. Subcultures tend to develop in large organizations to reflect common problems, situations, or experiences that members face. If organizations had no dominant culture and were composed only of numerous subcultures, the value of organizational culture as an independent variable would be significantly lessened.

It has become increasingly popular to differentiate between strong and weak cultures. The argument is that strong cultures have a greater impact on employee behavior and are more directly related to reduced turnover. A strong culture is characterized by the organization's core values being both intensely held and widely shared. The more members who accept the core values and the greater their commitment to those values, the stronger the culture is. A strong culture demonstrates high agreement among members about what the organization stands for.

3 What value does an organization's culture bring to the organization? How can it's culture hinder organizational effectiveness?
Answer - Organizational culture has a boundary-defining role; that is, it creates distinctions between one organization and others. It conveys a sense of identity for organization members. Culture facilitates the generation of commitment to something larger than one's individual self-interest. Culture is the social glue that helps hold the organization together by providing appropriate standards for what employees should say and do. Finally, culture serves as a sense-making and control mechanism that guides and shapes the attitudes and behavior of employees.

Culture is a liability when the shared values do not agree with those that will further the organization's effectiveness. This is most likely to occur when the organization's environment is dynamic. When the environment is undergoing rapid change, the organization's entrenched culture may no longer be appropriate.

4 What are the possible origins of an organization's culture?
Answer - An organization's current customs, traditions, and general way of doing things are largely due to what it has done before and the degree of success it had with those endeavors. The ultimate source of an organization's culture is its founders. The organization's culture results from the interaction between the founders' biases and assumptions and what the original members learn subsequently from their own experiences.

5 As the president of a medium-sized but growing company you have become concerned that your existing organizational culture be maintained during the growth. What could you direct your managers to do that would help maintain the current culture?
Answer - Once a culture is in place, practices within the organization act to maintain it by exposing employees to a set of similar experiences. An organization's human resource practices reinforce its

culture. Three forces play a particularly important part in sustaining a culture--selection practices, the actions of top management, and socialization methods. The explicit goal of the selection process is to identify and hire individuals who have the knowledge, skills, and abilities to perform the jobs within the organization successfully. The actions of top management have a major impact on an organization's culture. What they say and how they behave establish norms that filter down through the organization. No matter how good a job the organization does in recruiting and selection, new employees are not fully indoctrinated in the organization's culture. The most critical socialization stage is at the time of entry into the organization. Socialization has three stages--pre-arrival, encounter, and metamorphosis. Exhibit 16-2 depicts this process.

6 What could you do to transmit your organizational culture to your new employees?
Answer - Students can offer several tools but should address some of the following. Stories contain a narrative of events about the organization's founders, rule breaking, rags-to-riches successes, reductions in the workforce, relocation of employees, reactions to past mistakes, and organizational coping. These stories anchor the present in the past and provide explanations and legitimacy for current practices. Rituals are repetitive sequences of activities that express and reinforce the key values of the organization, what goals are most important, which people are important and which are expendable. Material symbols convey messages to new employees. Messages can also be conveyed by material symbols bestowed on executives. Many organizations and units within organizations use language as a way to identify members of a culture or subculture.

7 If a company wanted to reshape its culture what factors might hinder the change? What might assist the change?
Answer - Because an organization's culture is made up of relatively stable characteristics, it's difficult to change. It develops over many years and is rooted in deeply held values. A number of forces maintain a given culture.

- Written statements about the organization's mission and philosophy.
- The design of physical spaces and buildings.
- The dominant leadership style.
- Historical selection criteria, past promotion practices, entrenched rituals.
- Popular stories about key people and events, etc.

Conditions for effective cultural change.

- A dramatic crisis exists or is created. This is the shock that undermines the status quo and calls into question the relevance of the current culture.
- A surprising financial setback, the loss of a major customer, or a dramatic technological breakthrough by a competitor.
- Turnover in leadership. New top leadership, which can provide an alternative set of key values, is usually needed to make cultural change work.
- Young and small organization. Cultural change is more likely to take if the organization is both young and small.
- Weak culture. The more widely held a culture is and the higher the agreement among members on its values, the more difficult it will be to change.

8 As the leader of your organization, what steps might you encourage that would foster an ethical climate?
Answer - An organizational culture most likely to shape high ethical standards is high in risk tolerance, low to moderate in aggressiveness, and focuses on means as well as outcomes. If the culture is strong and supports high ethical standards, it should have a very powerful and positive influence on employee behavior. There are a number of practices for creating a more ethical culture.

- Be a visible role model--Employees will look to top-management behavior as a benchmark for appropriate behavior.

- Communicate ethical expectations---An organizational code of ethics should state the organization's primary values and the ethical rules that employees are expected to follow.
- Provide ethical training--Use training sessions to reinforce the organization's standards of conduct, to clarify what practices are and are not permissible, and to address possible ethical dilemmas.
- Visibly reward ethical acts and punish unethical ones--Performance appraisals of managers should include a point-by-point evaluation of how their decisions measured against the organization's code of ethics.
- Provide protective mechanisms--The organization needs to provide formal mechanisms so that employees can discuss ethical dilemmas and report unethical behavior without fear of reprimand.

9 What is the relationship between organizational culture and national culture?
Answer - National culture must be taken into account if accurate predictions are to be made about organizational behavior in different countries. The research indicates that national culture has a greater impact on employees than does their organization's culture. This conclusion has to be qualified to reflect the self-selection that goes on in hiring.

10 In what way(s) does an organization's culture create a diversity paradox for managers?
Answer - Socializing new employees who, because of race, gender, ethnic, or other differences, are not like the majority of the organization's members. This creates what we call the paradox of diversity. Management wants new employees to accept the organization's core cultural values. But at the same time, management wants to openly acknowledge and demonstrate support for the differences that these employees bring to the workplace. The dilemma--organizations hire diverse individuals because of the alternative strengths these people bring to the workplace, yet these diverse behaviors and strengths are likely to diminish in strong cultures as people attempt to fit in. Management's challenge in this paradox of diversity is to balance two conflicting goals:

EXERCISE

<u>What Does Our Culture Tell Us About Us?</u>

The purpose of this exercise is to increase students' awareness of organizational culture and enhance their ability to read the "signs" of organizational culture as they enter new organizations.

1. This may be done individually or in pairs.
2. Do in class. Create a list of 15 "signs" that reveal an organization's culture.
   - Refer students to the text or give a mini-review lecture.
   - Have students brainstorm a list of these "signs."
   - Create a common set of 15 "signs" that will help students identify:
     - the strength of the organizational culture.
     - norms and expectations.
     - what events, activities, or people sustain the existing culture.
     - key stories, rituals, material symbols, and language specific to an organizational culture.
     - the degree of ethicality of an organization's culture.
3. Outside of class. Students should pick an organization to examine--social group, the college/university, a workplace, etc.
   - Students are to evaluate that organization's culture in terms of the list of signs and draw a conclusion as to the nature of its culture.
4. Students should report their findings and conclusions in class either in written or oral form. If oral, limit each presentation to 10 minutes.
5. Conclude with a general class discussion about organizational culture and how what they learned will help them in their job searches and careers and in choosing where to work.

CHAPTER 17 - ORGANIZATIONAL CHANGE AND DEVELOPMENT

CHAPTER OBJECTIVES

After reading this chapter, students should be able to:

1. Describe the forces that act as stimulants to change.
2. Define planned change.
3. Summarize Lewin's three-step change model.
4. Explain sources of resistance to change.
5. List techniques for overcoming resistance to change.
6. Define organizational development (OD).
7. Identify symptoms of work stress.
8. Summarize sources of innovation.

LECTURE OUTLINE

I. FORCES FOR CHANGE
  A. Six forces
    1. Exhibit 17-1 summarizes all six
    2. Nature of the workplace
      a) Adjustments to a multicultural workforce
      b) HRM policies and practices have to change in order to attract and keep this more diverse workforce.
      c) Spending on training to upgrade reading, math, computer, and other skills of employees
    3. Technology
      a) The substitution of computer control for direct supervision, resulting in wider spans of control
      b) Sophisticated information technology is also making organizations more responsive.
    4. Economic shocks
      a) Hong Kong real estate prices have dropped more than 30 percent.
      b) South Korean financial system has nearly collapsed.
    5. Competition
      a) Competitors are as likely to come from across the ocean as from across town.
      b) Established organizations need to defend themselves against both traditional competitors who develop new products and services and small, entrepreneurial firms with innovative offerings.
    6. Social trends
      a) In the 1970s and 1980s point to changes for organizations to make in the 1990s
        (1) The trend in marriage and divorce increased the number of single households and demand for housing by singles.
    7. World politics
      a) Not even the strongest proponents of globalization could have imagined how world politics would change in recent years.
        (1) The fall of the Berlin Wall and the reunification of Germany
        (2) Iraq's invasion of Kuwait
        (3) The breakup of the Soviet Union

II. MANAGING PLANNED CHANGE
  A. Examples
    1. A small retail women's clothing store becoming a nonsmoking environment.

2. A major automobile manufacturer spent several billion dollars to install state-of-the-art robotics.
   a) Since the new equipment would dramatically change jobs and since management anticipated considerable employee resistance to the new equipment, executives were developing a program to help people become familiar with the equipment and to deal with any anxieties they might be feeling.
3. Of the above scenarios only the second scenario described a planned change.
   a) We're concerned with change activities that are proactive and purposeful, intentional, and a goal-oriented activity.
4. Goals of planned change
   a) It seeks to improve the ability of the organization to adapt to changes in its environment.
   b) It seeks to change employee behavior.
5. To survive an organization must respond to changes in its environment. Introduction of work teams, decentralized decision making, and new organizational cultures are examples of planned change directed at responding to changes in the environment.
6. Planned change also is concerned with changing the behavior of individuals and groups within the organization.
7. Change agents can be managers or nonmanagers, employees of the organization, or outside consultants.
   a) For major change efforts, internal management often will hire outside consultants to provide advice and assistance.
   b) Outside consultants usually have an inadequate understanding of the organization's history, culture, operating procedures, and personnel.
   c) Outside consultants also may be prone to initiating more drastic changes--which can be a benefit or a disadvantage--because they do not have to live with the repercussions after the change is implemented.
   d) Internal staff specialists or managers, when acting as change agents, may be more thoughtful (and possibly cautious) because they must live with the consequences of their actions.

III. TWO VIEWS

A. Introduction

1. View one. The organization is like a large ship traveling across the calm Mediterranean Sea to a specific port. Every once in a while, however, a storm will appear, and the crew has to respond. Implementing change in organizations should, therefore, be seen as a response to a break in the status quo and needed only in occasional situations.
2. View two. The organization is more akin to a 40-foot raft than to a large · ship. Rather than sailing a calm sea, this raft must traverse a raging river made up of an uninterrupted flow of permanent white-water rapids. Change is a natural state, and managing change is a continual process.

B. 'The "Calm Waters" Simile

1. This simile used to dominate the thinking of practicing managers and academics.
   a) Exhibit 17-2, Kurt Lewin's three-step change process describes it.
      (1) Successful change requires unfreezing the status quo.
      (2) Changing to a new state.
      (3) Refreezing the new change to make it permanent.
      (4) The status quo can be considered an equilibrium state.
2. Unfreezing can be achieved in one of three ways.
   a) The driving forces, which direct behavior away from the status quo, can be increased.

b) The restraining forces, which hinder movement from the existing equilibrium, can be decreased.

c) The two approaches can be combined.

3. Once unfreezing has been accomplished, the change itself can be implemented.
4. The new situation needs to be refrozen so it can be sustained over time.
   a) If not done there is a very strong chance the change will be short-lived and employees will revert to the previous equilibrium state.
   b) The objective of refreezing, then, is to stabilize the new situation by balancing the driving and restraining forces.
5. Lewin's three-step process treats change as a break in the organization's equilibrium state.

C. The "White-Water Rapids" Simile

1. This simile is consistent with uncertain and dynamic environments.
2. It is consistent with the trend of an industrial society moving to an information society.
   a) Example of attending a college with variable curriculum.
3. A growing number of managers accept that stability and predictability don't exist.
   a) Nor are disruptions in the status quo only occasional and temporary, followed by a return to calm waters.
   b) Many of today's managers face constant change, bordering on chaos.

D. Putting the Two Views in Perspective

1. More and more managers face a world of constant and chaotic change.
2. Few organizations today can treat change as the occasional disturbance in an otherwise peaceful world.
3. Most competitive advantages last less than eighteen months.

IV. RESISTANCE TO CHANGE

A. Introduction

1. Organizations and their members resist change.
2. In a sense, this resistance is positive.
   a) It provides a degree of stability and predictability to behavior.
   b) Resistance to change can also be a source of functional conflict.
   c) The down side to resistance to change is that it hinders adaptation and progress.
3. Resistance can be overt, implicit, immediate, or deferred.
   a) It is easiest to deal with resistance when it is overt and immediate.
   b) Implicit resistance efforts are subtle--loss of loyalty to the organization, loss of motivation to work, etc., --and hence difficult to recognize.
   c) Deferred actions cloud the link between the source of the resistance and the reaction to it.
      (1) A change may produce what appears to be only a minimal reaction at the time it is initiated but surfaces weeks, months, or even years later.
      (2) Or a single change by itself, has little impact. But it becomes the straw that breaks the camel's back.
4. Sources of resistance are individual and organizational but may overlap.

B. Individual Resistance

1. Five reasons why individuals may resist change.
   a) Habit. We're creatures of habit relying on habits or programmed responses.
   b) Security. People who have a high need for security are likely to resist change because it threatens their feeling of safety.

c) Economic Factors. The concern that changes will lower one's income. Fear they won't be able to perform the new tasks or routines to their previous standards, especially when pay is closely tied to productivity
d) Fear of the Unknown. Changes substitute ambiguity and uncertainty for the known.
e) Employees in organizations hold the same dislike for uncertainty.
f) Selective Information Processing. Individuals shape their world through their perceptions and they resist changing it.

C. Organizational Resistance
1. Organizations, by their very nature, are conservative and actively resist change.
2. Six major sources of organizational resistance
3. Structural Inertia. Organizations have built-in mechanisms to produce stability--the selection process, training, formalization, etc.
4. Limited Focus of Change. Organizations are made up of interdependent subsystems. You can't change one without affecting the others. Limited changes in subsystems tend to get nullified by the larger system.
5. Group Inertia. Group norms may act as a constraint.
6. Threat to Expertise. Changes may threaten the expertise of specialized groups.
7. Threat to Established Power Relationships. Redistribution of decision-making authority can threaten long-established power relationships within the organization.
8. Threat to Established Resource Allocations. Those who control sizable resources often see change as a threat.

D. Overcoming Resistance to Change
1. Six tactics
2. Education and Communication
   a) This tactic assumes that the source of resistance lies in misinformation or poor communication.
      (1) This approach works provided that the source of resistance is inadequate communication and that mutual trust and credibility characterize management-employee relations.
   b) Drawback is the time and effort it takes.
3. Participation
   a) It is difficult for individuals to resist a change decision in which they participated.
      (1) If the participants have the expertise to make a meaningful contribution, their involvement can reduce resistance, obtain commitment, and increase the quality of the change decision.
   b) It can result in a poor decision and consume a lot of time.
4. Facilitation and Support
   a) When employee fear and anxiety are high, employee counseling and therapy, new skills training, or a short paid leave of absence may facilitate adjustment.
   b) It is expensive, time consuming, and doesn't always work.
5. Negotiation
   a) Negotiation, as a tactic, may be necessary when resistance comes from a powerful source.
   b) It has potentially high costs and once a change agent negotiates to avoid resistance, he or she is open to the possibility of being "blackmailed."
6. Manipulation and Co-optation
   a) Manipulation is a covert attempt to influence. Twisting and distorting facts to make them appear more attractive, withholding undesirable information, or creating false rumors to get employees to accept a change are all examples of manipulation.

b) Co-optation, on the other hand, is a form of both manipulation and participation. It seeks to buy off the leaders of a resistance group by giving them a key role in the change decision.
c) Both manipulation and co-optation are relatively inexpensive and easy ways to gain the support of adversaries, but the tactics can backfire which may reduce the change agent's credibility to zero.

7. Coercion
   a) The application of direct threats or force on the resisters.
   b) The advantages and drawbacks of coercion are approximately the same as those mentioned for manipulation and co-optation.

V. MANAGING CHANGE THROUGH ORGANIZATIONAL DEVELOPMENT

A. Introduction
1. Organizational development refers to systematic, planned change.
2. OD is a term used to encompass a collection of change techniques or interventions, from organization-wide changes in structure and systems to psychotherapeutic counseling sessions with groups and individuals, undertaken in response to changes in the external environment that seek to improve organizational effectiveness and employee well-being.
3. Characteristics
   a) Built on humanistic-democratic values.
   b) Emphasizes the work team as the key unit.
   c) Emphasizes participation and collaborative management.
   d) An emphasis on changing the organization's culture.
   e) The use of behavioral scientists as change agents.
   f) A view of the change effort as an ongoing process.
4. OD techniques and interventions
   a) Structural
   b) Task-technology
   c) People-focused interventions

B. Structural Interventions
1. Structural OD interventions emphasize making organizations more organic and egalitarian.
2. Structural Reorganization
   a) Recent trends indicate that structures are becoming flatter, more decentralized, and more organic.
   b) Change agents favor flatter organizations.
      (1) They provide economic benefits.
      (2) Fewer vertical levels improve communication.
      (3) Wider spans of control typically give employees greater autonomy, since managers can't directly oversee their subordinates as closely.
   c) Decentralized decision making is a popular intervention favored by OD change agents.
   d) The trend in OD structural interventions has been toward organic organizations.
   e) These reorganizations are typically quite disruptive and threatening to the people affected. As a result, OD change agents favor employees' active participation.
3. New Reward Systems
   a) Change agents accept operant conditioning's notion that behavior is a function of its consequences.
   b) Organizations have done a poor job of linking rewards to employee performance.
   c) In recent years, organizations have moved to enact pay-for-performance' programs.

4. Changing Organizational Culture
    a) Those who argue that change is possible still realize that it's a long-term process.
    b) Many large and historically successful organizations have learned the hard way that cultures can become obsolete and create serious impediments for responding to a changing environment.
    c) The emphasis has moved toward making organizational cultures more flexible, more responsive, and more focused on customer needs, service, and quality.
    d) How? They're reorganizing; replacing and reassigning people in key positions; changing their reward systems; creating new stories, symbols, and rituals; and modifying their selection and socialization processes to hire and support individuals who will espouse the new values.

C. Task-Technology Interventions
1. These emphasize changing either the actual jobs that people do or the technological processes and tools they use to perform those jobs.
2. Job Redesign
    a) See chapter 14. Examples of job redesign interventions include job rotation, enlargement, enrichment, and autonomous work teams.
    b) Job redesign is similar to structural reorganization except, instead of focusing the change effort at the level of the organization, the focus is at the job level.
    c) Job redesign has been done along the lines suggested by the job characteristics model.
    d) Successful job redesign interventions using JMC share several qualities.
        (1) They take place in cultures that support employee autonomy and participation, have low formalization that allows flexibility in redesigning tasks, and either are nonunionized or have the support of the union.
3. Sociotechnical Systems
    a) Accomplishment of any task requires a technology and a social system.
        (1) The technology consists of the tools, techniques, procedures, skills, knowledge, and devices used by employees to do their jobs.
        (2) The social system comprises the people who work in the organization and their interrelationships.
        (3) Proponents argue that any successful work design must jointly optimize the social and the technological demands of the job.
    b) Originally introduced in the 1950s, this perspective was one of the first to recognize that the needs of both the organization and the individual employee had to be considered in the design of work.
    c) How applied?
        (1) Conceptualize work design as organizing groups of workers rather than individuals alone.
        (2) The various technologies that are within the feasible set for achieving the group's objectives can be evaluated to find the proper match.
4. Quality of Worklife
    a) A process by which an organization responds to employee needs by developing mechanisms to allow them to share fully in making the decisions that design their lives at work.
    b) Eight specific categories of interventions
        (1) Adequate and fair compensation
        (2) A safe and healthy environment
        (3) Jobs that develop human capacities
        (4) A chance for personal growth and security

(5) A social environment that provides personal identity, freedom from prejudice, a sense of community, and upward mobility
(6) Rights of personal privacy, dissent, and due process
(7) A work role that minimizes infringement on personal leisure and family needs
(8) Socially responsible organizational actions

5. Any comprehensive list of QWL programs would encompass job redesign, participative management, and flextime, etc.

D. People-Focused Interventions

1. The majority of OD intervention efforts have been directed at changing the attitudes and behaviors of organizational members through the processes of communication, decision making, and problem solving.
2. OD has emphasized five specific people-focused interventions: sensitivity training, survey feedback, process consultation, team building, and intergroup development.
3. Sensitivity Training
   a) Sensitivity training, laboratory training, encounter groups, or T-groups (training groups) all refer to a method of changing behavior through unstructured group interaction.
   b) Members discuss themselves and their interactive processes, the discussion is loosely directed by a professional behavioral scientist, and the group is process oriented.
   c) The objectives of the T-groups are to provide the subjects with increased awareness of their own behavior and how others perceive them, greater sensitivity to the behavior of others, and increased understanding of group processes.
   d) Specific results sought include increased ability to empathize with others, improved listening skills, greater openness, increased tolerance of individual differences, and improved conflict resolution skills.
4. Survey Feedback
   a) A tool for assessing attitudes held by organizational members, identifying discrepancies among member perceptions, and resolving these differences is the survey feedback approach.
      (1) All members in the organization or unit usually complete a questionnaire.
      (2) Organizational members may be asked to suggest questions or may be interviewed to determine what issues are relevant.
      (3) The data from this questionnaire becomes the springboard for identifying problems and clarifying issues that may be creating difficulties for people.
   b) An external change agent may advise the manager about the meaning of the responses to the questionnaire and may give guidelines for leading the organizational family in group discussion of the results.
   c) Finally, group discussion in the survey feedback approach should result in members' identifying possible implications of the questionnaire's findings.
5. Process Consultation
   a) The purpose of process consultation is for an outside consultant to assist a client, usually a manager, to perceive, understand, and act on process events with which he or she must deal.
      (1) These might include work flow, informal relationships among unit members, and formal communication channels.
   b) Process consultation is similar to sensitivity training but is more task-directed than sensitivity training.
   c) The consultant works with the client in jointly diagnosing what processes need improvement.

(1) Having the client actively participate in both the diagnosis and the development of alternatives enhances understanding of the process and the remedy and reduces resistance to the action plan chosen.

d) Importantly, the process consultant need not be an expert in solving the particular problem that is identified.

(1) If the specific problem uncovered requires technical knowledge outside the client and consultant's expertise, the consultant helps the client locate such an expert and then instructs the client in how to get the most out of this expert resource.

6. Team Building

a) Team building can be applied within groups (intragroup) or between groups (intergroup). Here, we emphasize the intragroup level and leave intergroup development to the next section.

b) Intragroup development concerns organizational families (command groups), committees, cross-functional teams, and task groups.

(1) The activities that form team building can typically include goal setting, development of interpersonal relations among team members, role analysis to clarify each member's role and responsibilities, and team process analysis.

(2) Basically team building attempts to use high interaction among group members to increase trust and openness.

c) It may be beneficial to begin by having members attempt to define the goals and priorities of the group.

d) Next, members can evaluate the group's performance, how effective is it in structuring priorities and achieving the goals.

e) Team building can also address the clarification of each member's role in the group. Still another team-building activity is to analyze key processes that go on within the team to identify the way work is performed and how these processes might be improved to make the team more effective.

7. Intergroup Development.

a) A major area of concern in OD is dysfunctional conflict between groups.

b) Intergroup development seeks to change the attitudes, stereotypes, and perceptions that groups have of each other.

c) A popular method emphasizes problem solving.

(1) Members of each group meet independently to develop lists of their perception of themselves, the other group, and how they believe the other group perceives them.

(2) The groups then share their lists, after which similarities and differences are discussed.

(3) Differences are clearly articulated, and the groups look for the causes of the disparities.

d) Once the causes of the difficulty have been identified, the groups can move to the integration phase and work to develop solutions that will improve relations between the groups.

e) Subgroups, with members from each of the conflicting groups, can now be created for further diagnosis and begin to formulate alternative actions that will improve relations.

VI. CONTEMPORARY ISSUES IN ORGANIZATIONAL CHANGE

A. Work Stress

1. Stress is a dynamic condition in which an individual is confronted with an opportunity, constraint, or demand related to what he or she desires and for which the outcome is perceived to be both uncertain and important.

2. Stress can be good or bad.
   a) It often helps athletes or stage performers achieve a superior performance in a critical situation.
   b) However, stress is more often associated with constraints and demands.
      (1) A constraint prevents you from doing what you desire.
      (2) Demands refer to the possible loss of something desired.
3. Symptoms of Stress
   a) Stress shows itself in a number of ways that may be subsumed under three general categories: physiological, psychological, and behavioral.
   b) Most of the early concern with stress was directed at physiological symptoms.
      (1) Research led to the conclusion that stress could create changes in metabolism, increase heart and breathing rates, increase blood pressure, bring on headaches, and induce heart attacks.
      (2) Physiological symptoms have the least direct relevance to managers.
   c) Of greater importance are the psychological symptoms.
      (1) Stress can cause dissatisfaction. Job-related stress can cause job-related dissatisfaction.
   d) Behavioral stress symptoms include changes in productivity, absence, and turnover, as well as changes in eating habits, increased smoking or consumption of alcohol, rapid speech, fidgeting, and sleep disorders.
4. Reducing Stress
   a) Not all stress is dysfunctional and stress can never be totally eliminated.
   b) In terms of organizational factors
   c) Begin with employee selection
      (1) Management needs to make sure that an employee's abilities match the requirements of the job.
      (2) Improved organizational communications will keep ambiguity-induced stress to a minimum.
      (3) Similarly, a goal-setting program will clarify job responsibilities and provide clear performance objectives.
      (4) Job redesign is also a way to reduce stress.
   d) Stress that arises from an employee's personal life creates two problems.
      (1) It is difficult for the manager to directly control.
      (2) There are ethical considerations--does the manager have any right to intrude?
      (3) Employee counseling can provide stress relief.
      (4) Offering a time management program for employees whose personal lives suffer from a lack of planning and organization that in turn, creates stress.
      (5) Still another approach is organizationally sponsoring physical activity programs.

B. Stimulating Innovation
1. 3M Company example
   a) A reputation for being able to stimulate innovation over a long period of time.
   b) It's stated objective is that 30 percent of its sales are to come from products less than four years old.
   c) In one recent year alone, 3M launched more than 200 new products.
2. Characteristics of innovative organizations.
   a) We group them into structural, cultural, and human resource categories.
3. Structural Variables
   a) Organic structures positively influence innovation because they facilitate the flexibility, adaptation, and cross-fertilization that make the adoption of innovations easier.

b) Long tenure in management is associated with innovation.
c) Innovation is nurtured where there are slack resources.
d) Interunit communication is high in innovative organizations where there is a high use of committees, task forces, cross-functional, and other mechanisms that facilitate interaction across departmental lines.

4. Cultural Variables
   a) They encourage experimentation.
   b) They reward both successes and failures. They celebrate mistakes.
   c) Such cultures extinguish risk taking and innovation.
5. Human Resource Variables
   a) Innovative organizations actively train and develop their members to keep them current.
   b) They offer high job security and they encourage individuals to become champions of change.
   c) Once a new idea is developed, champions of change actively and enthusiastically promote the idea, build support, overcome resistance, and ensure that the innovation is implemented.
6. Summary
   a) 3M as a premier product innovator
      (1) Highly decentralized
      (2) Idea champions are created and encouraged.
      (3) The company encourages its employees to take risks.
      (4) The company still continues to be a model of corporate stability.

C. Creating a Learning Organization

1. A learning organization is an organization that has developed the continuous capacity to adapt and change.
2. Most organizations engage in what has been called single-loop learning.
   a) When errors are detected, the correction process relies on past routines and present policies.
3. Learning organizations use double-loop learning.
   a) When an error is detected, it's corrected in ways that involve the modification of the organization's objectives, policies, and standard routines.
   b) Double-loop learning challenges deep-rooted assumptions and norms within an organization.
4. Exhibit 17-3 summarizes the five basic characteristics of a learning organization.
5. Proponents of the learning organization envision it as a remedy for the three fundamental problems--fragmentation, competition, and reactiveness.
   a) Fragmentation based on specialization creates "walls" and "chimneys" that separate different functions into independent and often warring fiefdoms.
   b) An overemphasis on competition often undermines collaboration.
   c) Reactiveness misdirects management's attention to problem solving rather than creation.
6. A model learning organization is exemplified by the characteristics described in Exhibit 17-3.
   a) Think of a learning organization as an ideal to strive toward rather than a realistic description of structured activity.
7. Learning organizations draw on OB concepts.
   a) TQM
   b) Organizational culture
   c) The boundaryless organization

d) Functional conflict
e) Transformational leadership

8. Three suggestions for creating a learning organization.
   a) Establish a strategy--Management needs to make explicit its commitment to change, innovation, and continuous improvement.
   b) Redesign the organization's structure--Flattening the structure, eliminating or combining departments, and increasing the use of cross-functional teams reinforces interdependence and reduces boundaries between people.
   c) Reshape the organization's culture--risk-taking, openness, and growth characterize learning organizations. Management sets the tone for the organization's culture by what it says (strategy) and what it does (behavior).

VII. IMPLICATIONS FOR MANAGERS

1. The need for change encompasses almost all of the concepts within organizational behavior--attitudes, perceptions, teams, leadership, motivation, organizational design, and the like.
2. If environments were perfectly static, if employees' skills and abilities were always up to date and incapable of deteriorating, and if tomorrow was always exactly the same as today, organizational change would have little or no relevance to managers. But the real world is turbulent, requiring organizations and their members to undergo dynamic change if they are to perform at competitive levels.
3. In the past, managers could treat change as an occasional disturbance in their otherwise peaceful and predictable world. Such a world no longer exists for most managers. Today's managers are increasingly finding that their world is one of constant and chaotic change. In this world, managers must continually act as change agents.

SUMMARY

1 Today's business environment is marked by change, change driven by primarily by six forces: the changing nature of the workplace, technology, economic shocks, domestic and global competition, new social trends, and world politics.

2 While all businesses face various types of change, we are concerned with change activities that are proactive and purposeful, intentional, and a goal-oriented activity. Planned change seeks to improve the ability of the organization to adapt to changes in its environment.

3 There are two primary views of organizational change; 1) implementing change in organizations is a response to a break in the status quo and needed only in occasional situations, and 2) change is a natural state, and managing change is a continual process.

4 Kurt Lewin proposed a three-step change process to describe the "calm waters" simile of change. 1) Successful change requires unfreezing the status quo. 2) Changing to a new state. 3) Refreezing the new change to make it permanent. The status quo can be considered an equilibrium state. Lewin's three-step process treats change as a break in the organization's equilibrium state.

5 Both experience and research show that organizations and their members resist change. In a sense, resistance is positive. This resistance can be overt, implicit, immediate, or deferred. Sources of resistance are individual and organizational but may overlap. There are five reasons why individuals may resist change and six major sources of organizational resistance.

6 Managers have six tactics they can use to overcome resistance to change; education and communication, employee participation, facilitation and support, negotiation--when resistance comes from a powerful source--manipulation and co-optation, and coercion--the application of direct threats or force on the resisters.

7 Organizational development (OD) is a term used to encompass a collection of change techniques or interventions, from organization-wide changes in structure and systems to psychotherapeutic counseling sessions with groups and individuals, undertaken in response to changes in the external

environment that seek to improve organizational effectiveness and employee well-being. It uses three categories of interventions: structural, task-technology, and people-focused interventions.

8 While there are any number of contemporary issues in organizational change we focus on stress. Work stress is a dynamic condition in which an individual is confronted with an opportunity, constraint, or demand related to what he or she desires and for which the outcome is perceived to be both uncertain and important. It can be good or bad. Stress shows itself in a number of ways that may be subsumed under three general categories: physiological, psychological, and behavioral.

9 As part of change, innovation is critical. Innovative organizations are characterized by structural, cultural, and human resource innovations. Organic structures positively influence innovation because they facilitate the flexibility, adaptation, and cross-fertilization that make the adoption of innovations easier. Cultural innovation encourages experimentation and rewards both successes and failures. They celebrate mistakes. And, innovative organizations actively train and develop their members to keep them current.

10 A new type of innovative organization is the learning organization, an organization that has developed the continuous capacity to adapt and change. Proponents of the learning organization envision it as a remedy for the three fundamental problems--fragmentation, competition, and reactiveness. A model learning organization is exemplified by the characteristics described in Exhibit 17-3.

DISCUSSION QUESTIONS

1 You are preparing to address your stockholders at the company's annual meeting. Your topic is "The Changing Business Environment." What changes would you talk about with your stockholders?
Answer - Note that Exhibit 17-1 summarizes all six. 1) Nature of the workplace--Adjustments to a multicultural workforce. 2) Technology--The substitution of computer control for direct supervision and the growth of sophisticated information technology are also making organizations more responsive. 3) Economic shocks. 4) Competitors are as likely to come from across the ocean as from across town. 5) New social trends. 6) Dramatic changes in world politics--not even the strongest proponents of globalization--could have imagined how world politics would change in recent years.

2 Define planned change.
Answer - It seeks to improve the ability of the organization to adapt to changes in its environment and it seeks to change the behavior of individuals and groups within the organization. Planned change involves change agents who can be managers or nonmanagers, employees of the organization, or outside consultants.

3 What is a change agent and who might fulfill that role in a planned change?
Answer - A change agent drives and guides a planned change effort. Change agents can be managers or nonmanagers, employees of the organization, or outside consultants. For major change efforts, internal management often will hire outside consultants to provide advice and assistance. Outside consultants usually have an inadequate understanding of the organization's history, culture, operating procedures, and personnel. Outside consultants also may be prone to initiating more drastic changes--which can be a benefit or a disadvantage--because they do not have to live with the repercussions after the change is implemented. Internal staff specialists or managers, when acting as change agents, may be more thoughtful (and possibly cautious) because they must live with the consequences of their actions.

4 Summarize Lewin's three-step change model.
Answer - Organizational change is based in two views; that it is a response to a break in the status quo and that it is a natural state, and managing change is a continual process. Lewin's three-step change process relates to the first view of change.

- Successful change requires unfreezing the status quo.

- Changing to a new state.
- Refreezing the new change to make it permanent.

The status quo can be considered an equilibrium state. Lewin's three-step process treats change as a break in the organization's equilibrium state. Unfreezing can be achieved in one of three ways: 1) the driving forces, which direct behavior away from the status quo, can be increased, 2) The restraining forces, which hinder movement from the existing equilibrium, can be decreased, or 3) the two approaches can be combined. Once unfreezing has been accomplished, the change itself can be implemented. The new situation needs to be refrozen so it can be sustained over time. If not done there is a very strong chance the change will be short-lived and employees will revert to the previous equilibrium state.

5 Why do individuals and organizations resist planned change efforts?
Answer - individuals resist change because of:

- Habit. We're creatures of habit relying on habits or programmed responses.
- Security. People who have a high need for security are likely to resist change because it threatens their feeling of safety.
- Economic Factors. The concern that changes will lower one's income. Fear they won't be able to perform the new tasks or routines to their previous standards, especially when pay is closely tied to productivity.
- Fear of the Unknown. Changes substitute ambiguity and uncertainty for the known.
- Employees in organizations hold the same dislike for uncertainty.
- Selective Information Processing. Individuals shape their world through their perceptions and they resist changing it.

While organizations, by their very nature, are conservative and actively resist change there are six major sources of organizational resistance.

- Structural Inertia. Organizations have built-in mechanisms to produce stability--the selection process, training, formalization, etc.
- Limited Focus of Change. Organizations are made up of interdependent subsystems. You can't change one without affecting the others. Limited changes in subsystems tend to get nullified by the larger system.
- Group Inertia. Group norms may act as a constraint.
- Threat to Expertise. Changes may threaten the expertise of specialized groups.
- Threat to Established Power Relationships. Redistribution of decision-making authority can threaten long-established power relationships within the organization.
- Threat to Established Resource Allocations. Those who control sizable resources often see change as a threat.

6 Name six tactics for overcoming resistance to change, why you use each, and any drawbacks to the techniques.
Answer - 1) Education and communication--this tactic assumes that the source of resistance lies in misinformation or poor communication. This approach works provided that the source of resistance is inadequate communication and that mutual trust and credibility characterize management-employee relations. However it takes time and effort. 2) Participation--it is difficult for individuals to resist a change decision in which they participated. If the participants have the expertise to make a meaningful contribution, their involvement can reduce resistance, obtain commitment, and increase the quality of the change decision. However, it can result in a poor decision and consume a lot of time. 3) Facilitation and support--when employee fear and anxiety are high, employee counseling and therapy, new skills training, or a short paid leave of absence may facilitate adjustment. It is expensive, time consuming, and doesn't always work. 4) Negotiation--may be necessary when resistance comes from a powerful source. Unfortunately, it has potentially high costs and once a change agent negotiates to avoid resistance, he or she is open to the possibility of being "blackmailed." 5) Manipulation

and co-optation. Manipulation is a covert attempt to influence. Co-optation, on the other hand, seeks to buy off the leaders of a resistance group by giving them a key role in the change decision. Both manipulation and co-optation are relatively inexpensive and easy ways to gain the support of adversaries, but the tactics can backfire reducing the change agent's credibility may drop to zero. 6) Coercion--the application of direct threats or force on the resisters. The advantages and drawbacks of coercion are approximately the same as those mentioned for manipulation and co-optation.

7 What are the basic assumptions underlying organizational development (OD) change efforts?
Answer - Organizational development refers to systematic, planned change. OD is a term used to encompass a collection of change techniques or interventions, from organization-wide changes in structure and systems to psychotherapeutic counseling sessions with groups and individuals, undertaken in response to changes in the external environment that seek to improve organizational effectiveness and employee well-being. It is characterized by:

- being built on humanistic-democratic values.
- emphasizing the work team as the key unit.
- emphasizing participation and collaborative management.
- an emphasis on changing the organization's culture.
- the use of behavioral scientists as change agents.
- a view of the change effort as an ongoing process.

8 What are three categories of interventions available to management and what does each emphasize?
Answer - 1) Structural OD interventions emphasize making organizations more organic and egalitarian. 2) Task-technology interventions emphasize changing either the actual jobs that people do or the technological processes and tools they use to perform those jobs. 3) People-focused interventions--the majority of OD intervention efforts have been directed at changing the attitudes and behaviors of organizational members through the processes of communication, decision making, and problem solving. OD has emphasized five specific people-focused interventions: sensitivity training, survey feedback, process consultation, team building, and intergroup development.

9 You are leading an internal change team in your company. Your goal is a more flexible, more organic organization, where employees are empowered. What type of intervention would you implement and why?
Answer - Students should choose a structural intervention. Structural OD interventions emphasize making organizations more organic and egalitarian. They could choose from one of the following specific tactics.

- Structural Reorganization--Recent trends indicate that structures are becoming flatter, more decentralized, and more organic.
- New Reward Systems--Change agents accept operant conditioning's notion that behavior is a function of its consequences.
- Changing Organizational Culture-- Many large and historically successful organizations have learned the hard way that cultures can become obsolete and create serious impediments for responding to a changing environment.

10 Why should managers be sensitive to work stress and how can they reduce it?
Answer - Work stress is a dynamic condition in which an individual is confronted with an opportunity, constraint, or demand related to what he or she desires and for which the outcome is perceived to be both uncertain and important. Stress can be good or bad. Stress shows itself in a number of ways that may be subsumed under three general categories: physiological, psychological, and behavioral. Not all stress is dysfunctional and stress can never be totally eliminated. Managers can reduce stress by careful employee selection. Management needs to make sure that an employee's abilities match the requirements of the job.

11 What distinguishes an innovative organization from more traditional organizations?
Answer - The characteristics of innovative organizations can be grouped into structural, cultural, and human resource categories.

- Structural Variables--organic structures positively influence innovation because they facilitate the flexibility, adaptation, and cross-fertilization that make the adoption of innovations easier.
- Cultural Variables--encouraging experimentation, rewarding both successes and failures. They celebrate mistakes. And, such cultures extinguish risk taking and innovation.
- Human Resource Variables--innovative organizations actively train and develop their members to keep them current. They offer high job security and they encourage individuals to become champions of change.

12 What is a learning organizations? Why are they the future of organizational change?
Answer - A learning organization is an organization that has developed the continuous capacity to adapt and change. Most organizations engage in what has been called single-loop learning. When errors are detected, the correction process relies on past routines and present policies. A learning organizations use double-loop learning. When an error is detected, it's corrected in ways that involve the modification of the organization's objectives, policies, and standard routines. Double-loop learning challenges deep-rooted assumptions and norms within an organization. Exhibit 17-3 summarizes the five basic characteristics of a learning organization. Proponents of the learning organization envision it as a remedy for the three fundamental problems--fragmentation, competition, and reactiveness. a) Fragmentation based on specialization creates "walls" and "chimneys" that separate different functions into independent and often warring fiefdoms. b) An overemphasis on competition often undermines collaboration. c) Reactiveness misdirects management's attention to problem solving rather than creation. Think of a learning organization as an ideal to strive toward rather than a realistic description of structured activity. Learning organizations draw on OB concepts.

13 What steps can top management take toward making their companies learning organizations?
Answer - Three suggestions for creating a learning organization.

- Establish a strategy--Management needs to make its commitment to change, innovation, and continuous improvement explicit.
- Redesign the organization's structure--Flattening the structure, eliminating or combining departments, and increasing the use of cross-functional teams reinforces interdependence and reduces boundaries between people.
- Reshape the organization's culture--Risk-taking, openness, and growth characterize Learning organizations. Management sets the tone for the organization's culture by both what it says (strategy) and what it does (behavior).

EXERCISE

Overcoming Resistance

Students will learn that sometimes necessary change is unwanted and resisted and that resistance must be overcome if the organization is to change, grow, and succeed. You can use this as a double exercise. First, to strategize how to overcome resistance. Or, second, and more complex, you can use it to have students think through the whole change process and create alternative courses of action--other change efforts that might help the college/university solve its problem in another way.

1. Propose the following scenario [or one of your own that is more relevant to your situation] to the class:

Situation

Due to massive cutbacks in both federal and state support (or alumni gifts) your college/university must make some significant changes that will affect revenue and cash flow. The institution had anticipated a budget increase this year in order to hire more faculty, reduce class sizes, and improve academic programs. Instead funding was cut.

They are mandating the following:

- All freshmen and sophomores must live on campus in dorms. (To increase occupancy.)
- There will be Saturday classes. (To increase utilization of space.)
- All faculty will have their teaching loads increased by one class per semester. (To reduce the need for additional faculty.)
- All classes must have a minimum of 15 enrollments or they will be canceled. All introductory courses will be taught as large lecture sections. (To reduce the need for faculty and increase the "profit margin" per class.)
- Students must pay a $250 per semester parking fee to have a car on campus and a $100 per semester security fee. (To pay for parking facilities and campus police.)
- All majors with less than 100 students will either be consolidated or eliminated. (To focus resources on larger majors.)

2. As a class, brainstorm what type of resistance is likely to arise from these changes and from what constituencies.
3. Consolidate the specific examples of resistance into 5-6 categories.
4. Discuss what strategies might be effective in overcoming each category of resistance.
5. In addition, discuss what other ways the college/university might address the problem.

Tips

1. Students will begin by arguing about the specific changes. Students will want to argue that the changes shouldn't be made or that these are stupid, etc. Help them focus on the fact that as managers they will have to support and implement changes with which they do not agree.
2. Next students will start talking about the kind of resistance and focus on specific acts--protests, demonstrations, angry letters, etc. Help them think about the constituencies, who have a vested interest in these changes besides students and faculty.
3. Students should begin by going back to the basic problem and assumptions.
   - Basic problem, insufficient money.
   - Assumption, solve the problem by spending less.
4. Then students should think about the particular needs represented by the various "stakeholders."
   - What does the administration need?
   - What does the faculty need?
   - What do students need?
5. Students reference their solutions, alternatives, and overcoming resistance strategies to text content.